IMAGES
of America

BIG CYPRESS NATIONAL PRESERVE

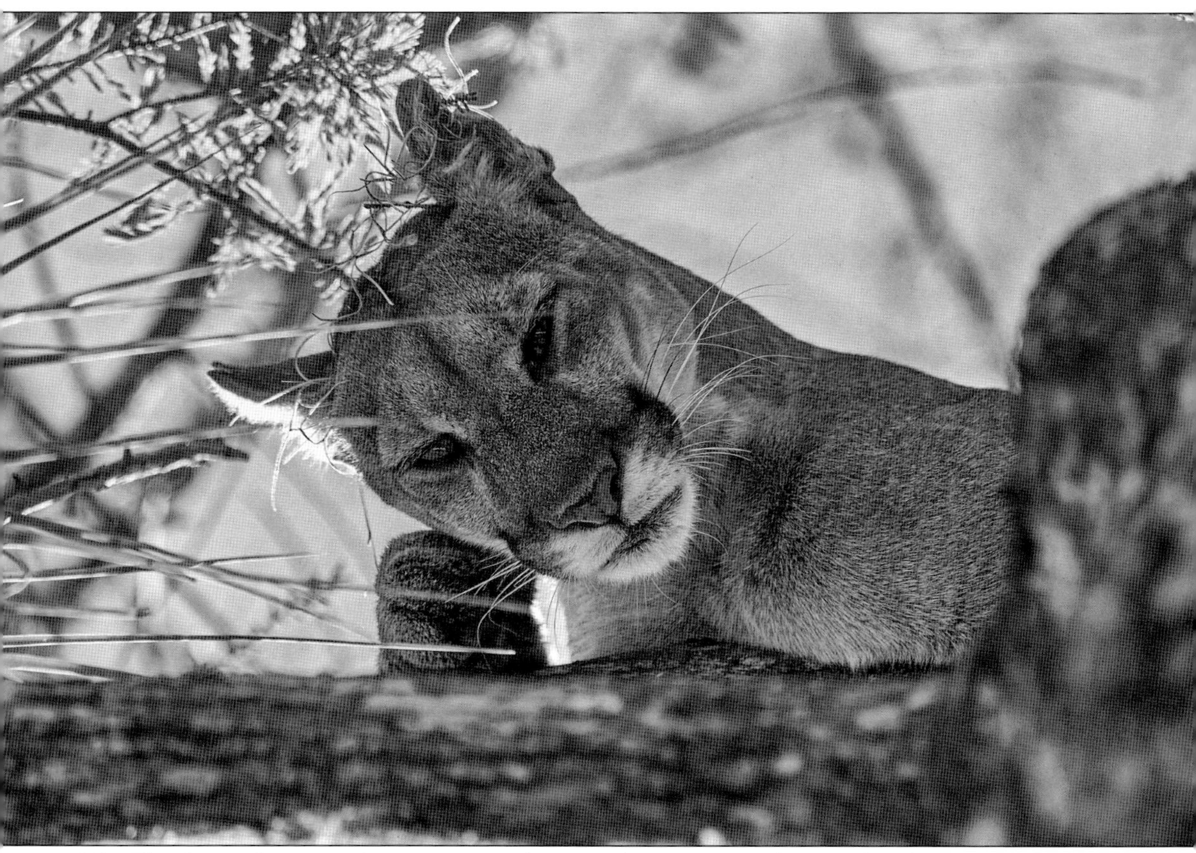

The Florida panther is Big Cypress National Preserve's iconic animal. Considered nearing extinction in the 1970s with its last population center in the Big Cypress Swamp, coordinated management to reduce threats, improve reproduction, and protect lands, including the preserve and nearby Florida Panther National Wildlife Refuge, have resulted in an amazing recovery. This panther, FP-220 (shown as a kitten on page 127), shows the success of these efforts. (Courtesy of Ralph Arwood.)

On the Cover: In April 1923, the self-appointed Tamiami Trail Blazers set out from Fort Myers, intending to traverse the route of the unfinished Tamiami Trail to Miami. The 10 cars, 23 men, and tractor faced a roadless Big Cypress Swamp. Wandering widely well off the road's future route and presumed lost by the public, surviving cars finally emerged after nearly three weeks to great national publicity. (Courtesy of State Library and Archives of Florida, Florida Memory.)

IMAGES
of America

Big Cypress National Preserve

James A. Kushlan and Kirsten Hines

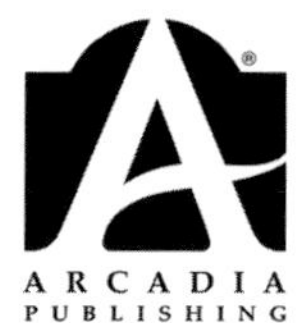

ISBN 978-1-4671-6298-2
Hardcover ISBN 978-1-5402-9962-8

Published by Arcadia Publishing
Charleston, South Carolina

Printed in the United States of America

Library of Congress Control Number: 2025947340

For all general information, please contact Arcadia Publishing:
Telephone 843-853-2070
Fax 843-853-0044
E-mail sales@arcadiapublishing.com

Visit us on the Internet at www.arcadiapublishing.com

Contents

Acknowledgments 6

Introduction 7

1. A Land Apart: The Cypress 11
2. Living with the Swamp: Indigenous Peoples and Early Settlers 25
3. Taming the Swamp: Roads, Canals, and Developers 41
4. Preserving the Swamp: The 1960s, an Airport, and a Preserve 81
5. People and the Swamp: The Big Cypress National Preserve 97

Acknowledgments

We thank the Big Cypress National Preserve and its leadership, Tom Forsyth and Pedro Ramos, for encouraging this project. Kirsten Hines was NPS Artist-In-Residence in the preserve in 2020; this book is a result. We thank the many who provided suggestions, information, and access to images, including Ralph Arwood; Cesar Beccara; Cynthia Guerra; David and Kathy McDonald; Martin Pate; John Sheldon; Jannatul Ahmed (American Museum of Natural History); Michelle Hanson, Deb Jansen, Matthew McCollister (Big Cypress National Preserve); Ron Middlebrook (Centerstream Publishing); Jennifer Guida (Collier County Museums); Elina Garrison, Jessica Pernell (Florida Fish and Wildlife Conservation Commission); Jennifer Green (Florida Museum of Natural History); Ashley Trujillo, Sebastian Saavedra (HistoryMiami Museum); Jennifer Cicero (Marco Island Historical Society); Georgen Charnes (Martin Digital History); Cesar Bracamonte (Miami-Dade Public Library System); Thomas Lockyear (Museum of the Everglades); Ryan Pettigrew (Richard Nixon Presidential Library and Museum); Bonnie Ciolino, Adam Palumbo, Michael Lorusso (South Florida Collections Management Center); Dixon Gutierrez (State Library and Archives of Florida); Stefania Eleni Papadopulos (University of Miami Libraries). We appreciate contributions of reviewers of earlier drafts, including Cesar Beccara, Tom Forsyth, Jennifer Green, and Thomas Lockyear.

Key to Courtesy Lines

AMNH	American Museum of Natural History
BICY	Big Cypress National Preserve, National Park Service
BPL	Boston Public Library, Digital Commonwealth
CCM	Collier County Museums
CP	Centerstream publishing, Fiddler's Curse
EFWE	Edison & Ford Winter Estates
FLMNH	Florida Museum of Natural History
FN	Formulanone, Flickr
FWC	Florida Fish and Wildlife Conservation Commission
HMM	HistoryMiami Museum
KH	Kushlan Hines Collection
LOC	Library of Congress
MCPL	Monroe County Public Library, Florida Keys History Center
MDPLS	Gleason Waite Romer Photographs, Miami-Dade Public Library System
MMP	MikesMegapixels, Panoramio
MP	Southeastern Archaeological Center, NPS, Painting by Martin Pate
NPG	National Portrait Gallery, Smithsonian Institution
NPS	National Park Service Archives at Harper's Ferry Center
NYPL	New York Public Library
OPN	Open Parks Network
RA	Ralph Arwood
RNPL	Richard Nixon Presidential Library and Museum
SFCMC	South Florida Collections Management Center, NPS
SFCMC-GP	South Florida Collections Management Center, Photo by Gustave Pellerin
SLAF	State Library and Archives of Florida, Florida Memory
UF	University of Florida Digital Collections
UM	Special Collections, University of Miami Libraries, Coral Gables, FL
UPENN	University of Pennsylvania Museum of Archaeology & Anthropology
USF	Digital Commons at the University of South Florida
USFWS	United States Fish and Wildlife Service, National Digital Library
USNA	United States National Archives

INTRODUCTION

The Big Cypress Swamp—or simply "the Cypress"—is indeed big, covering 2,400 square miles, over 1,000 of which have been set aside as the Big Cypress National Preserve. A responsibility of the National Park Service, the preserve is about the size of Rhode Island; the original Big Cypress Swamp is twice the size. It is big.

The Big Cypress Swamp is indeed a land of cypress trees, populated by bald cypress and smaller pond cypress (also called scrub and dwarf cypress). Bald cypress lived with the dinosaurs; a modern tree may be 700 years old. Beyond cypress, pinelands, hardwood hammocks, dry and wet prairies, and estuarine mangrove swamps complete the landscape. Differences in elevation among these communities measure scant inches. The Big Cypress Swamp is a complex mosaic comprised of plants and animals, some of which are highly endangered.

The Big Cypress Swamp is indeed a swamp, a highly seasonal swamp at that. Summer-fall rain inundates the land from inches to several feet, then trickles seaward over unnoticeable gradients and into the groundwater. The rest of the year, the swamp dries up, flow stops, saltwater moves up the estuaries, alligators retreat to their ponds and caves, waterbirds feed on trapped fish, cypress seeds germinate in damp soil, and fires burn. But they burn in both seasons by lightning, historically by Native Americans and pioneers, and now purposely by highly trained resource management crews. The Cypress both floods and burns.

The Big Cypress Swamp was historically a land of abundant fish and wildlife, home to Florida panthers, Florida black bears, locally adapted white-tailed deer, alligators, snakes, pig frogs, migratory birds, and waterbirds, the white ibis being historically most abundant. Locally called curlews or Chokoloskee chicken, white ibis were a staple of pioneer cook pots. James Kushlan, an author of this book, studied white ibis for his doctoral thesis. Tarpon mingled with Florida bass in estuarine rivers. Bays and coast provided pinfish and mullet; beds of clams, oysters, and whelks; edible manatee; and marketable sea turtles.

These were the natural resources supporting the swamp's Indigenous peoples, whose occupancy dates back multiple thousands of years, even to before the pause in sea-level rise that made the place a swamp. In the 16th century, the Spanish gave names to the local mound-dwelling people and the places they lived— Calusa, Muspa, and Tequesta. Mostly residing coastally, they used interior swamps seasonally. Maintaining a surprising independence during the Spanish colonial centuries, their numbers and culture inevitably eroded. Then, others moved into Florida from the north, fostering a culture that would eventually be called Seminole. The US government spent several decades attempting to remove these people from Florida. Moving ever farther south, they resisted and persisted in small numbers, yet unconquered, in the Big Cypress and Everglades. In this inaccessible refuge, they adapted to swamp living, isolating in dispersed, independent, family-oriented encampments perched on patches of higher ground in the swamp called tree islands. Other settlement was slow in coming. Cuba-derived, semipermanent, Spanish-speaking fishing communities developed along the coast. The Civil War little touched the region, although its cracker cattle became crucial to feeding the South. Special southern troops, the Cow Cavalry, wrangled cattle into Georgia. Key West locals and northern refugees moved to the region to farm the ancient mounds, salt fish, and catch turtles for that Union-held town.

With war's end, the region's isolation and resources reencouraged a slow arrival of settlers, American pioneers wanting new opportunities, health-seekers needing a mild climate, Seminole and Civil War veterans, and renegades hiding from troubles they had elsewhere, all in the isolation of the nation's last frontier. Communities developed slowly. Transport and communication were by boat along the coast. In the swamp, canoes, canoe-like skiffs, and wading were the ways to move about in the wet season. In the dry season, it remained a hard-walking place by foot, horseback, or ox cart. While the North was experiencing its Gilded Age, in the Big Cypress, Seminoles lived in open-sided, palm-thatched shelters called chickees, and settlers lived in driftwood and tar paper shacks, both sensible and serviceable accommodations but a far cry from Victorian mansions in the North.

Big Cypress pioneers fed themselves and families by hunting, fishing, farming, making moonshine and charcoal, smuggling, and moving from place to place, many leaving little trace of their time in the Cypress. Drinking water was a key to settlement, obtained by traveling upriver, accessing shallow surface aquifers, artesian wells, swamp water, and eventually rain-catching cisterns. Hurricanes repeatedly destroyed family dreams. Hunting produced food and trade goods—cash was scarce, the economy ran mostly on egret plumes and alligator hides. Subsistence and market farming took hold along the coast, especially on the ancient mounds, producing marketable winter vegetables and cane syrup. From the 1870s, trading posts serviced both settlers and Seminoles, some seeding persistent towns—Chokoloskee, Immokalee, and Everglades City. (The town sequentially was named Allen's Place, Everglade, Everglades, and Everglades City, although the real, often-mentioned Everglades marsh lay 30 miles east. So as to avoid confusion, the town will typically be referred to as Everglades City, albeit sometimes anachronistically.) Hurricane tides and sea-level rise eventually drove market farming inland. Local farming made the national map when a grapefruit grove was carved out of Deep Lake Strand. To get the fruit to northern markets, a small railroad was run to a coastal settlement, which became Everglades City. Commercial net fishing expanded, and a clam-harvesting dredge created a wage-paying industry for the locals. Packinghouses managed commercial farm produce; boats hauled fish, turtles, cane, syrup, and vegetables to Key West.

Pioneer life began to wane when the Cypress and much of its surroundings were purchased by one man, Barron Gift Collier, who bought the Deep Lake citrus operation in 1922, then most of the region and Everglades City, to become his development headquarters. A road from Miami to Tampa, the Tamiami Trail, changed everything. Its story is that of Collier, who bought up 1.3 million acres and that of multifaceted Miami developer James F. Jaudon, who secured several hundred thousand acres. Collier's 1923 publicity stunt of sending a brigade of cars called the Tamiami Trail Blazers across the swamp to Miami fixed the trail in the public's and the Florida legislature's consciousness (see cover). That year, Collier bartered to establish a county in his name for completing the trail, which he did in 1928 along with a road and railroad to Immokalee and beyond. The car era arrived in the Cypress, never to depart. Tamiami Trail changed the Seminole and settler ways of life, land uses, and fundamentally the South Florida environment itself. It famously opened seasonally flooding swamps for sale to developers, idealistic sugarcane and citrus farmers, and unwary investors nationwide.

Everglades and Cypress Seminoles moved their family camps from the seasonally flooded swamp to the higher roadside. Some joined the tourist trade, turning their camps into "Indian Villages." Local and nonresident hunters now could more easily access the swamp, especially using swamp buggies and airboats that could go places in minutes that used to take hours, days, or not at all. Learning from pioneers, second-generation backwoodsmen developed a hunting- and camp-oriented, cracker, "gladesman" tradition in the Cypress. Commercial fishing was increasingly focused on game-fish tourism, and fishermen became guides. Deer, alligators, raccoons, turkey, and waterbirds were hunted, but increasingly, less for subsistence or trade than for sport hunting.

By 1923, Baron Collier had his own county, his county seat, and a compliant county commission to issue bonds. Collier built up the once-tiny settlement with a port, lumber mill, bank, stores, hotels, restaurants, railroad depot, fishing boats and guides, and real estate opportunities. Jaudon's company sold off its real estate options in the southern Big Cypress and Pinecrest, which serially developed and declined idiosyncratically over the decades. Agriculture turned to vegetable farming in the mucky marshes, which profitably shipped winter vegetables by train to northern markets. Farming towns of Immokalee and Ochopee attracted workers, residents, and businesses. The Depression brought hard times for residents, hanging on while new arrivals sought escape and self-reliance in the backcountry. World war followed, and lumbering expanded during and after the war in Big Cypress's seemingly endless cache of trees. Lumber company towns, Copeland by the Lee Tidewater Cypress Company and Jerome by the C.J. Jones Company, prospered until they had cut all the commercially useful trees by the 1950s and moved on. In the 1940s, oil was found under the swamp.

Everglades National Park, dedicated in 1947, had a region-wide impact. As land was acquired in the southern Big Cypress and Ten Thousand Islands, restrictions and enforcement followed, altering the way of life of locals. At the same time, the Florida Game and Freshwater Fish Commission increasingly regulated hunting and fishing. In places, buggy access became trespassing, alligator hunting became poaching, bird rookeries were off limits, deer had a hunting season, and nighttime fire-hunting became illegal. Also in 1947, a flood control district was established to tame South Florida's wetlands, rearranging water flows and building impoundments in the previously contiguous and confluent watersheds of the Everglades and Big Cypress Swamp.

Seminoles and Miccosukee continued their deep relationship with the Cypress, living there and using the land in traditional ways. Deprived of a state-designated reservation in the southern Cypress, reservation land in the northern Cypress was accepted, as was, many years later, compensation for lost treaty land. But the Big Cypress Swamp was eyed by others. Transported by swamp buggies, half-tracks, and airboats, sportsmen claimed sites in the swamp, building temporary shelters and later permanent cabins for hunting and for experiencing a backwoods lifestyle. Starting in 1960, about 112,000 acres of the Big Cypress's Picayune and Fakahatchee Strands were carved up into 800 miles of road and 180 miles of drainage canals to develop the southern Golden Gate Estates. Alligator Alley, initially derisively named, opened in 1968, crossing 50 miles of the Big Cypress. Sportsmen's clubs, environmental groups, longtime local users, and the tribes took notice of conservation challenges developing in the swamp.

The future of the Big Cypress Swamp came into broader notice in 1968, when the Dade County Port Authority began constructing a 39-square-mile, six-runway intercontinental, supersonic airport—the Everglades Jetport. While Dade and Collier Counties quickly secured land through eminent domain, planning for the Everglades Jetport had slipped beneath the notice of potentially concerned citizens, agencies, and water managers. Miccosukees had traditional ceremonial sites taken over. The jetport, intending to service 50 million passengers annually, would have spurred intensive and extensive development, expressways, and rapid transit. A wide consortium of conservationists, the tribes, hunters, off-road vehicle (ORV) enthusiasts, and influential people in the federal and state governments came to oppose the idea. Opponents came together as the Everglades Coalition to speak as one voice on the jetport controversy. Marjorie Stoneman Douglas became its public face. Reports by the Department of the Interior and the National Academy of Sciences concluded the inevitability of severe damage to Everglades National Park downstream. The academy recommended that Big Cypress become a natural water conservation area. Owing to these concerns and the cancellation of Boeing's supersonic jet development, construction ended in 1970 with the Everglades Jetport Pact, leaving one relic 10,500-foot runway for practice.

Pres. Richard Nixon proposed creating a "Big Cypress National Freshwater Reserve." On October 11, 1974, the Big Cypress National Preserve was established with responsibility assigned to the National Park Service. This was a victory for the conservation community and for public participation in such national decisions—and it was a great compromise. This was not to be a typical national park, but a new concept. A federally protected area in which recreational, consumptive, and cultural activities, as legislated by Congress, would continue. These included hunting and fishing in coordination with the state, oil extraction in that most subsurface rights were retained, cattle grazing, ORV use, existing private land ownership, and traditional and customary uses by the Miccosukee and Seminole people.

Over the years, other portions of the Big Cypress Swamp surrounding the preserve came under state, federal, and tribal management, accumulating over one million protected acres. These include Fakahatchee Strand Preserve State Park, Picayune Strand State Forest, Florida Panther National Wildlife Refuge, and Ten Thousand Islands National Wildlife Refuge. Other Big Cypress reserves include Okaloacoochee Slough State Forest, Corkscrew Swamp Sanctuary, Corkscrew Regional Ecosystem Watershed, Rookery Bay National Estuarine Research Reserve, and the Green Heart of the Everglades Management Area. In 1988, about 146,000 acres of Addition Lands were added to the preserve. The Alligator Alley Reservation of the Miccosukee tribe of Indians of Florida and Big Cypress Reservation of the Seminole tribe of Florida bracketed the preserve's northeastern borders. To the south and southwest lie the 1.5 million acres of Everglades National Park, and to the east are over 800,000 acres of South Florida's water conservation areas, containing most of the remnant Everglades marsh, over much of which the Miccosukee tribe has a perpetual lease for traditional activities. As a result, much of the greater Big Cypress Swamp came under legal protection and management.

The National Park Service slowly assumed management of its preserve. It was not easy. The federal government set out to acquire land, much of it initially from the state and supportive Collier interests. Preserve policies regarding camps on unowned land, access rules, and the state's hunting regulations met with local resistance. The preserve wrote resource management plans taking into consideration multiple uses, impacts of ORVs, over-drainage, and effects of fire suppression. Big Cypress's endangered species were of special concern, particularly the once abundant Florida panther that, when the preserve was established, teetered on the brink of extinction, a crashing population of endangered Cape Sable seaside sparrow, and poaching threats to plants such as the increasingly scarce ghost orchid. The preserve continued to manage new threats, such as from invasive non-native plants and the insatiable Burmese python, while protecting natural resources and expanding opportunities for visitors.

During the over 50 years since the preserve's establishment, visitor use of the Big Cypress increased markedly and diversified as more people sought the outdoors. Adding to traditional hunting, private camps, and airboat and swamp buggy use were activities such as hiking, including the southern leg of the Florida National Scenic Trail; swamp slogging; paddling; biking; birding; wildlife watching; recreational vehicle (RV) and tent camping; and strolling the boardwalks. Informative programs by rangers and park volunteers and festivals such as the Swamp Heritage Festival, Wild Hog BBQ, and Everglades Seafood Festival shared Big Cypress swamp heritage stories. Owners retained cabins and backwoods lifestyles. Oil continued to be pumped. Vintage buildings were repurposed. Annually, about a million people visit the Big Cypress National Preserve to experience its forests and prairies; noble cypress trees and gnarled cypress knees; orchids and alligators; seasonal and resident birds, including its great diversity of waterbirds; and, if very lucky, a Florida panther.

One

A Land Apart

The Cypress

For millennia, Indigenous peoples, followed by Seminoles and pioneer settlers, were supported by the Big Cypress Swamp's natural resources. Hunting, fishing, and gathering produced deer meat, bones, and antlers; alligator skin, bones, and teeth; waterfowl; ibis; turkey; quail; garfish; native tropical fruits; palm hearts; and flour-producing coontie roots. The historic Cypress was an optimal habitat for mammalian predators, including the Florida panther, the Florida black bear, bobcat, raccoon, otter, and, after the arrival of the Spanish, European hogs. During settler times, panthers were so common as to require constant vigilance. Egrets numbered in the tens of thousands and white ibis, likely, in hundreds of thousands. Cottonmouths and other water snakes plied the waters; diamondback and pygmy rattlesnakes were in the tree islands.

The swamp is more water than land for much of the year. For all its history but the past century, it was impenetrable in the wet season except by canoe and later by skiff, poled by knowledgeable locals. The Cypress is an uneven place underlain by karstic limestone that, in places, emerges through thin organic and marl soils. Lakes, potholes, and ponds are scattered about. The sloughs and strands follow elongated channels etched in the limestone below. Water is the Cypress's primary natural resource and the rationale for the national preserve's creation. The preserve depends primarily on local rainfall but also on runoff from the north. Spring rainfall raises water levels throughout the swamp; water flows ever so slowly from higher levels to lower, imperceptibly mostly. The Cypress's two sub-basins drain toward the Everglades to the east and the Gulf to the southwest. In winter and spring, rains stop, water evaporates, shallow parts of the swamp dry out, aquatic fauna concentrate where water remains, prairie fires burn, and the swamp regenerates itself.

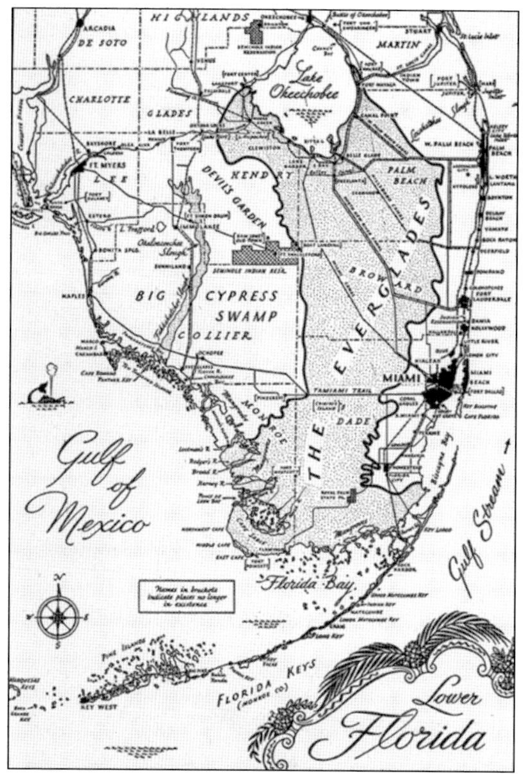

The Big Cypress Swamp historically occupied much of southwestern Florida, as seen at left. To the north is the Immokalee Rise, the highest elevation in the region. The 60-mile-long Okaloacoochee Slough and Corkscrew Strand form the Big Cypress's north and northwestern edges. The northern reaches of the Big Cypress and beyond have been much changed by farming, ranching, and development. The Big Cypress National Preserve now encompasses much of the remaining swamp (below) while western portions are protected by such reserves as the Fakahatchee Strand Preserve State Park, Florida Panther National Wildlife Refuge, and Picayune Strand State Forest. The Everglades marsh is to the east, its northern portion confined by levees into Water Conservation Area 3A. Everglades National Park abuts the south and wraps around to encompass Big Cypress's estuary, the Ten Thousand Islands. (Left, SFCMC; below, USNA.)

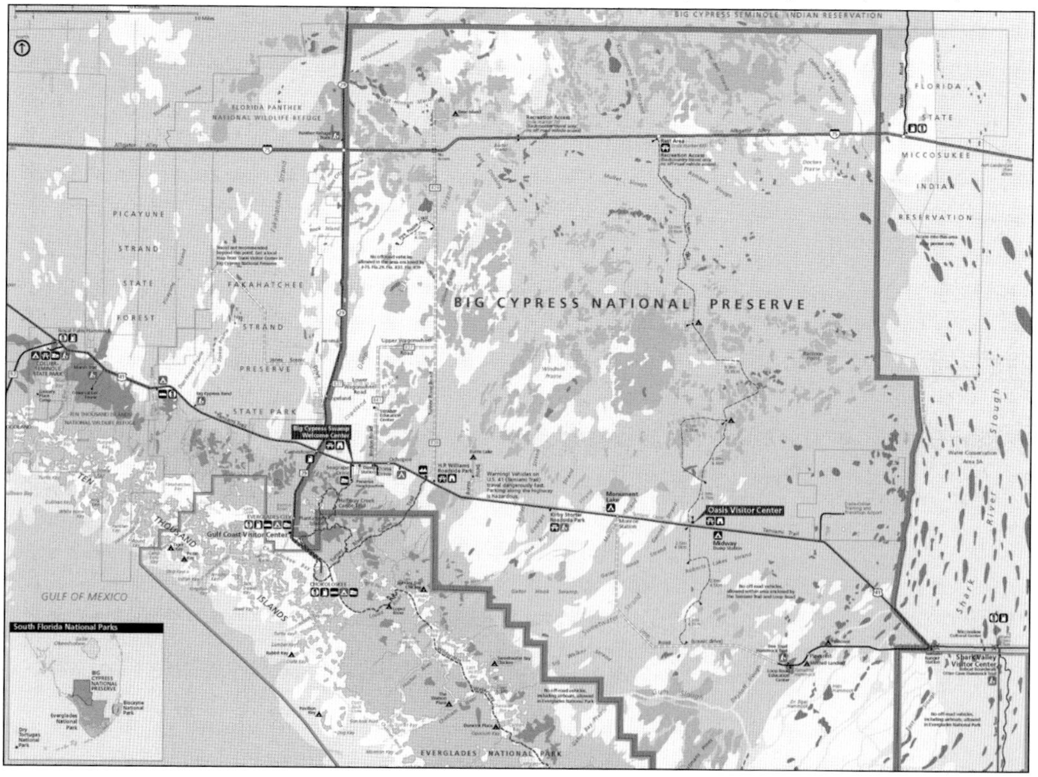

Cypress trees cover about a third of the Big Cypress National Preserve. Old and large bald cypress trees grew in peat-filled solution features, including deeper drainageways such as Fakahatchee, Okaloachoochee, and Lostmans Slough, as well as in smaller sloughs such as Gator Hook and Roberts Lakes Strands. Cypress trees were extensively lumbered in the Big Cypress Swamp for their soft but durable wood through the late 1950s. At right is a 1917 photograph from the Fakahatchee with an embedded machete for scale. Below, although outside the Big Cypress, this 1929 image of "the Senator" in Longwood, Florida, shows how big the trees could get. It was once 165 feet tall, the tallest tree east of the Mississippi River. At the time of its demise in 2012, its trunk was 11 feet across. (Both, SLAF.)

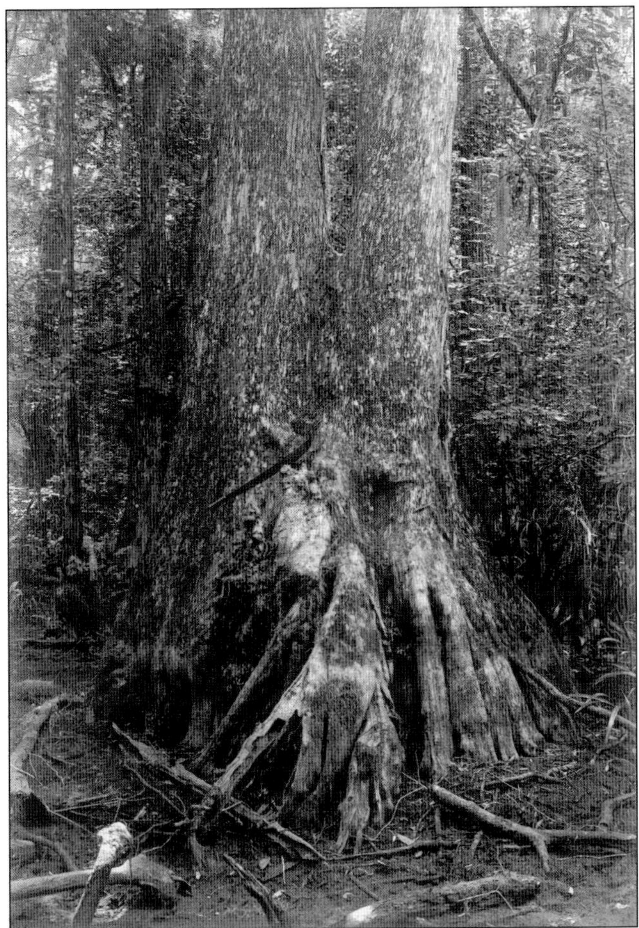

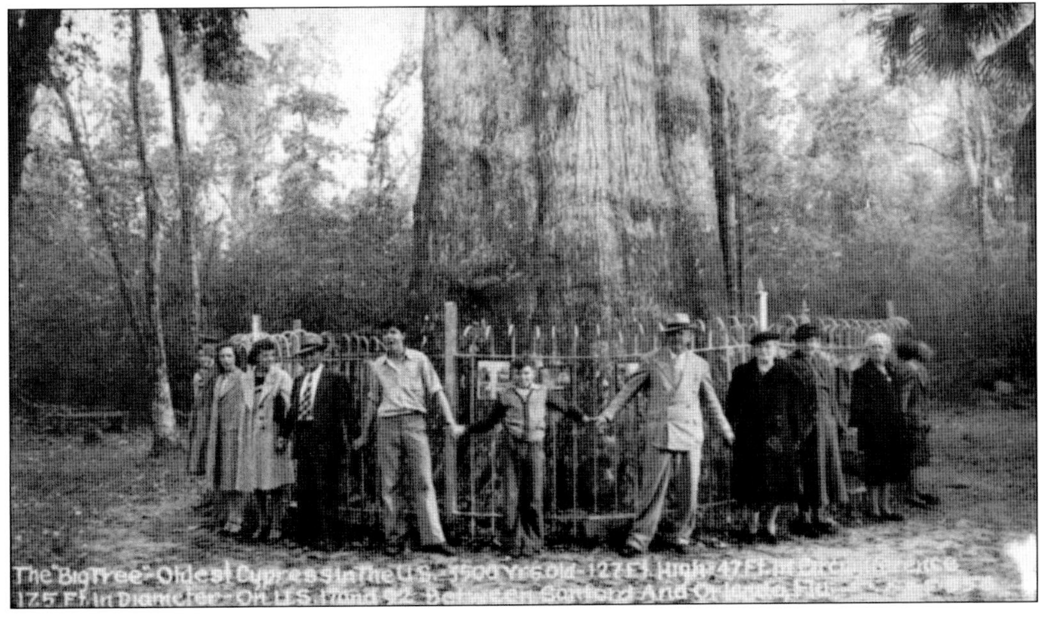

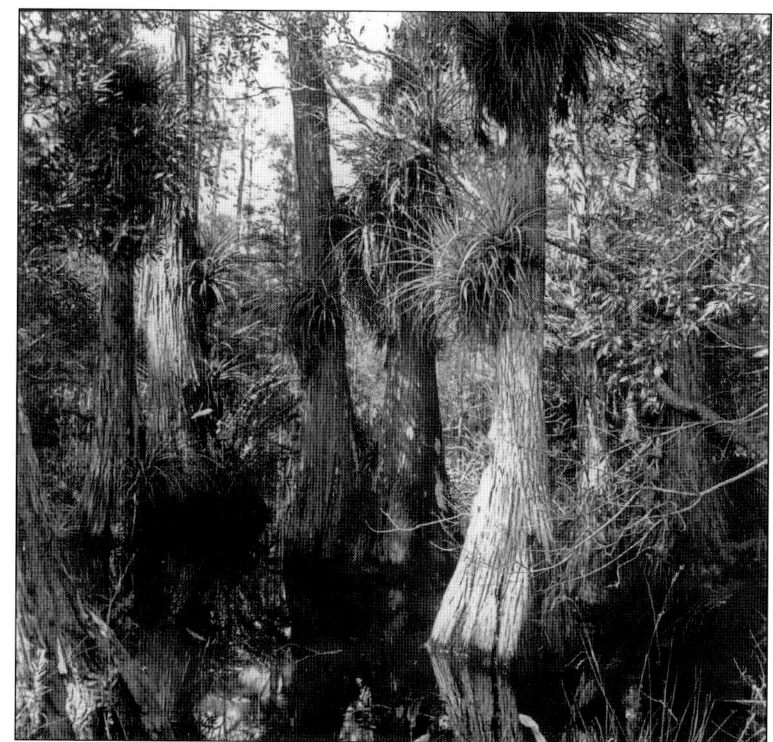

Cypress trees are so waterlogged that drying was required before lumbering. Temperate trees, they lose tiny leaf-lined branchlets during the winter dry season, leaving a "bald" crown. In the winter, naked gray trunks and branches extend to the horizon. Flaky bark supports lichens, ferns, orchids, and bromeliads, as shown in this 1942 image. Where the gray of lichens starts on the trunks marks the rainy season highwater mark. (SLAF.)

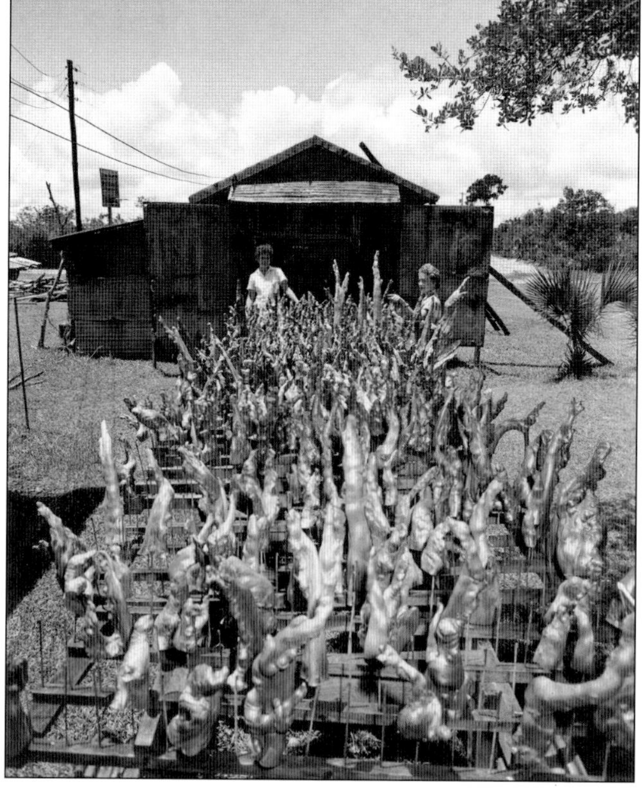

Swollen lower trunks called buttresses (previous image) and tangled roots hold strongly in wet soil. Cypress may have "knees" that grow from the roots above the high-water mark. They were once harvested for their entertaining shapes, becoming lamps and other novelties. From 1951 to 1998, Thomas Gaskins' Cypress Knee Museum in Palmdale (pictured) featured them. He quite literally "took the trees and put 'em in a tree museum." (SLAF.)

Cypress sloughs, also called strands, are moist, shaded, and diverse with orchids, bromeliads, ferns, maples, and other swamp plants (shown in this 1930s image). The largest trees grow in the deep peat in the strand's center, becoming shorter toward the outside. In wet seasons, sloughs are small streams. In dry seasons, the outer edges dry, but interior ponds, strung like beads down the flow-way, usually continue to hold water. (MDPLS.)

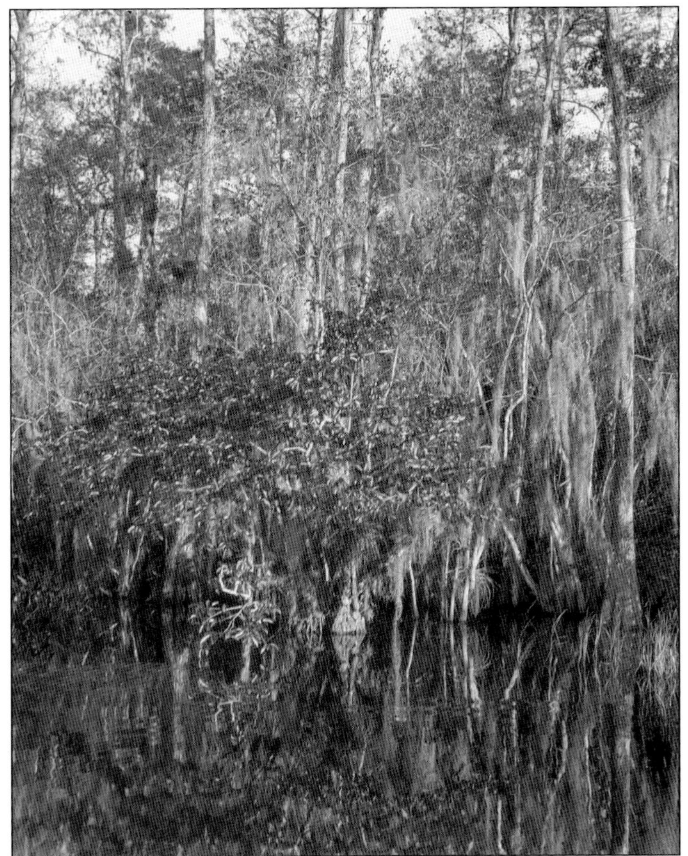

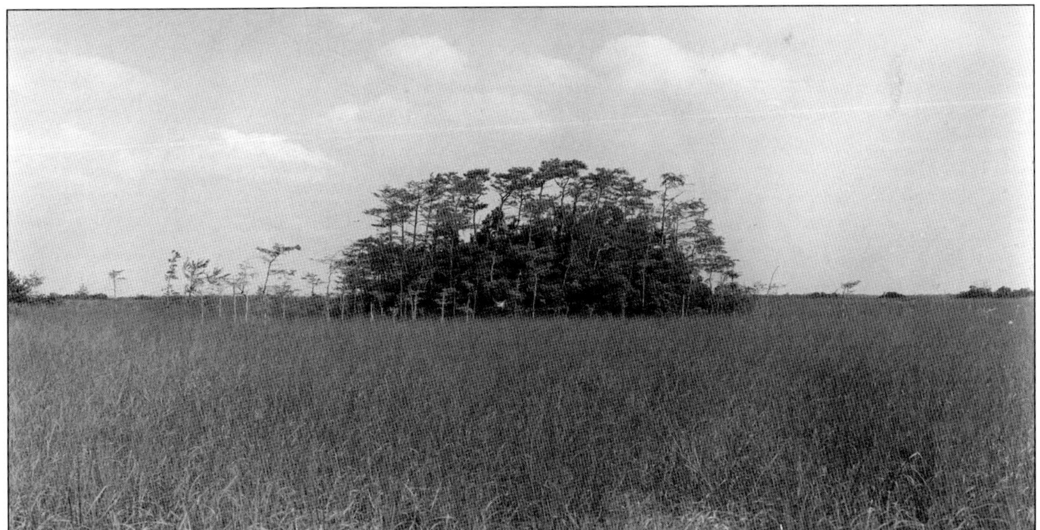

Cypress domes give the landscape a uniquely patterned texture. The shape is created by the larger trees toward the center and progressively shorter trees towards the edges, blending into the more sparsely treed swamp surrounding, as seen here. Other plants also may form heads, such as willow heads and bayheads. These circular features usually occupy depressions in the limestone or soil and may have a pond in the center. (SFCMC.)

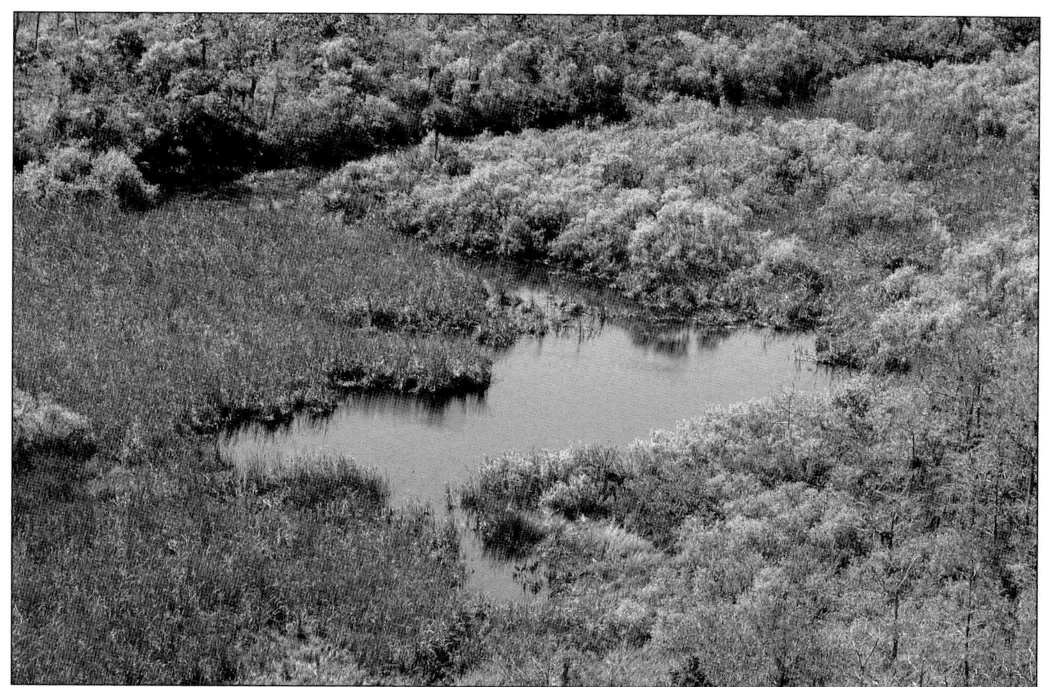

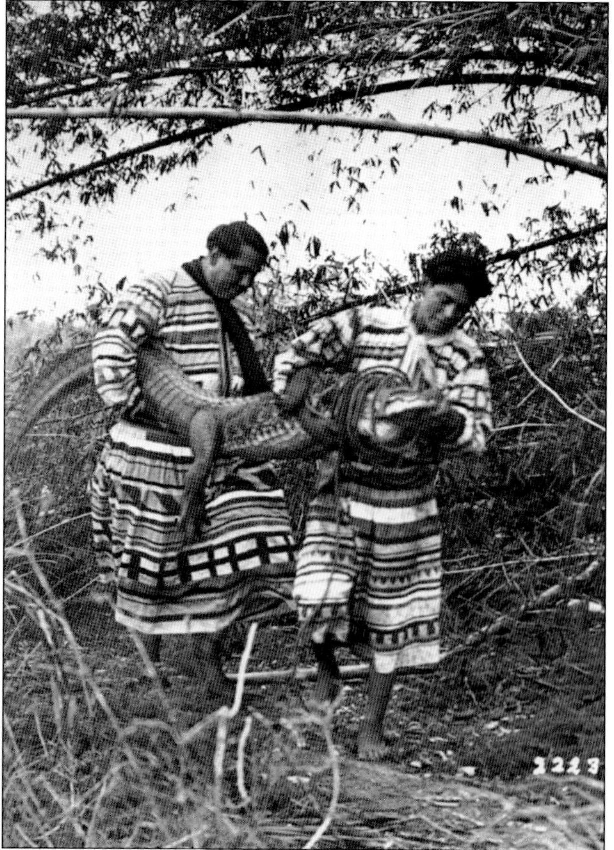

Ponds are one of the Big Cypress's more distinctive and ecologically important features. Alligators dig and maintain "gator holes" and attached caves, as James Kushlan, an author of this book, demonstrated in the 1970s. Ponds naturally provided the deepest water and, in dry season, usually stayed wet as the surrounding swamp dried, providing food and refuge for wildlife. In the dry season, a distinctive plant, fire flag, signaled their location for gator-hide hunters. (SFCMC-GP.)

Alligators were hunted in the Cypress for as long as humans were around. Calusa used bones, teeth, and dermal scutes. Settlers and Seminoles (shown in the 1920s) hunted them for their tradeable hides when confined to gator holes and caves in the dry season or by spotlight at night in the wet season. Gator hunting continued long after they were legally protected, but populations recovered, becoming abundant throughout the swamp. (SLAF.)

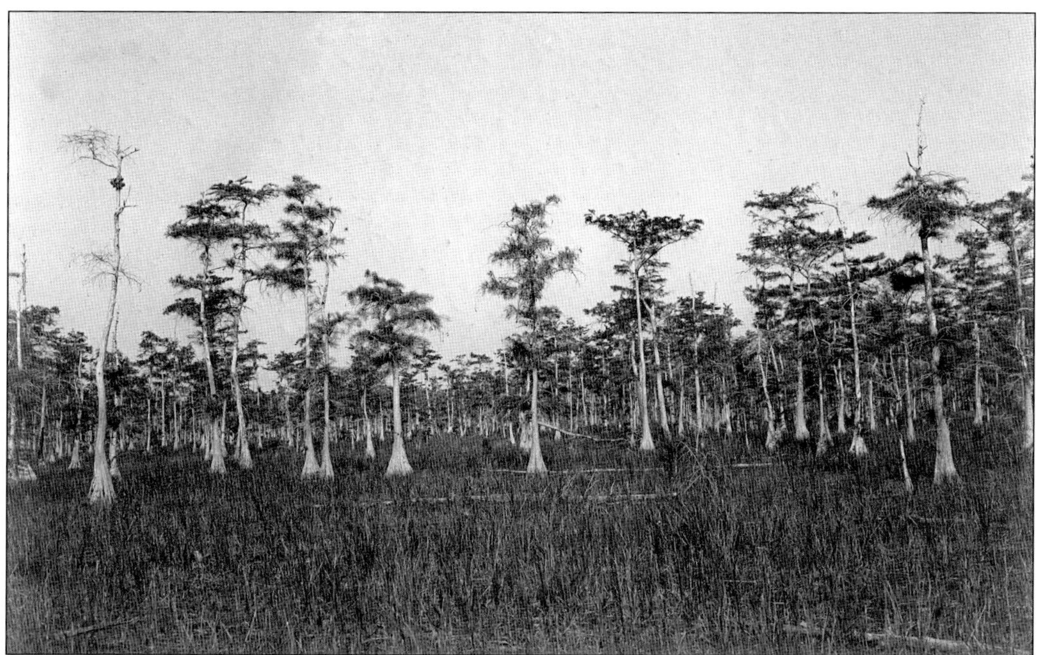

Much of the Big Cypress is covered by relatively short, thin pond cypress trees. Too skinny for lumber, historically, they provided excellent construction poles. Trees are rather widely spaced, as in this 1917 photograph. Pond cypress may flood for only half the year. Its sparse canopy provides conditions for ground plants, including orchids, grasses, sedges such as sawgrass, and plants particularly characteristic of this habitat. (SLAF.)

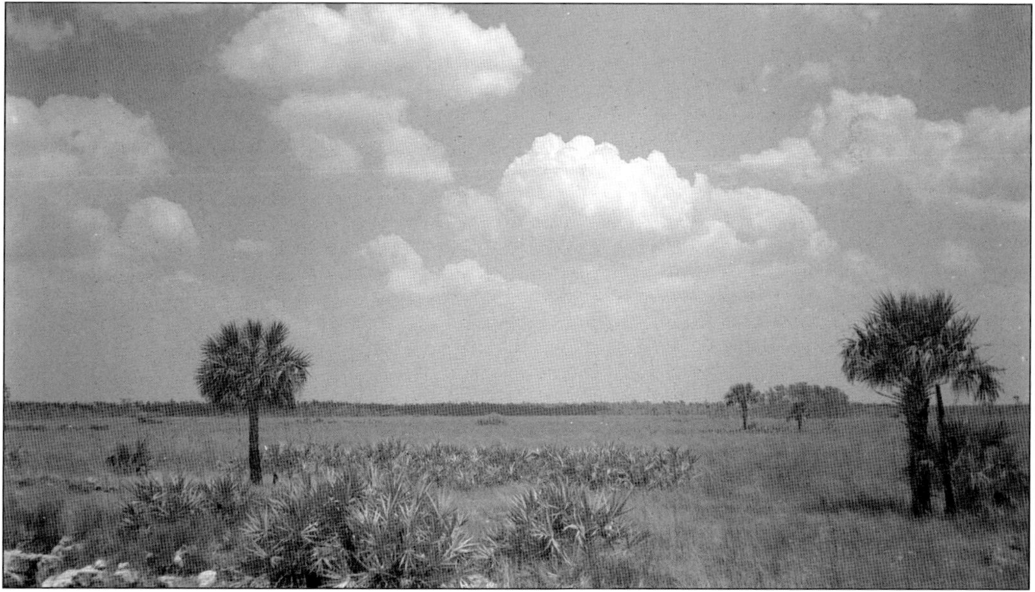

Grasslands vary from seasonally flooded marshes to drier prairies. Prairies burn naturally every few years. Historically, Seminoles, cattlemen, and hunters "fired" prairie grass to provide new growth for cattle or deer, to ease travel, and to reduce fuel. Marshes have such aquatic plants as sawgrass, cattails, and spikerush. Tall sabal (or cabbage) palms and shorter saw palmetto are common, as shown in this 1951 Big Cypress image. (MDPLS.)

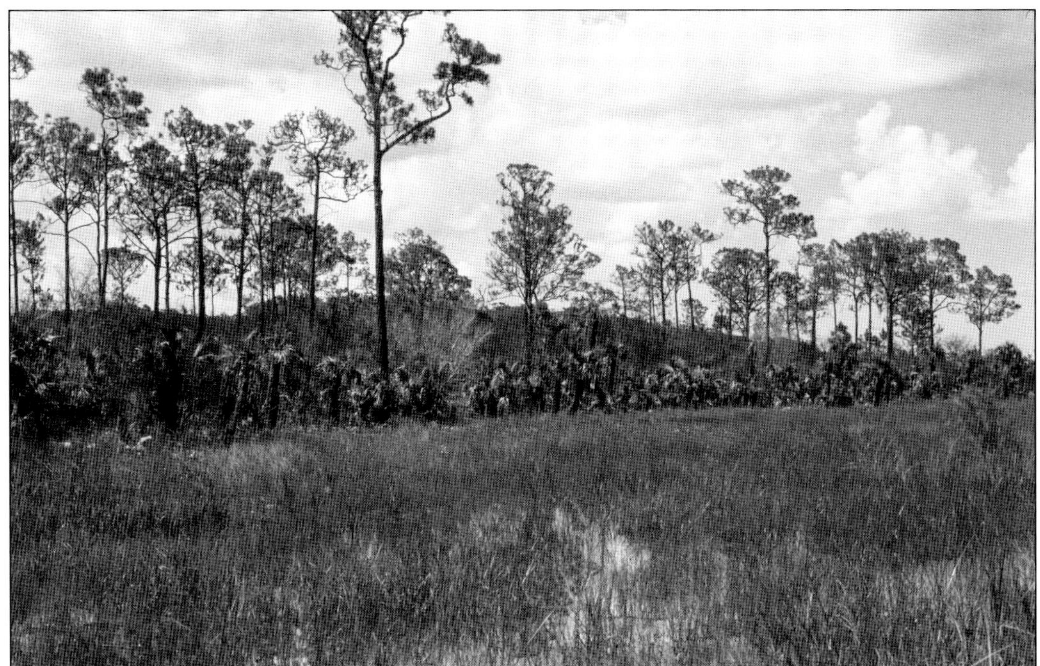

Native Big Cypress slash pines are adapted to intermittent flooding, as shown in this image. Pines occur on extensive islands in the swamp or scattered on slightly elevated patches surrounded by prairies or scrub cypress with an understory of saw palmetto, grasses, and herbs. Into the 1950s, they were heavily lumbered for their dense wood. (OPN.)

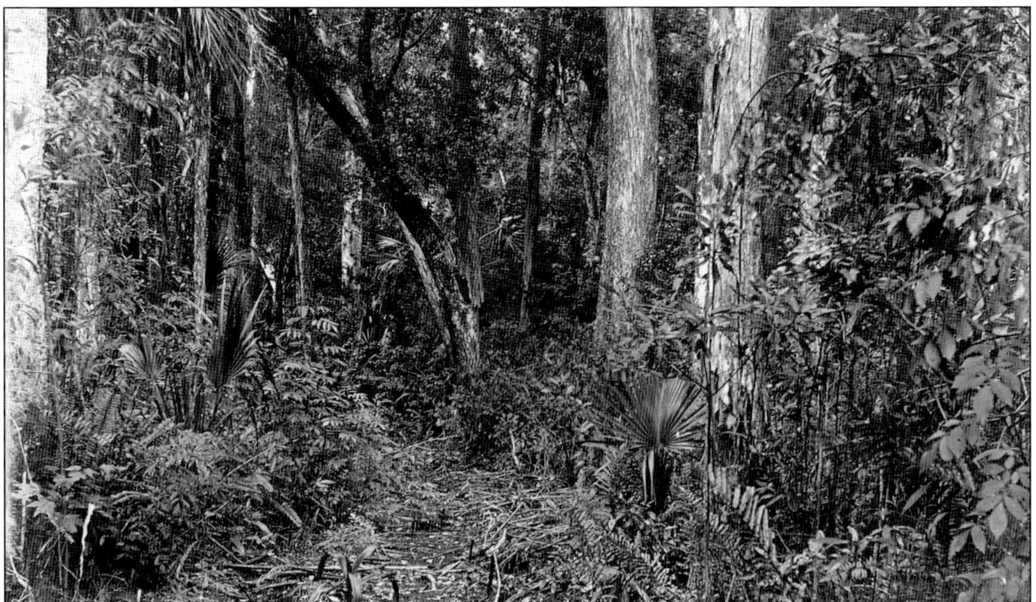

Hammocks provided ideal locations for camps for Seminoles and settlers and Calusa before them. They are hardwood forests of oaks, palms, tropical trees such as gumbo limbo, vines, and a thick edge of swamp plants such as cocoplum and willow. They occur on the highest elevations that seldom flood and never burn. Critical wildlife habitats, hammocks are used by resting deer, nesting alligators, roosting waterbirds, raccoons, and pygmy rattlesnakes. (CCM.)

Honored by Seminoles and feared by early settlers, Florida panthers are the Big Cypress's iconic animal. By the 1970s, the population was believed to be only a few dozen animals, but it has made an impressive comeback under protection, management, and habitat preservation, including in the Big Cypress National Preserve. Considered an umbrella species, the Big Cypress Swamp remains the core of the Florida panther's remaining range. (SLAF.)

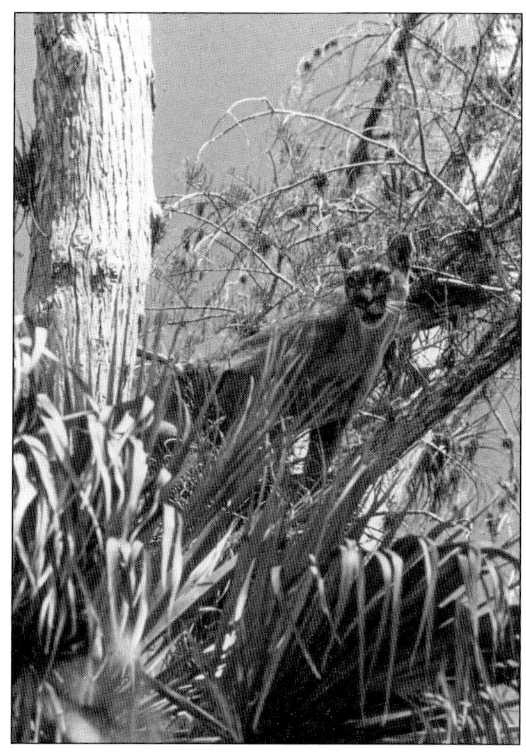

Historically, white-tailed deer have been central to Big Cypress's natural and human history. The native deer was small, adapted to South Florida and swamp-living, and immune to endemic diseases. They were a primary native prey for the Florida panther. Antlers and bones were used by Indigenous peoples, and hides formed the early Seminole trade economy. Meat fed settlers, and game attracted sport hunters, as shown in this 1954 image. (SLAF.)

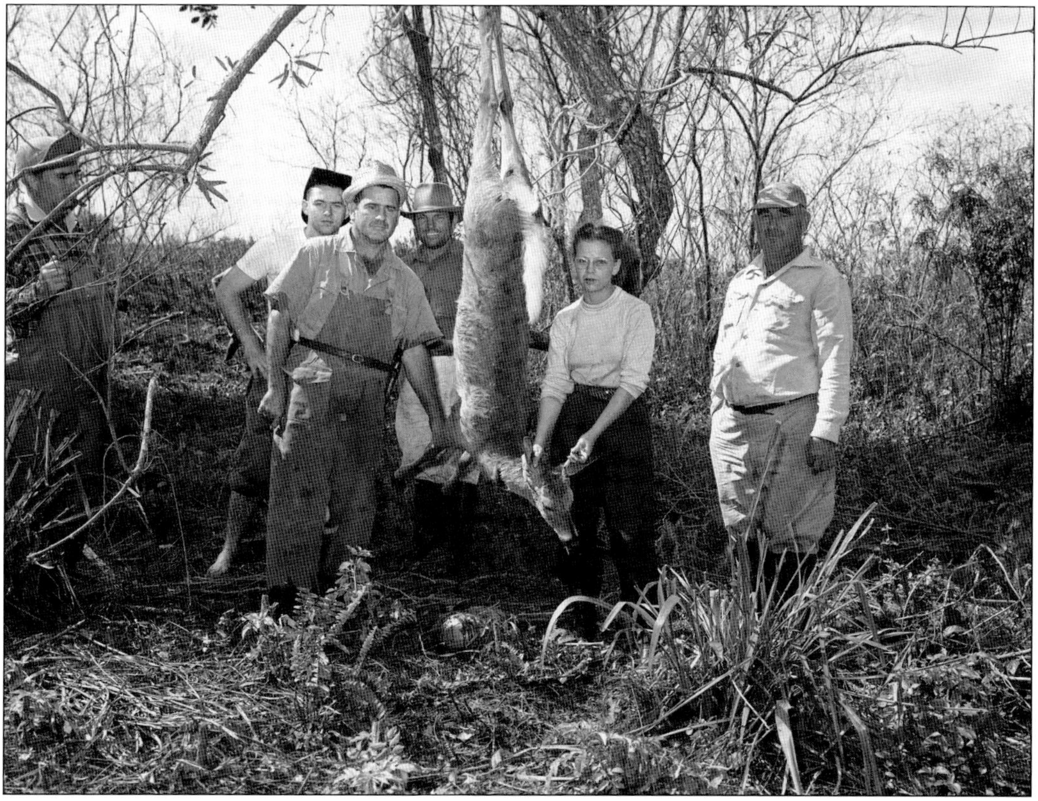

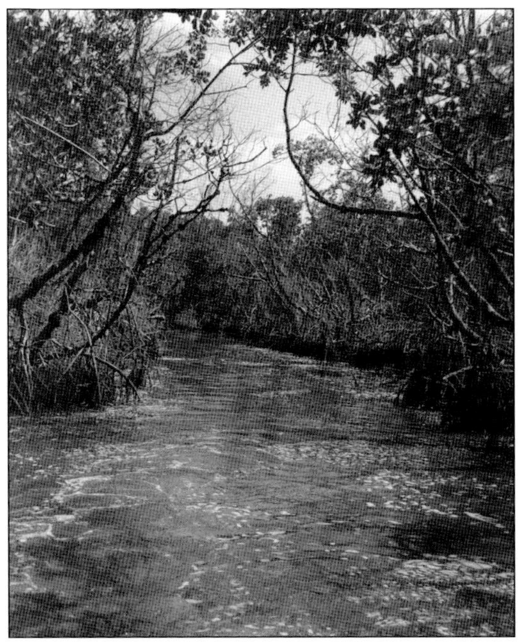

The Big Cypress's coastal rivers and islands are forested by salt-tolerant mangrove trees. Fresh waters of the wet season flow seaward through mangrove-lined rivers into the estuaries, as seen here. The dense, tangled, productive mangrove swamps were a historic economic engine providing birds, manatees, turtles, shellfish, and fish for food or sale. Calusa and then the pioneers settled primarily in this productive coastal zone rather than in the inland swamp. (OPN.)

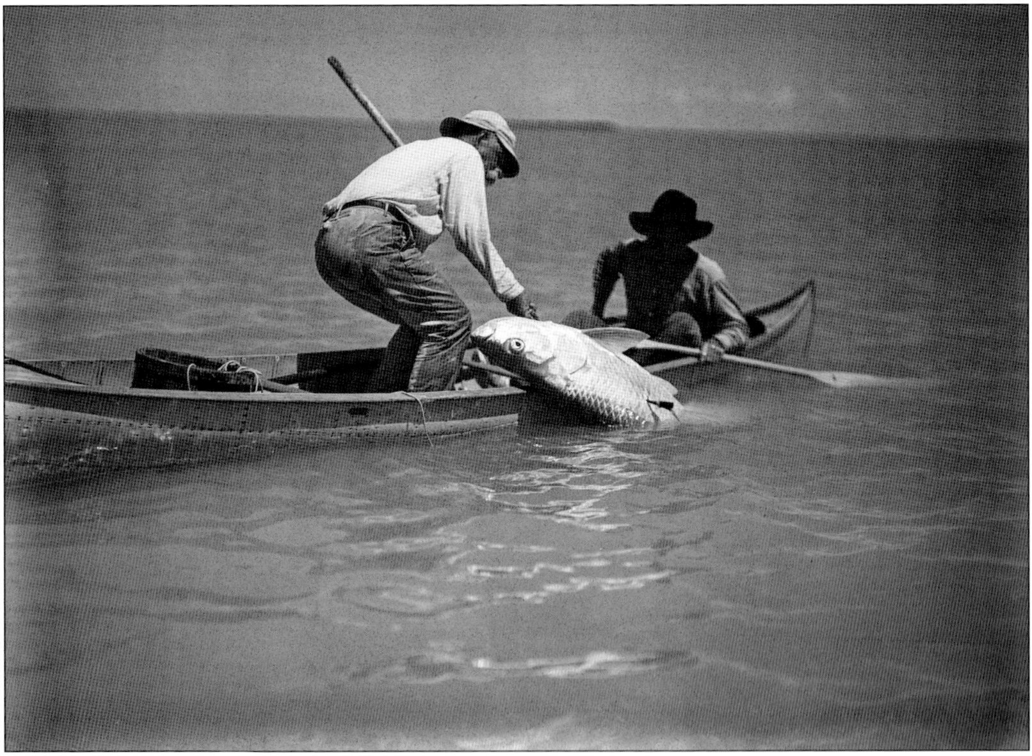

Starting in the late 1880s, tarpon, the silver king, became and remains a primary target of sport fishers in the Big Cypress's estuaries. This early-1900s image shows Big Cypress exploring author A.W. Dimock landing a tarpon in his canoe. Tarpons are one of the marine species that ascend mangrove-lined rivers into the freshwaters of the Big Cypress. Snook similarly became a targeted species in the 1940s. (AMNH.)

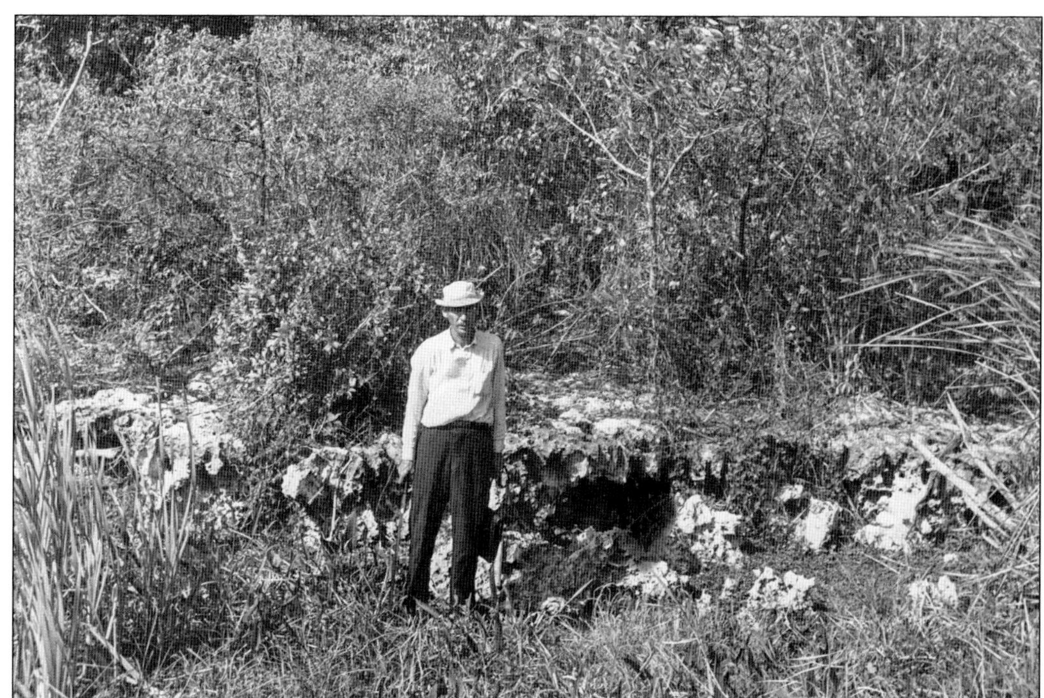

Rock in the Big Cypress is never far below a veneer of sand, marl, or peat, often sticking out, as shown in this 1942 image from near Pinecrest. Most exposures are of the Tamiami Formation from an oceanic deposit three to five million years old—a mostly hard, irregularly weathered, sandy limestone. Caloosahatchee Marl is two million years old, and Miami limestone is 130,000 years old. The rock elevates Big Cypress slightly above the Everglades. (SLAF.)

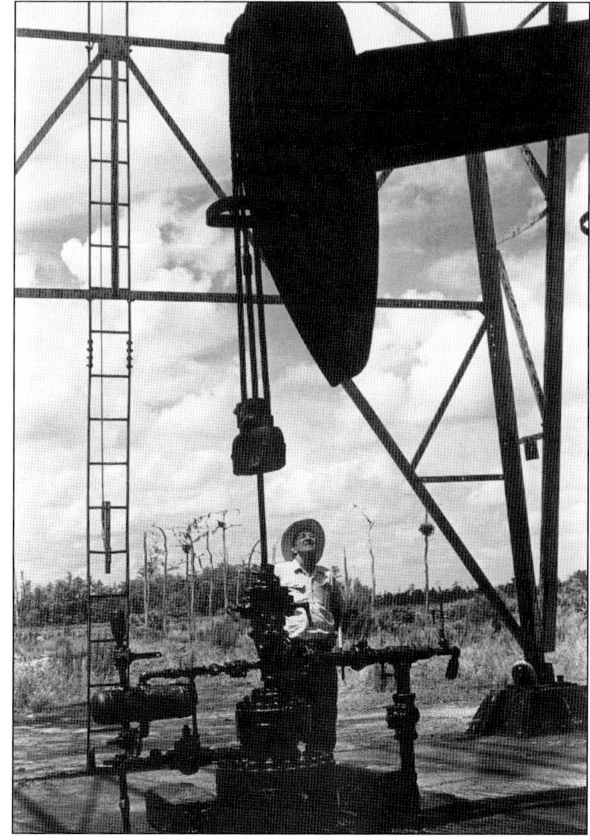

The sedimentary limestone below the Big Cypress Swamp extends downward for almost three miles. In 1943, oil was found south of Immokalee at Sunniland Field. A pumpjack is seen here. The petroleum derives from marine algae living in tidal shoals and on reefs during the Cretaceous Period, over 100 million years ago. The reservoir of gas and oil is about two miles below the swamp's surface. (SLAF.)

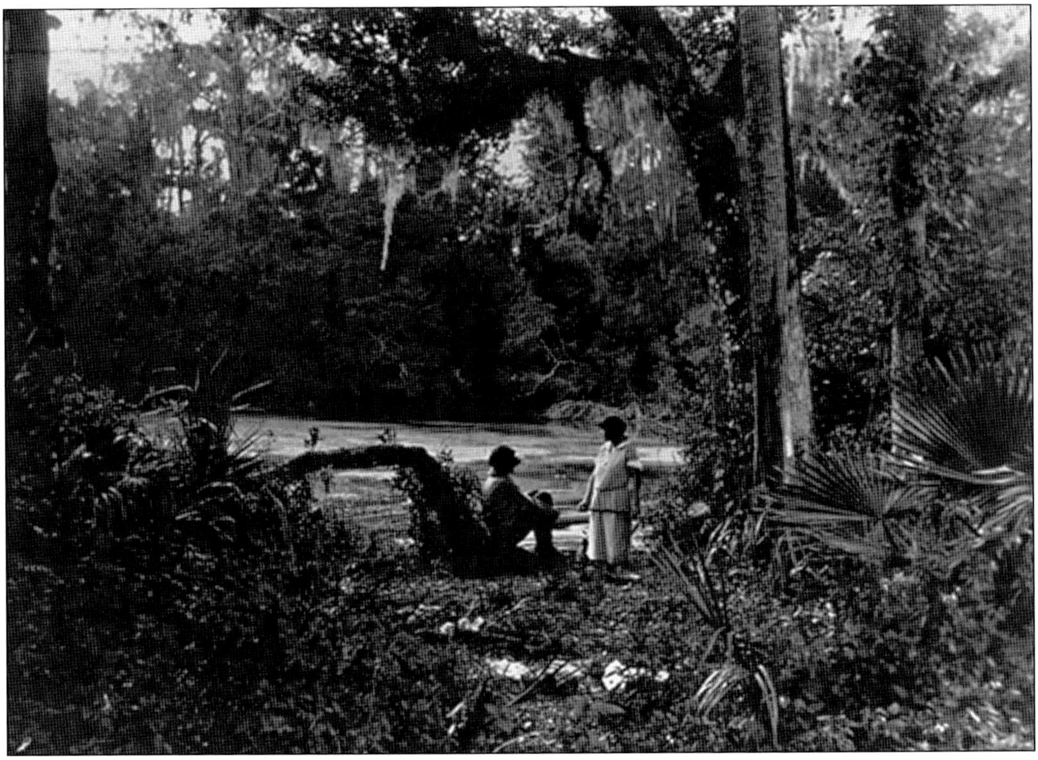

Deep Lake (shown here around 1905) and its high, fertile hammock and pineland were historically a home for Seminoles and a site of Big Cypress's early agriculture. At 90 feet, it is by far the deepest lake in South Florida; nearby Tarpon Lake is 60 feet deep. Such lakes formed by rainfall eroding the rock when sea levels were much lower, creating Big Cypress's current karst topography. (SFCMC.)

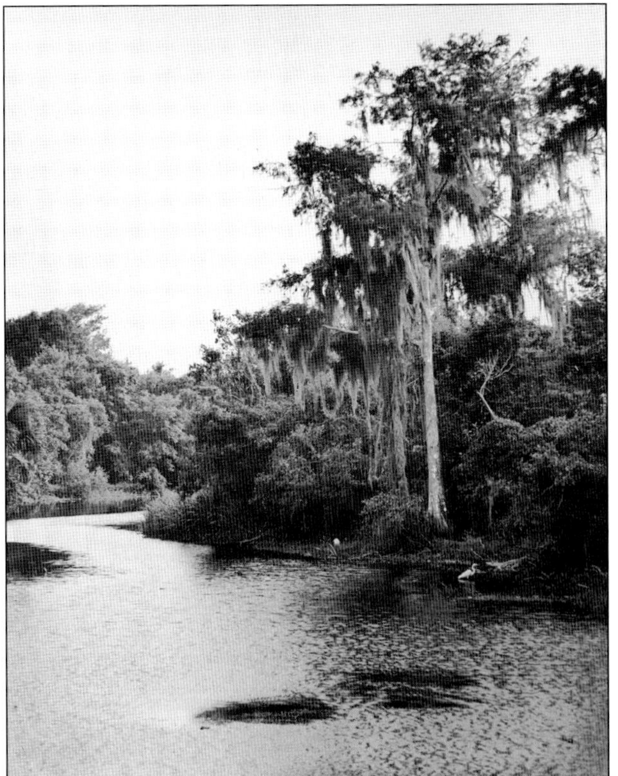

Water is the lifeblood of the Big Cypress Swamp. Its waters flow to the southern Everglades and Everglades National Park and to its estuaries. This image shows Turner River, one of Big Cypress's distributary rivers, in 1939. Over 50 inches of rain fall annually, 70 percent in the wet season. Terrestrial and aquatic plants and animals found there must adapt to swamp living, as must humans. (OPN.)

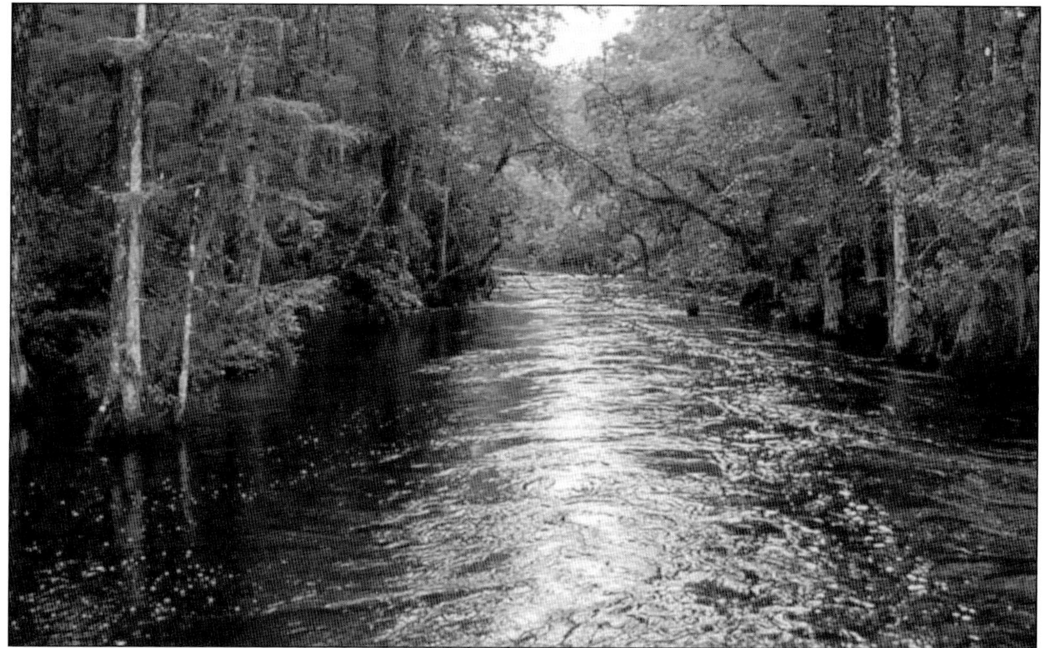

From before the time of the Calusa, the Cypress has experienced its cycle of wet and dry seasons, as illustrated here by the Sweetwater Strand in the two seasons. The spring-summer rainy season brings afternoon thundershowers and, less frequently, tropical storms, which repeatedly have destroyed homes and farms but renew the swamp. Through the wet season, water is relatively deep and moves downgradient and through sloughs, as seen above. Through the winter-spring dry season, water depths decline. Water movement decreases and then ceases (below). Toward the end, water may remain only in the deepest ponds. Some years are wetter; some are drier. In drought years, much of the swamp may be without surface water for months. (Both, SFCMC.)

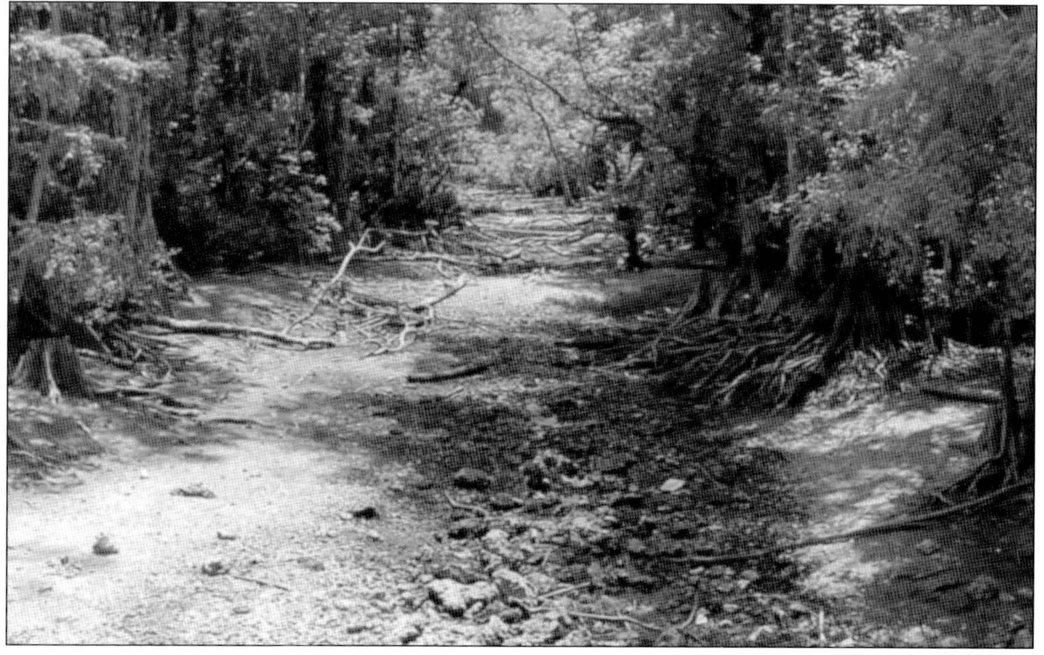

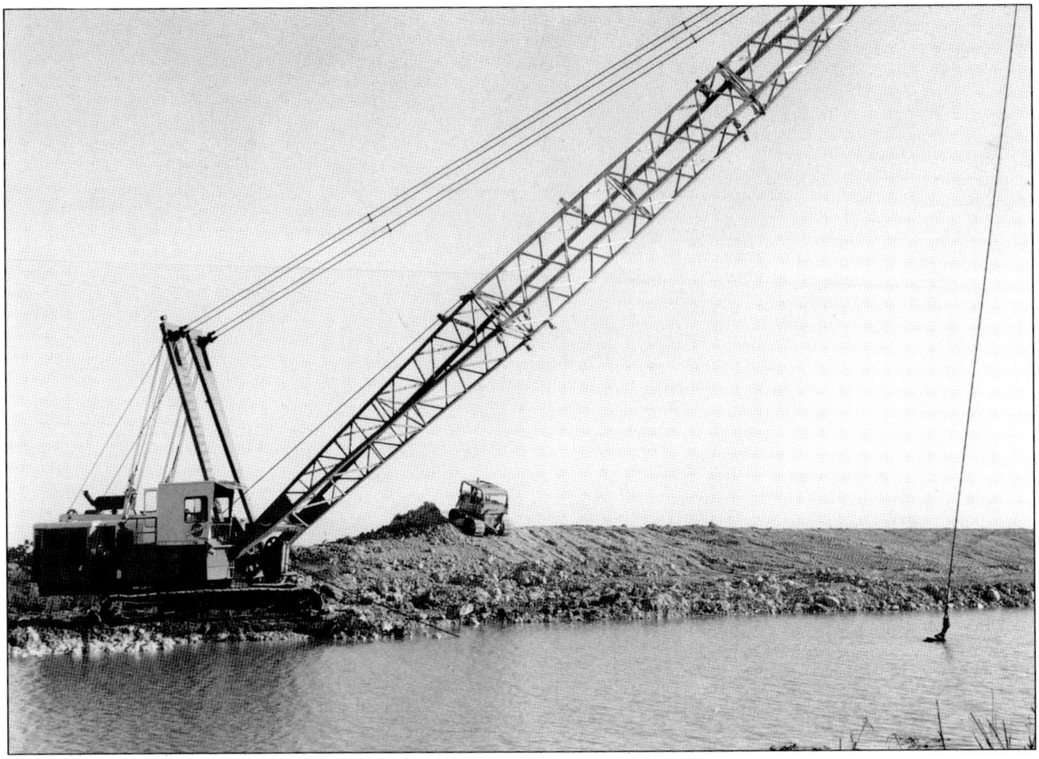

Most of Big Cypress's water comes from rain over the swamp, where it remains, drains below ground, or, when high enough, moves slowly downgradient. However, canals and attendant levees altered historic hydrology patterns in some of the Big Cypress by the early 19th century, as pictured above. Whether to provide land for development, beds for roads, or water management, canals diverted, controlled, and usually accelerated natural water flows. Water management levees purposely intercepted and directed flows, including from the Big Cypress to the Everglades. Others were dug to drain the swamp, affecting freshwater flows to the estuary. Below, canals provided access to the swamp and its fish and wildlife that would have been difficult, if not impossible, before. Due to drainage and levees, depending on location and year, wet seasons might be deeper and dry seasons drier. (Above, OPN; below, SLAF.)

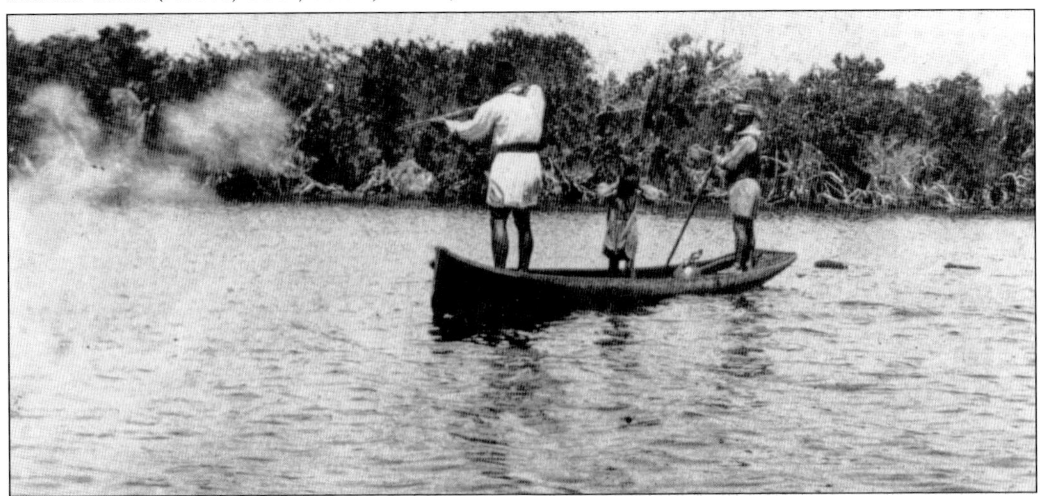

Two

Living with the Swamp

Indigenous Peoples and Early Settlers

By 15,000 years ago, nomadic Paleo-Indian hunters inhabited a dry South Florida. As Pleistocene megafauna went extinct and the climate grew generally wetter, people classified by archeologists as Archaic cultures settled into coastal and inland villages as wet-dry climate cycles fluctuated. About 5,000 years ago, South Florida's great wetlands started developing, as did tree islands, serving as permanent and temporary village sites. From 500 CE, people of the Big Cypress region, now identified as the Glades culture, lived in mound-based settlements at Turner River, Chokoloskee, and Marco and inland around Lake Okeechobee. They used inland swamps for resource harvesting. In the 1500s, the Spanish named chiefdoms and places, Calusa to the north of the Big Cypress, Muspa in the Ten Thousand Islands (by then absorbed into Calusa culture), and Tequesta in the eastern and southern Big Cypress eastward across the Everglades.

Although the people held off total Spanish domination for a century, in the 1600s, populations and social cohesiveness diminished. Survivors coalesced against English-enticed Creek slavers, moved southward, or assimilated with Cuban fishers. In the 1700s to early 1800s, Miccosukee-speaking people and those of the Muskogee Confederation chose to move into essentially vacant northern Florida. By the 1760s, these diverse Florida Indians were collectively called Seminoles in English. Once Spain ceded Florida in 1821, the United States commenced its Indian removal policy. Years of war followed, first in the north and then ever deeper south. By most accounts, fewer than a thousand Seminoles remained in 1858, with many isolating in the Cypress and Everglades.

During and after the Civil War, American settlers began occupying the coast. Meanwhile, Seminoles had adapted to swamp living, settling on tree islands. Pioneer life included fishing, hunting, farming, distilling, and smuggling. Starting in the 1870s, trading posts developed, and Seminoles slowly rejoined the economy. Settlements developed at Chokoloskee, Halfway Creek, Turner River, and Allen's Place (later Everglades City). The pioneer lifestyle became increasingly unsustainable due to soil and game depletion, exploitative commercial fishing, game laws protecting plume birds, and the regulation of other hunting. The 1910 hurricane destroyed homesites and salted fields. World War I, Prohibition, and the Depression followed, ending the pioneer era.

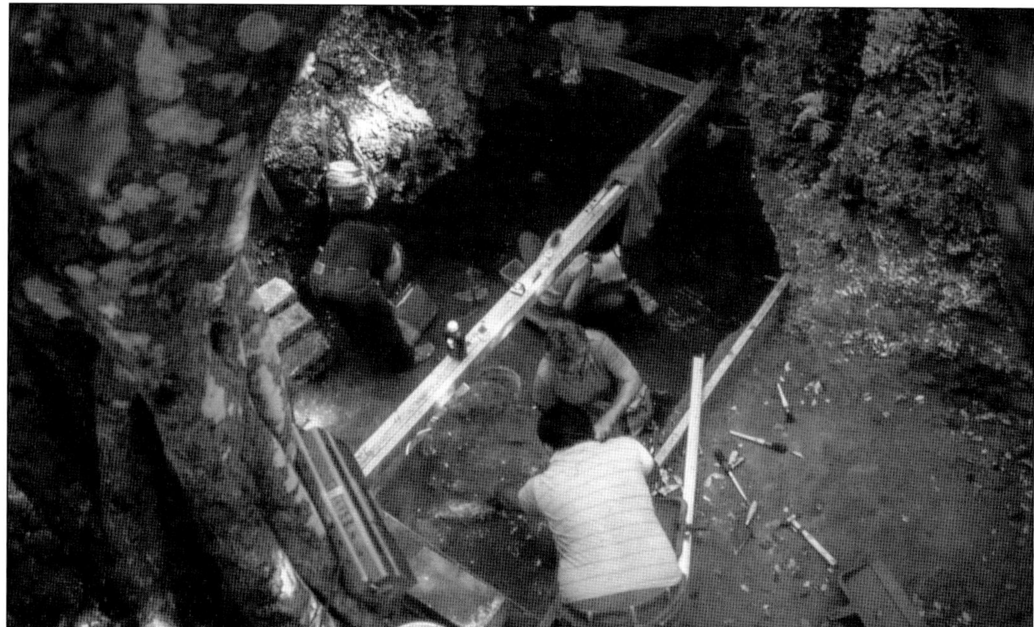

People lived in South Florida over 10,000 years ago, although local evidence of mobile, big-game-hunting Paleo-Indians is slim; half their range is submerged under the Gulf and mobile camps preserved poorly. A solution hole near Miami (pictured) revealed human evidence with Pleistocene megafauna—bison, camels, dire wolves, mastodons, and saber-toothed cats. As the sea level rose, the climate became wetter, megafauna disappeared, wetlands developed, and people gathered in settlements. (HMM.)

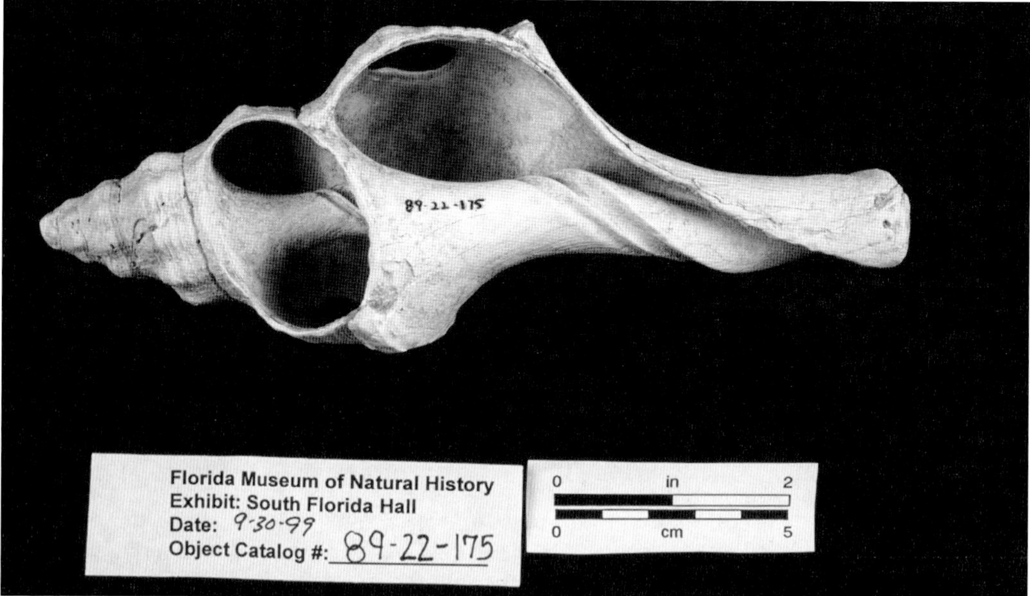

By 5,000 years ago, the climate had become similar to that of recent periods, although it was experiencing multi-decadal-long rainfall variation. People of the Archaic period created settlements along the coast and on inland tree islands. Horr's Island at Marco is a 6,700-year-old settlement on shell mounds, including a shell-outlined ceremonial ground—the largest known town of the Archaic people in South Florida. This conch shell hammer from the island is from 1100–1300 CE. (FLMNH.)

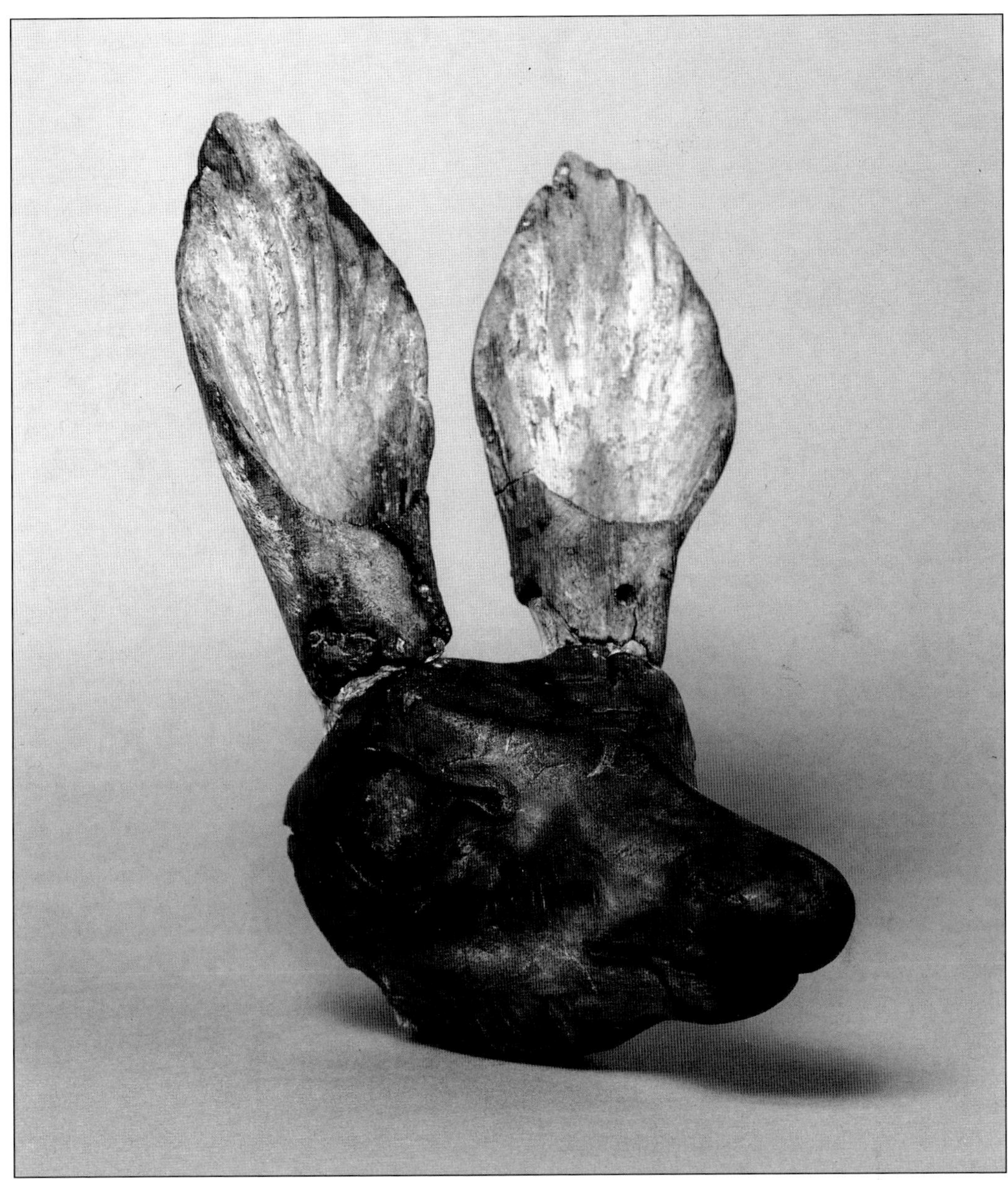

By 2,500 years ago, the Late Archaic people of southwest Florida were a well-settled hunting-gathering-fishing culture using shell, bone, wood, and ceramics. Permanent sites featured elevated residential, ceremonial, and burial mounds. Mounds and tree islands supported temporary and permanent camps and villages. For example, a town near the mouth of Turner River encompassed 30 acres of constructed shell mounds successively used over time. Mounds continued upriver just past today's Tamiami Trail. Black Hills mounds on the Barron River were made of shell and black dirt. Farther inland, Bear Island mounds were sand. Over 450 archeological sites are identified within the Big Cypress National Preserve. By 500 CE, the regional Glades cultures included the Indigenous Muspa and Calusa people in the western Big Cypress and Tequesta in the eastern. Chokoloskee and Marco were examples of large settlements. In 1896, a Pre-Calusa site on Marco built on stilts yielded the famous Key Marco cat and wooden deer figurehead (pictured). (UPENN.)

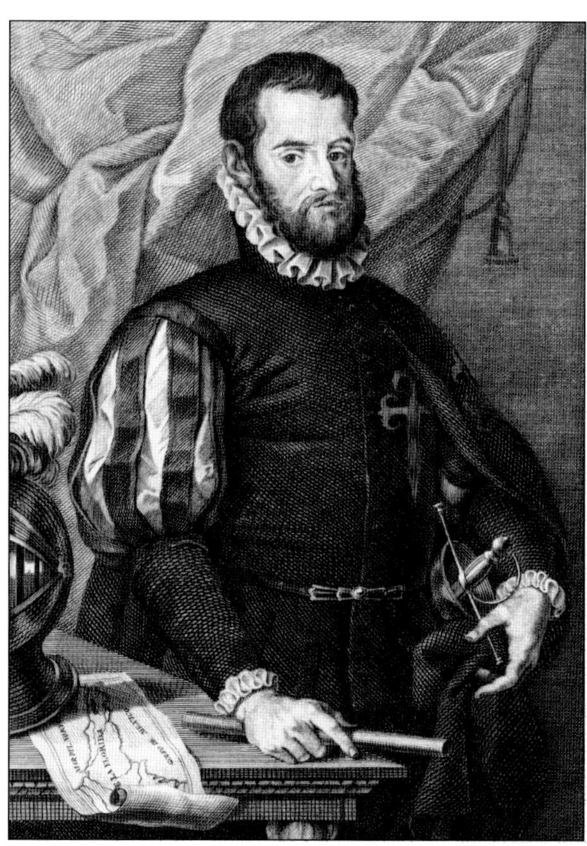

By the 1300s, Muspa and Tequesta were Calusa tributaries. The Calusa people defeated Juan Ponce de Leon's 1521 colonization attempt and later politically managed Pedro Menendez's (pictured) 1566 diplomatic incursions. Southwest Florida's people maintained their identity and autonomy within Spanish Florida for over 100 years, but in the 1600s, colonial disruption, disease, both northward and southward emigration, and slavers reduced their populations. The Muspa chief actually moved to Cuba in 1711. (LOC.)

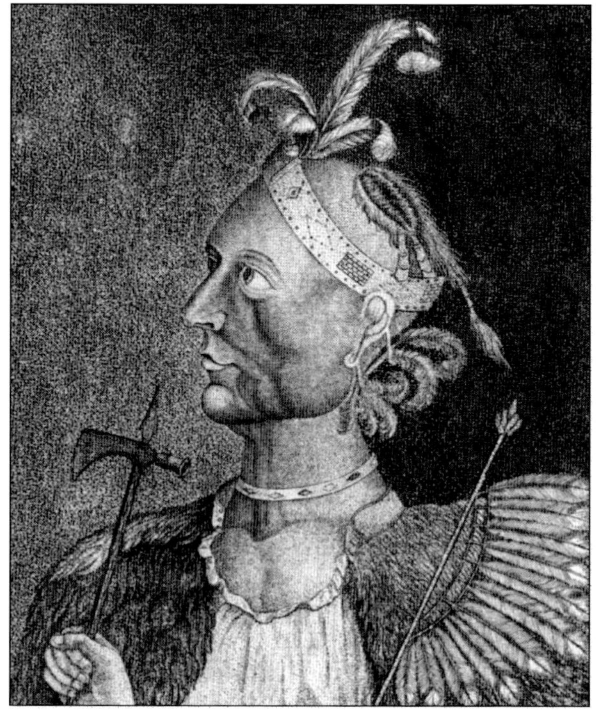

Remnants remained scattered in South Florida's swamps, gathered for protection, and over time amalgamated with other Native Americans and Cuban fishing communities. Meanwhile, diverse people, including Miccosukee-speaking Oconee people, moved into north Florida, unoccupied and abandoned by Spanish authorities. Deer-hunting parties soon ranged as far as Big Cypress. In the 1700s, leaders Ahaya (Cowkeeper) and Mico Chlucco (Long Warrior), seen here, achieved international fame through the writings of William Bartram. (LOC.)

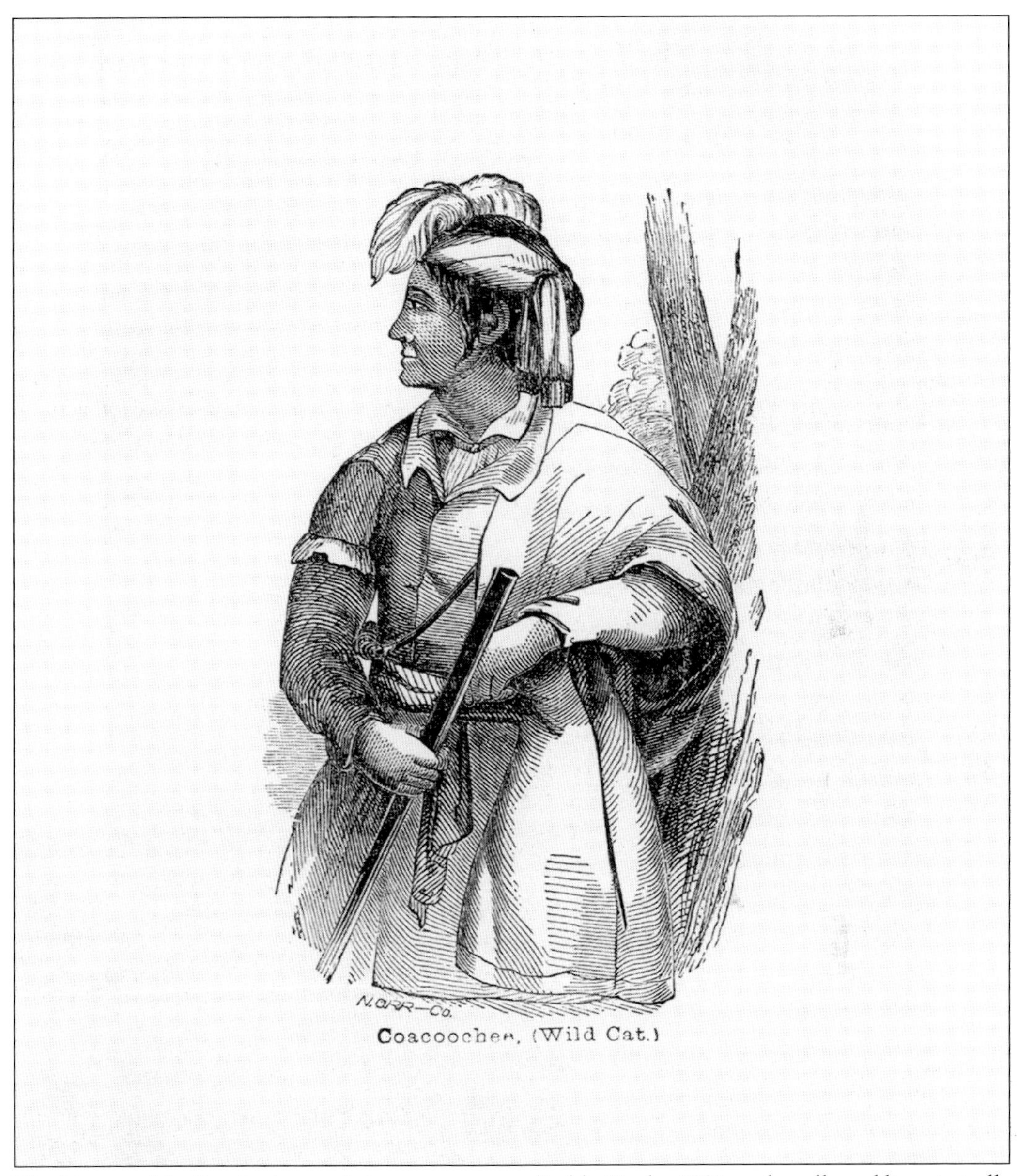

The history of the Seminole people is not very generalizable. By the 1760s, culturally and linguistically diverse Florida Indians coalesced into a people that came to be referred to in English as Seminoles. Additional Muskogean-speaking people joined earlier immigrants following the 1814 Red Stick War. They continued to engage in the colonial economy, trading corn, rice, cattle, and leather, and in the global economy for deerskins and plumes. American militia and then the Army, aided by other Creeks, invaded the north Florida Indian and allied Black communities in 1817. The US government pursued Indian removal, Seminoles resisted, war erupted in 1835, and survivors shifted southward. After the Battle of Okeechobee, Coacoochee (Wildcat), seen here, withdrew into the Big Cypress. Pursuing, the Army established Fort Keais, Fort Harrell, and other fortifications; temporary depots; camps; and trails through the Big Cypress. Patrols penetrated deeply, destroying homes and gardens. Hostilities ended in 1842; Coacoochee accepted exile. Over 6,000 Seminoles were exiled or killed; almost 1,500 troops died. (NYPL.)

Only a low number of Seminoles were left. The 1839 Macomb Truce designated a homeland of 2.5 million acres in southwest Florida, but American intrusions in the reserved lands caused war to erupt again in the Big Cypress. Holata Micco (Billy Bowlegs, pictured) led resistance as he had done throughout the previous warfare. But persistent Army patrols attacked known homesites and fields, including at Deep Lake and Royal Palm. (NPG.)

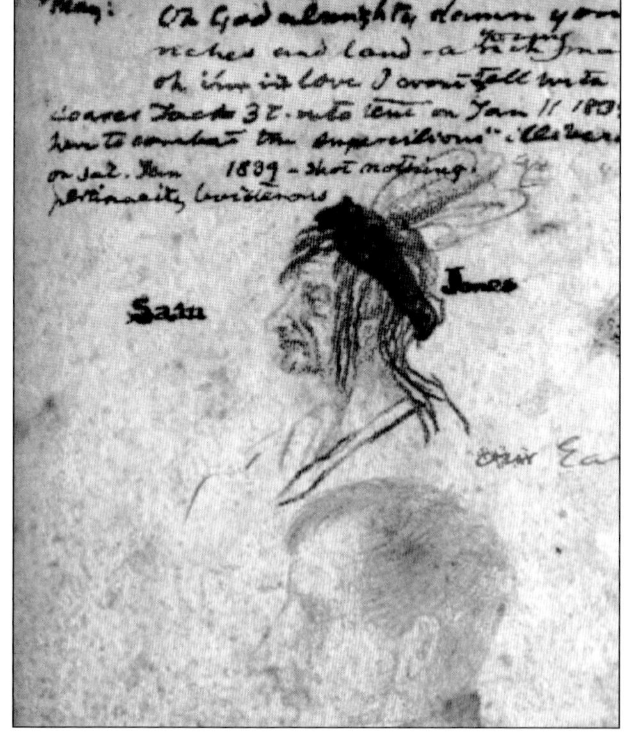

After Holata Micco's surrender in 1858, Abiaka (Sam Jones), who had led his people from the eastern Everglades to the Big Cypress, and about 100 others refused to go. This sketch is from Army assistant surgeon Ellis Hughes's diary. Avoiding contact with Whites for several decades (officially with the government for nearly a century), they created a family-camp-based swamp culture, revived traditional activities, and resisted imposed efforts toward assimilation. (USF.)

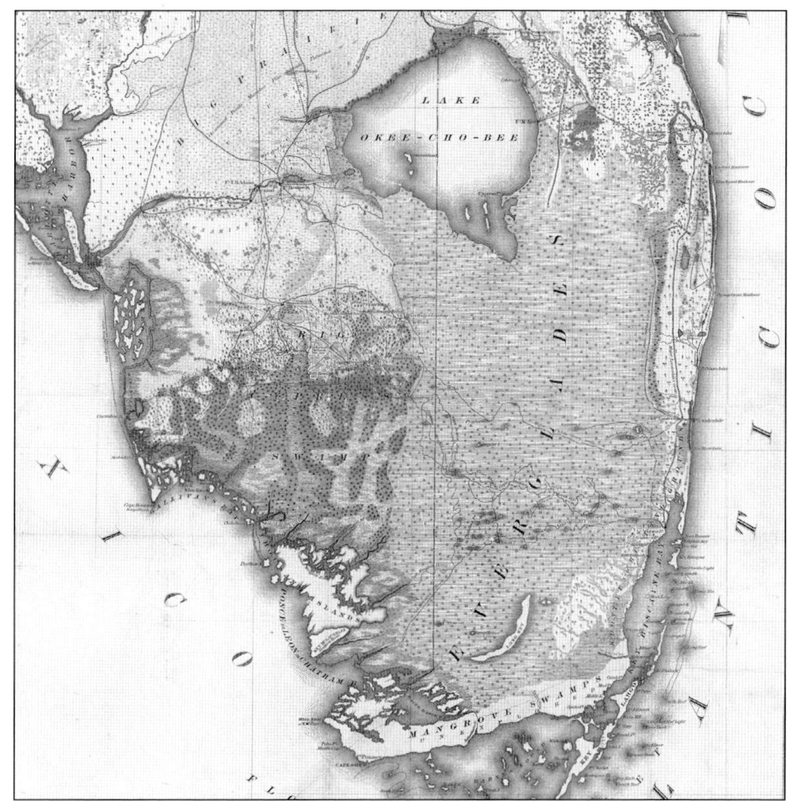

In the last engagement of the war, Capt. John Parkhill followed Turner River into the Fakahatchee, where he was killed—he gets a statue at the state capitol. The Army learned much. By 1856, a synthesis map provided clear descriptions of the Big Cypress Swamp and trails (pictured). Soldier Albert Canova wrote that the Big Cypress islands were as fertile as the Nile. No longer was the Cypress unknown. (USNA.)

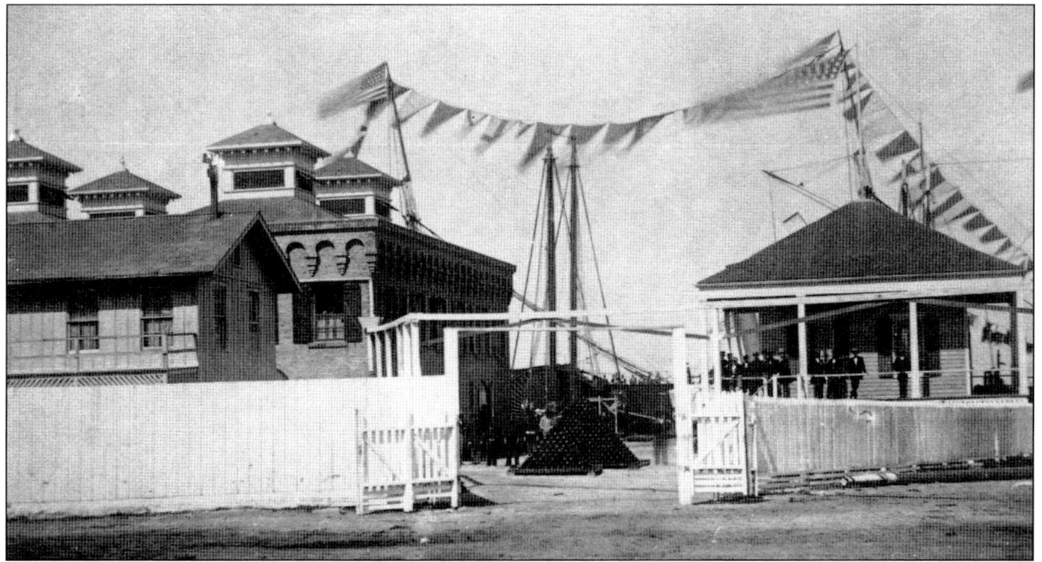

During the Civil War, Key West remained under Union control (the Naval headquarters are seen here in 1865) and needed food. Dick Turner, Captain Parkhill's guide, returned to farm the ancient mounds, giving Turner River its name. John Weeks, William A. Smith, then Charles W. Hendry, and in 1873, Key West mayor William Smith Allen established farms along what became the Allen River, the location becoming known as Allen's Place. (MCPL.)

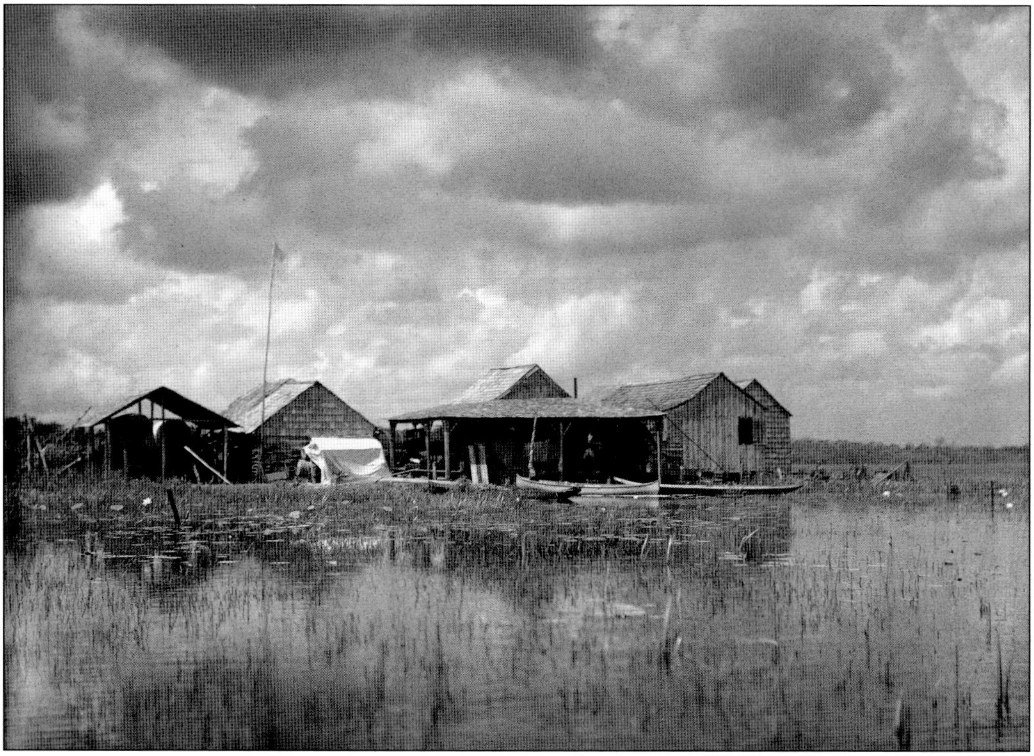

Sugarcane, winter vegetables, plumes, pelts, and hides needed market access; people needed goods. In a cashless society, trading posts met the demand. In 1885, English ship-deserter, self-renamed William H. Brown, built Boat Landing for canoe access east of Immokalee, trading for plumes and alligator hides by the thousands. He sold out to the Episcopal Church in 1908; missionary doctor Edwin Goodhand took over, the place becoming called Godden's Landing. (AMNH.)

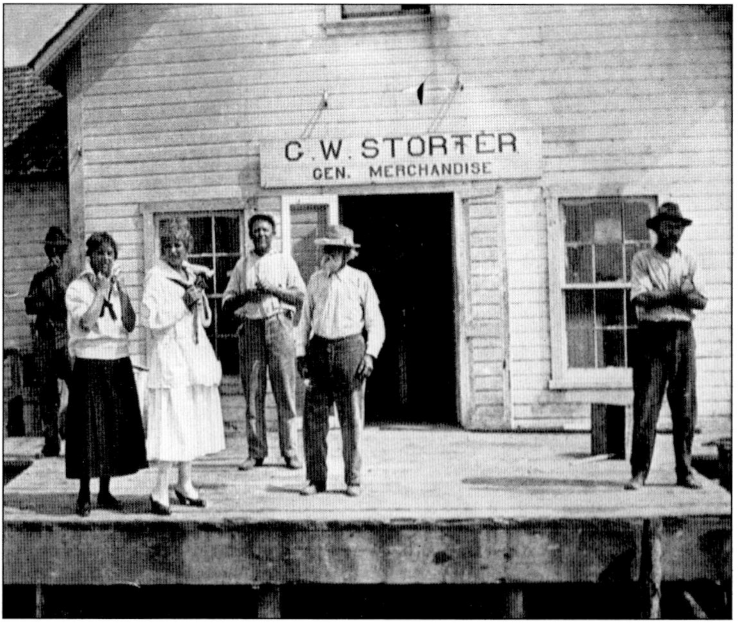

Bill Collier established a trading post at Marco. Joe Wiggins's posts were successively at Wiggins Pass, Allen River, and Broad River. He also farmed the black dirt mounds. George Storter Jr. purchased William Allen's farm and built his post (pictured), which became a long-lived gathering spot; the town became Everglades City. Storter produced sugarcane and syrup and provided maritime transport services, including mail. Others farmed Halfway Creek. (SLAF.)

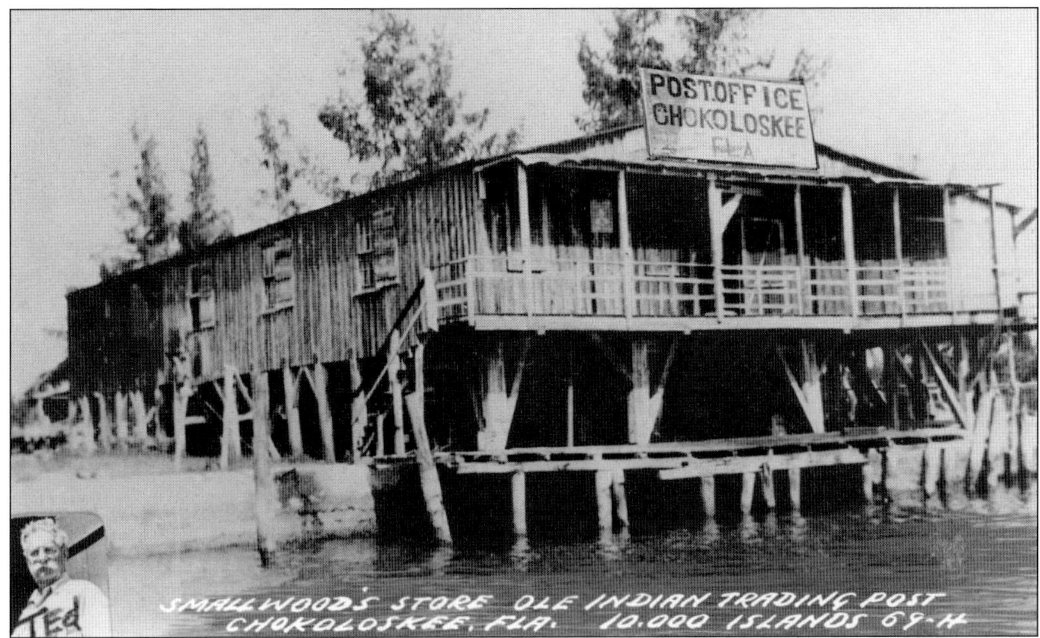

Key West's Santini family settled on Chokoloskee, farmed, fished, caught turtles, and operated boat services. In the late 1880s, C.G. McKinney opened a store, farmed, and in later years wrote amusingly for the newspaper. Ted Smallwood bought Santini's claim, opening a trading post at his house, later in a still-remaining building (pictured). Vegetables, syrup, tropical fruit, hides, plumes, turtles, salted fish, and charcoal were transported by boat and sold in Key West. (CCM.)

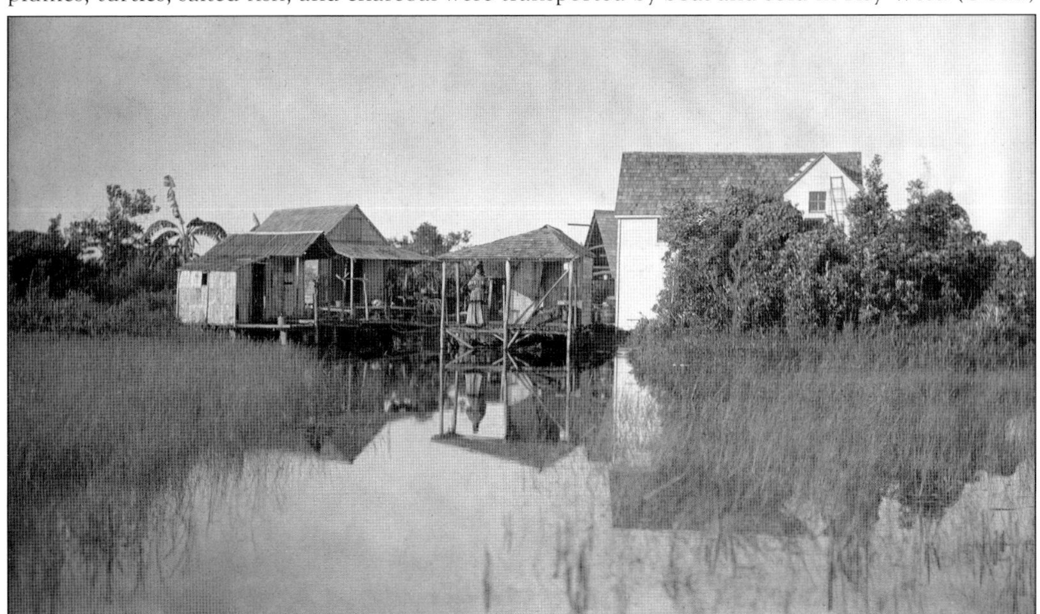

Charlie Tigertail built a trading post in the southern Big Cypress, convenient for local Indian families but hard to get to from the coast. He constructed sturdy board buildings (pictured) and partnered with Ted Smallwood, becoming somewhat famous. A.W. Dimock featured his store in his novel *Dick in the Everglades*. Seminoles increasingly visited trading posts for necessary supplies such as bullets, cornmeal, and cloth. (AMNH.)

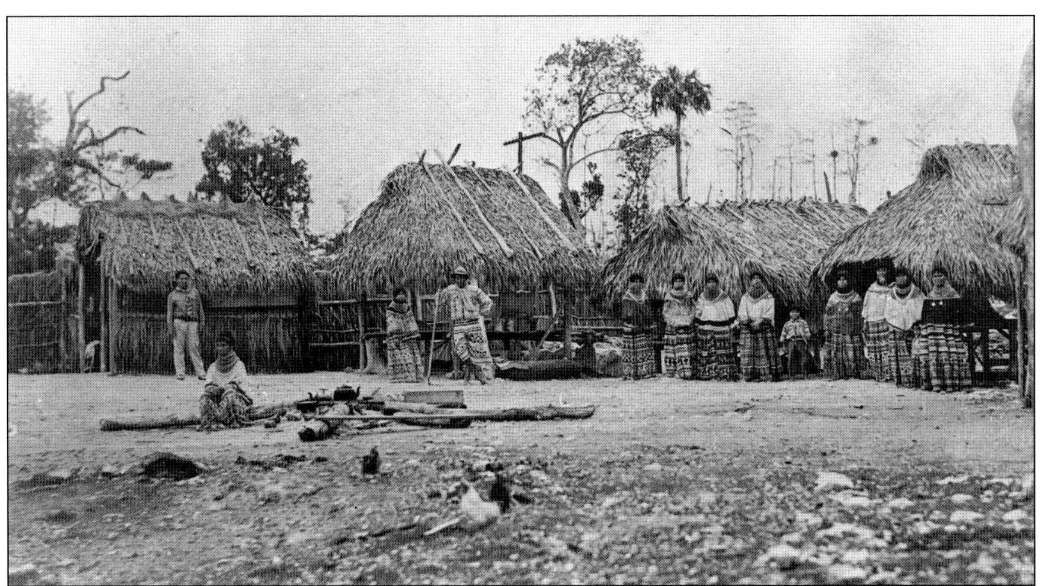

Seminoles lived in maternally based settlements, often on swamp tree islands. Their characteristic buildings, chickees, were palm-thatched, sometimes wall-less cabins, on pond-cypress poles (above). This wartime design, rapidly built from on-site materials, proved well-adapted and persistent. Camp could be moved quickly if discovered or a death occurred. Different chickees were for cooking, storage, eating, or sleeping. Storage was in rafters, and sleeping was on an elevated shelf. Fire was kept going at the tips of radiating logs (below). Food included fry bread, corn, game, turtle, gar, wild fruits and sofkee, a soup or porridge traditional in southeastern cultures made from ground corn, later cornmeal from trading posts. Some Seminoles settled on reservation land near Lake Okeechobee and eastern Everglades pinewoods. People living in the southern Big Cypress tended to live more independently and traditionally, beginning political separation among Seminoles. (Both, SLAF.)

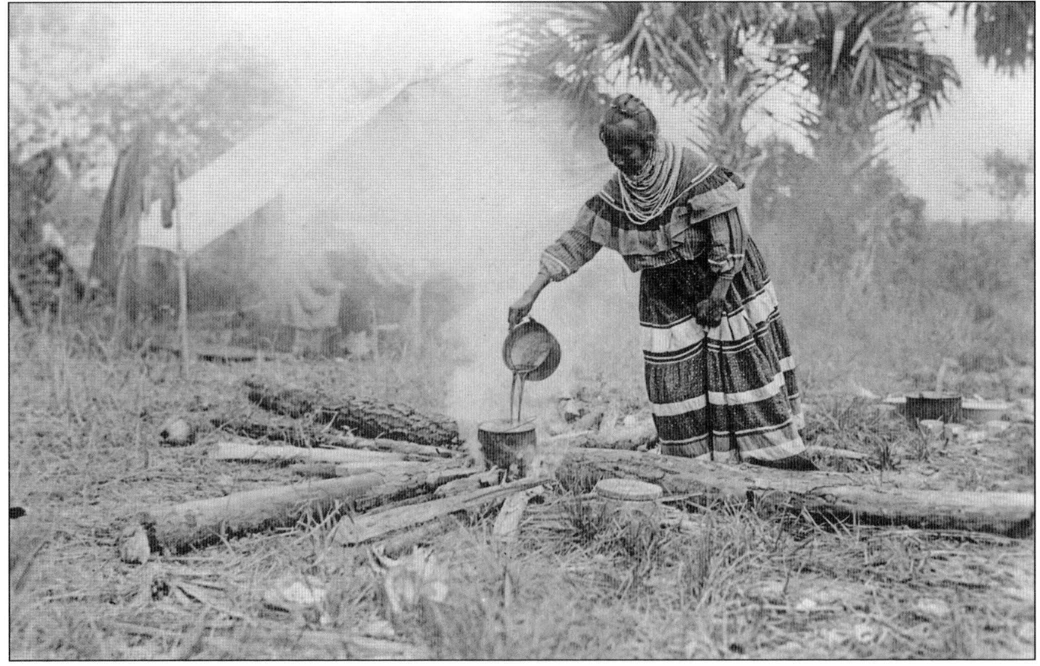

Canoes provided transportation. Tree island camps were located adjacent to deeper drainageways for wet-season canoe travel. Canoe-making techniques were not very different from those of the ancestral Calusa. Cypress logs were rough-hewn into shape, buried in mud for up to two years, dried, and hollowed out by burning and scraping to the correct thickness, determined by tapping sounds. The sharp bow parted thick vegetation. A rockered stern improved turning maneuverability, although dugouts—some 15 or more feet long—went better straight down the marsh than tightly turning. The aft overhang provided a platform for poling (right). Paddles were not used and sails infrequently. Dugouts were used for fishing, hunting, moving camp, hauling trade goods, and carrying family (below). (Both, SLAF.)

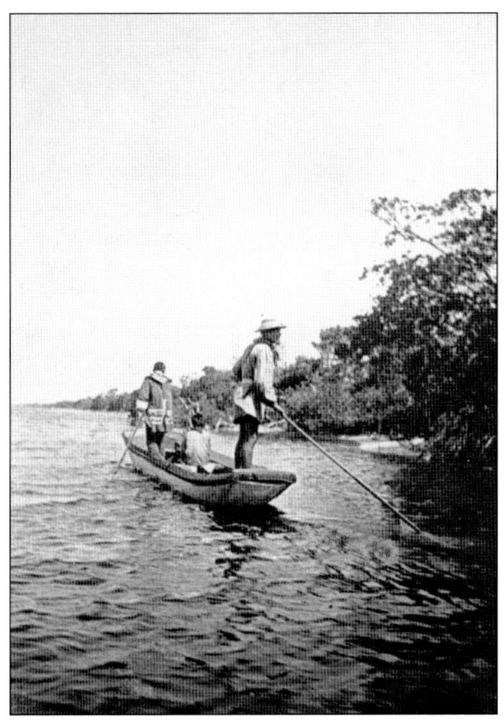

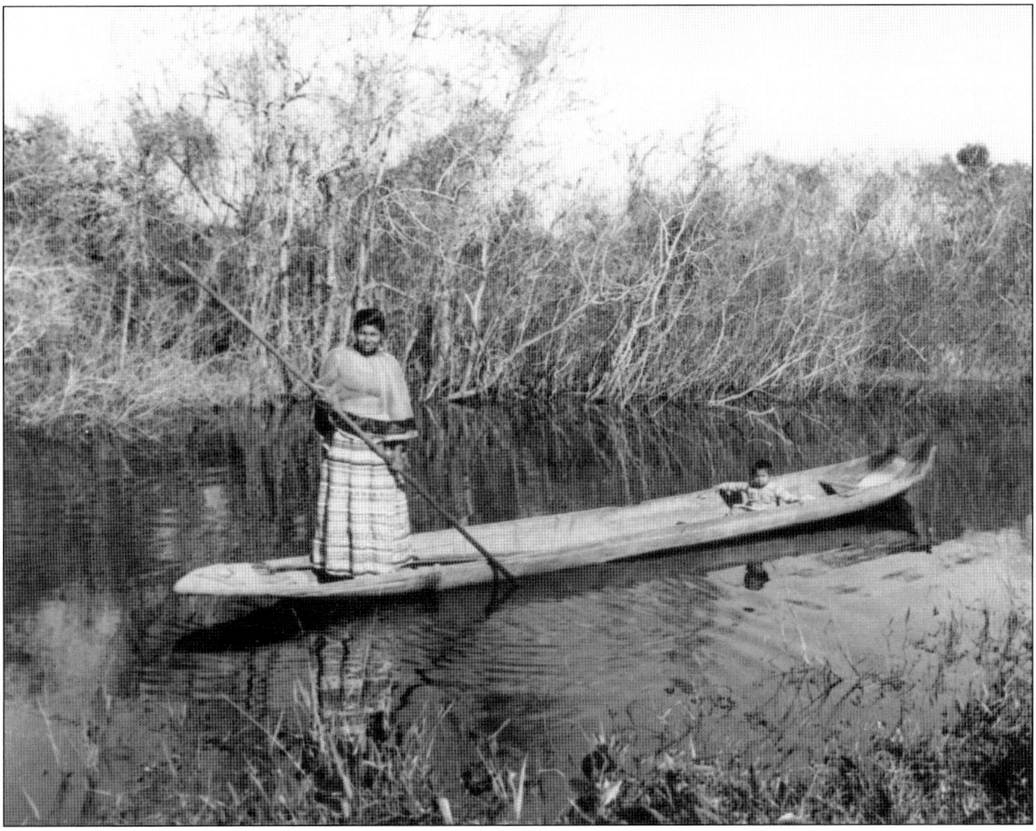

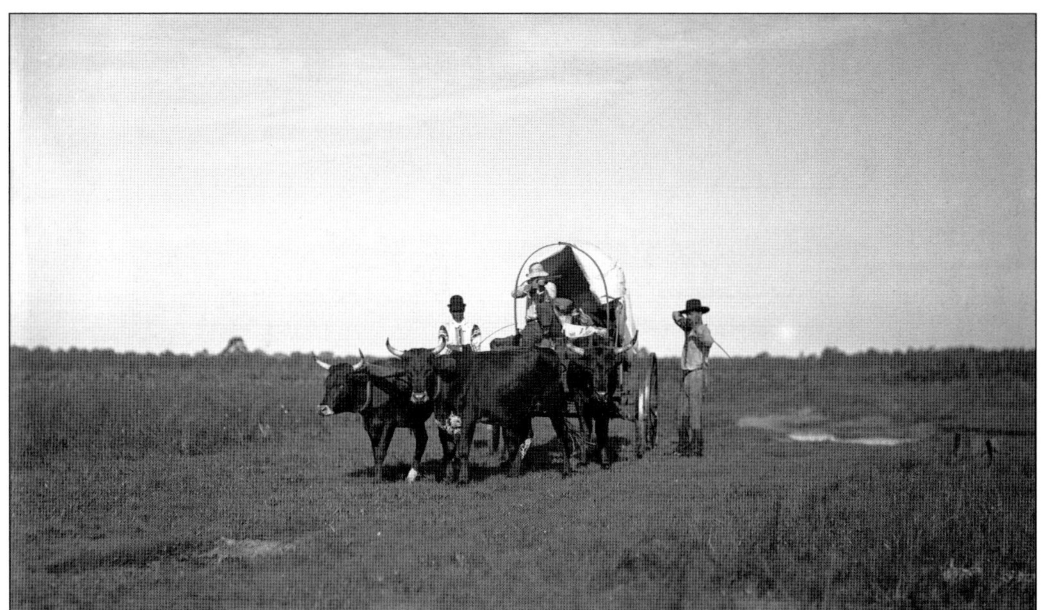

Much of the northern Big Cypress is prairie land. In the dry season, the sandy soil dries out, to an extent, allowing use of oxen-drawn carts (pictured), especially between Fort Myers and Immokalee and then southward. This was also a country for special horses and cattle. Swamp-adapted marsh tacky horses and Andalusian-derived cracker cattle spawned a free-range cattle industry critical to the southern Civil War effort and later for trade to Cuba. (AMNH.)

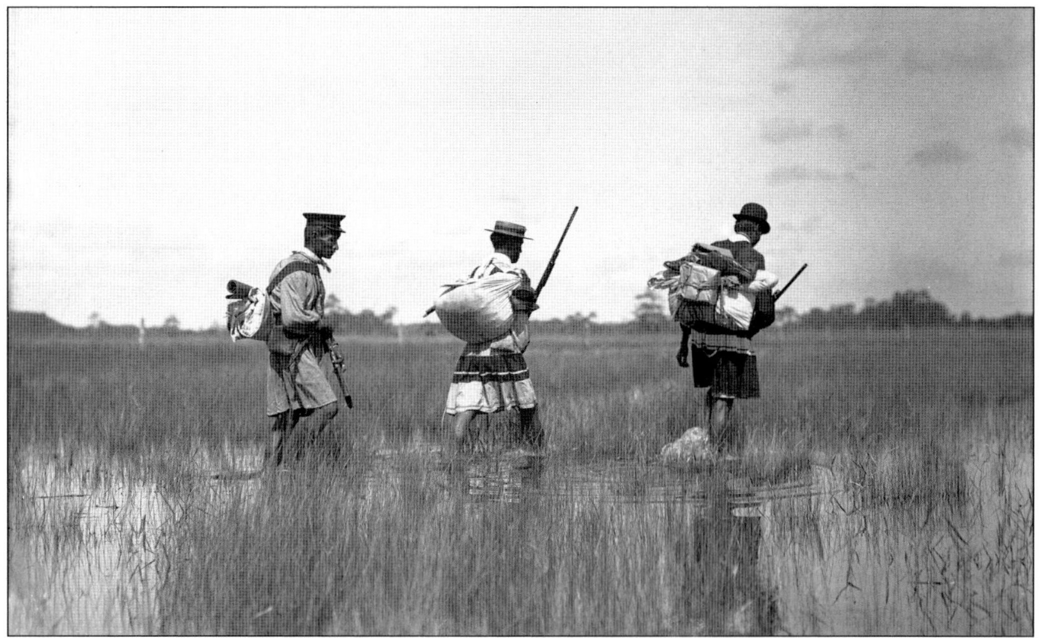

Walking was a primary way to get about the Big Cypress, whether in the dry season or wet. Great distances were hiked in moving among camps, settlements, trading posts, and hunting grounds. This 1910 image shows Seminoles leaving Boat Landing with their traded goods. Trips of 40 miles were regularly recorded, camping along the way. Hunters on foot sought deer, turkey, squirrels, raccoons, and alligators for food and for trade. (AMNH.)

Seminoles developed hammock horticulture on tree islands securely away from residential islands and hidden behind a privacy wall of shrubs and vines. Crops, jumbled together within limited space, included corn, beans, sweet potato, papaya, banana, citrus, and sugarcane. Seminole pumpkin (*chassa howitska*), a unique long-storage winter squash cultivar, vined into trees. Native plants—coontie root, fruit and heart of palm, cocoplum, and other fruit—were collected as available. (AMNH.)

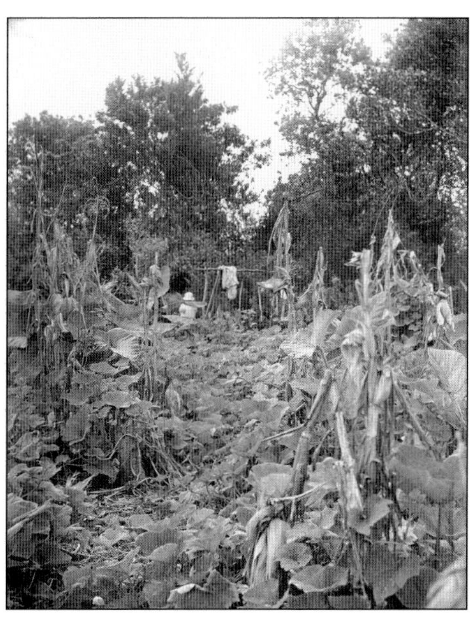

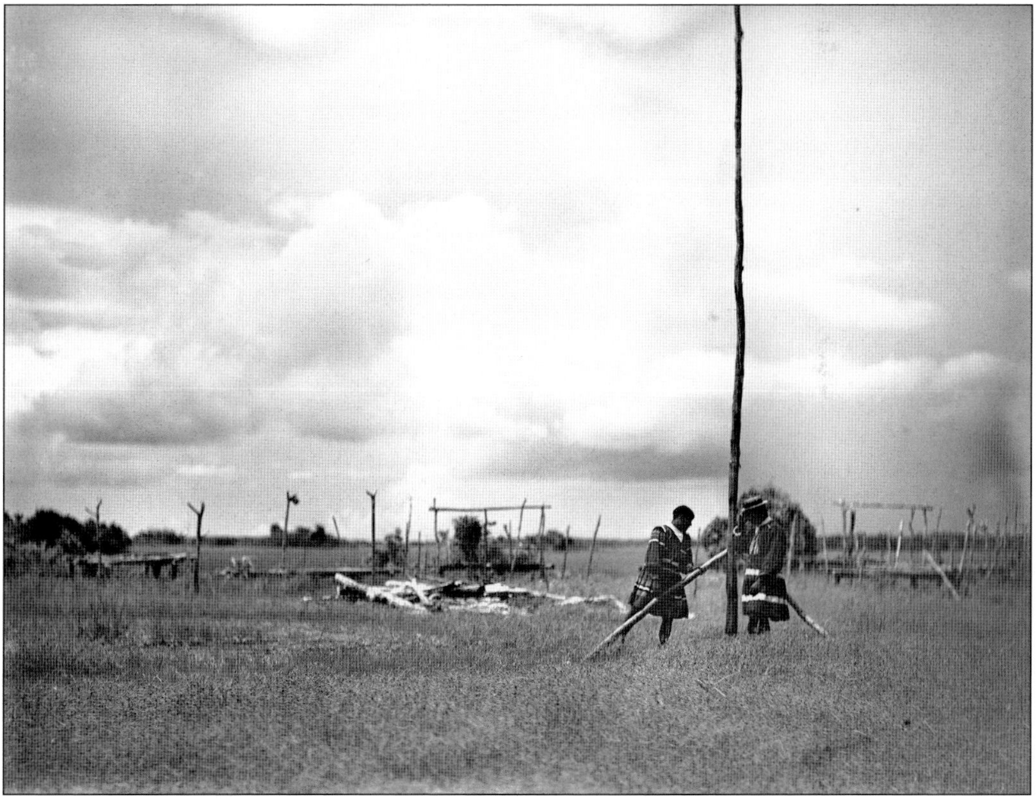

Tribal festivals were a central aspect of Seminole and more broadly of Mississippian culture, the annual Green Corn Dance being fundamental. Held at special, private sites in the Big Cypress, clans gathered to build shelters; create the year's ceremonial fire; celebrate the new year; stomp dance with leg rattles (historically box turtle shells and palmetto berries); and conduct purification, manhood, and judicial rites. This image shows preparing the site. (AMNH.)

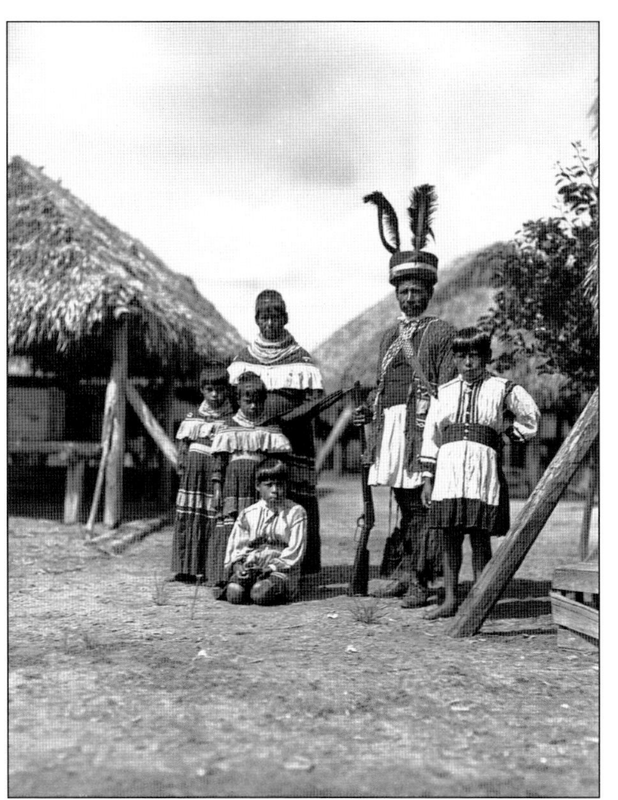

Seminole clothing evolved, taking a quantum leap when hand-operated sewing machines and calico became available at trading posts. Clothing styles were always highly decorative. The image at left shows Little Billy Conapatchie and his family dressed up for ethnographic expedition photographer Julian Dimock in 1910. Little Billy's wife shows her typical-for-the-time tower of beaded necklaces (collected from birth); floor-length, waist-high skirt; and cape, under which was a long-sleeved blouse. A.W. Dimock noted the region between the blouse and skirt was neglected. Women's hairstyles evolved over the decades. Men dressed formally wore a decorated turban, the longshirt (which evolved into the Seminole jacket), sashes, a belt, and leggings. The image below, from 1905, shows a feathered derby hat instead of a turban. The patchwork designs that developed are unique to Miccosukees and Seminoles. (Both, AMNH.)

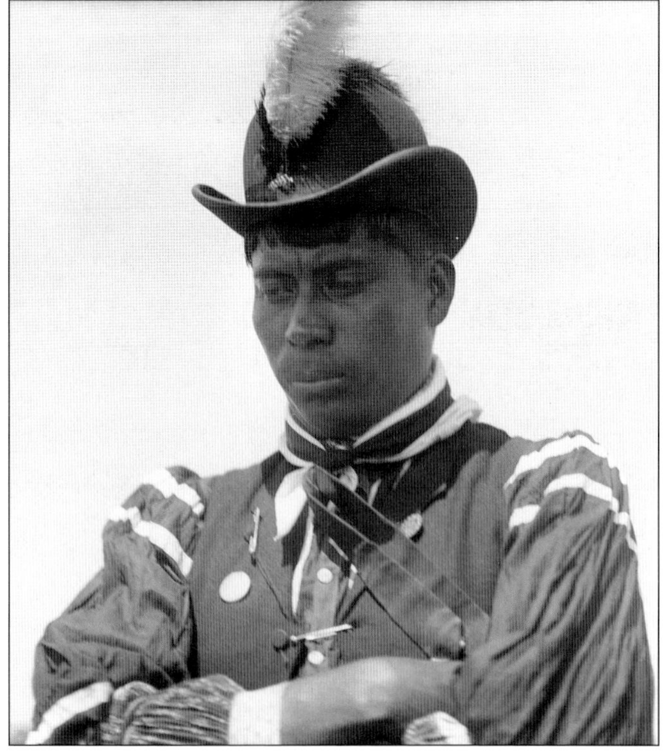

Pioneers came and went, only a few making it into recorded history. One of the authors' favorites was Ed Brewer, an outlaw, moonshiner, liquor purveyor to Indians, guide to Hugh Willoughby's Everglades crossing, and a failure in capturing Edgar Watson. People like Brewer did what they needed to in order to survive, market hunting being nearly universal. The most remunerative were egret plumes; the most reliable, alligator hides—and moonshine. (KH.)

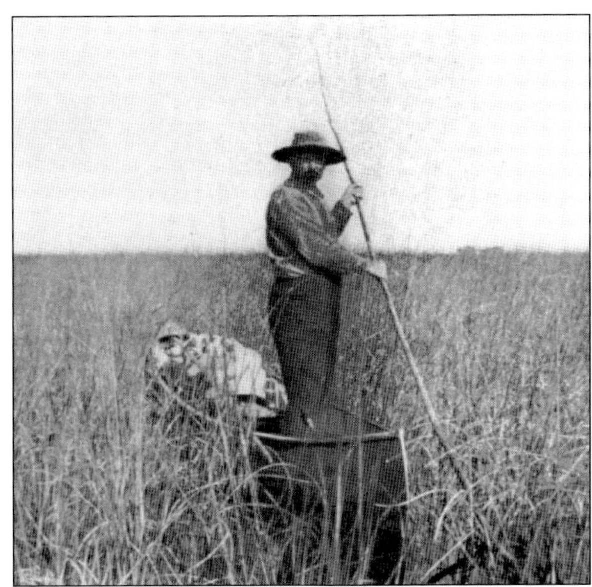

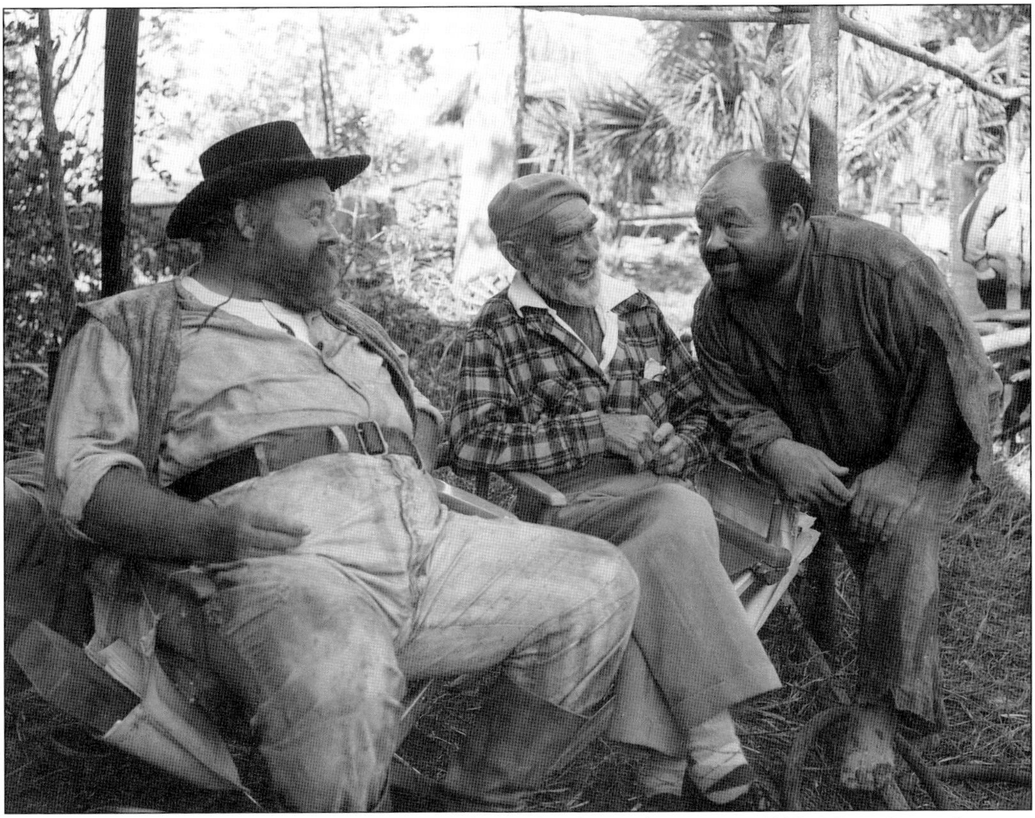

Hunting for valuable egret plumes devastated waterbird populations. In 1912, Rhett Green became warden for the miles-long Corkscrew rookery. Big Cypress plume hunting featured in the 1958 movie *Wind Across the Everglades*; Burl Ives (shown at left) was the plumer Cottonmouth. French plume hunter Jean Chevalier (called "Old Frenchman") also collected for museums. He was famous as a neighbor to an unfriendly Edgar Watson and for a namesake bay. (SLAF.)

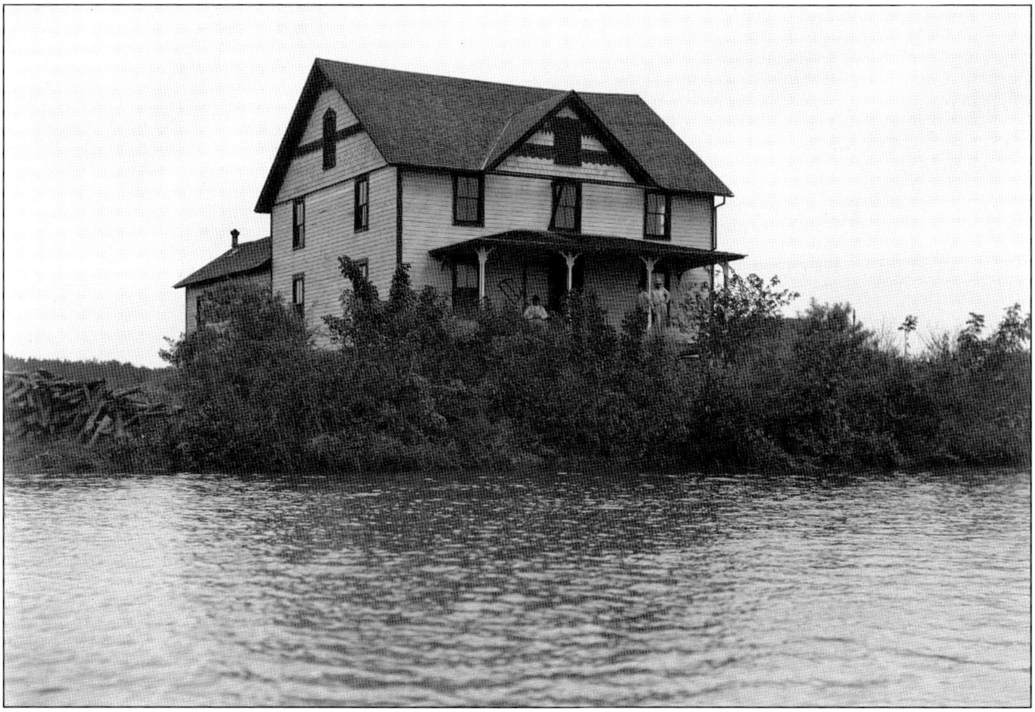

Pioneers claimed sites along the rivers, mostly seeking isolation inconvenient to law enforcement. Storied homesites included Sandfly Pass, Lopez River, Chatham Bend, Onion Key, Possum Key, and Lostmans. Persistently famous Edgar Watson (house shown above) was likely a fugitive and murderer, also a successful farmer of Island Pride Cane Syrup, associated with missing persons, shot dead by Chokoloskee neighbors, and fictionalized (sort of) by Peter Matthiessen in *Killing Mr. Watson*. (AMNH.)

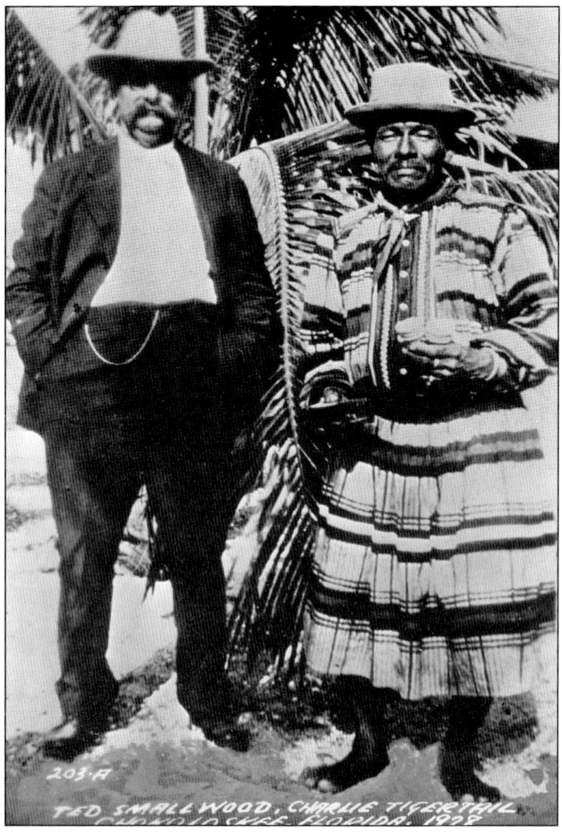

Watson's killing occurred next to Ted Smallwood's store; Mamie Smallwood had sold him wet shotgun shells. Ted Smallwood (left), who had a way of staying above the fray, was a central figure in the southern Big Cypress for decades, here posed with friend and fellow trading post operator Charlie Tigertail (right). Indicative of the future, Smallwood's store remains to be visited; Charlie Tigertail died running his new car into the Tamiami Trail canal. (SLAF.)

Three

Taming the Swamp

Roads, Canals, and Developers

Through the early 1900s, the Big Cypress remained a remote, nearly inaccessible, visitor-unfriendly, out-of-time sort of place. Transportation within remained by canoe, foot, horse, or oxen and to the outside world by boat coastally or trekking through wilderness. While the rest of the world modernized, the Cypress was a land apart, a last frontier. It would not stay that way long; roads, a railroad, and a land-seeking tycoon were coming to tame it.

Settlers of various sorts continued to discover the region. The citrus grove at Deep Lake brought big-time commercial farming and a port. Buying the grove and then the rest of the region, Barron Gift Collier took over, becoming Florida's largest landowner. Seminoles continued living in their island family camps, although increasingly providing their labor for farming, lumbering, and construction. Competing interests toiled to build a cross-state road through the Cypress. Collier, having had a new county established, assured Tamiami Trail's completion by 1928 as well as a railroad and a road to Immokalee and a town he renamed Everglades (now Everglades City).

Tamiami Trail brought huge changes. It drained some areas, flooded tree islands, blocked canoe routes, increased hunter and developer access, and enabled Seminoles to move to the non-flooding and transport-friendly roadside. Stores replaced trading posts, cars replaced canoes and glades skiffs, lumber mills felled the forests, and farming claimed seasonal marshes. These industries created new towns: Ochopee, Copeland, and Pinecrest.

New forms of transportation, such as airboats and swamp buggies, allowed deeper access to the swamp interior. Passing motorists and tourists tarried, spawning attractions such as roadside Indian Villages. Dedicated in 1947, Everglades National Park changed the rules for hunting, fishing, and other activities. Other reserves followed, such as Corkscrew Swamp Sanctuary in 1954. When accessible oil was discovered, extraction began in 1943. Many of the Cypress- and Everglades-dwelling Miccosukees achieved formal recognition by the federal government, and they and the Seminole tribe divided Big Cypress reservation lands while debating financial restitution for the historic loss of the rest of their lands. Meanwhile, Big Cypress development went big-time. Golden Gate Estates was marketed nationwide.

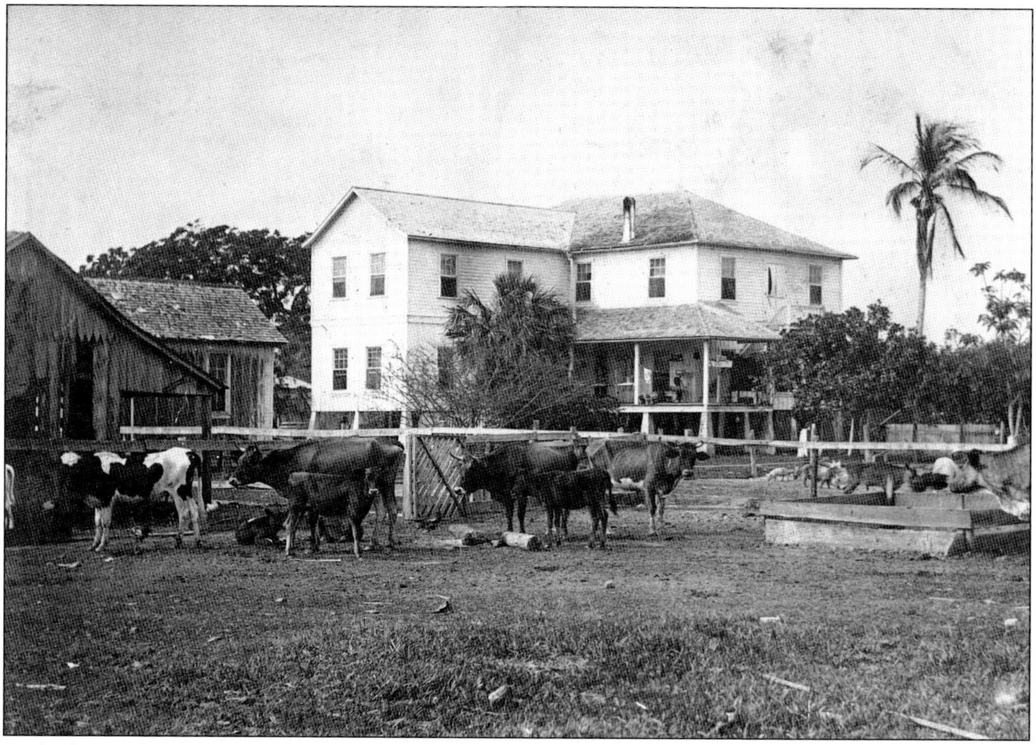

In the late 1800s and early 1900s, settlers continued arriving, many departing quickly, others lingering, some setting roots. Adventurers and vacationers appeared. The region remained dependent on boats plying coastal waters, trekking overland from Immokalee, or wading across the Okaloacoochee Slough. Trading posts at Chokoloskee and what was to become Everglades City (pictured) became their towns' nucleus. George Storter Jr. also began catering to visitors and sportsmen. (SLAF.)

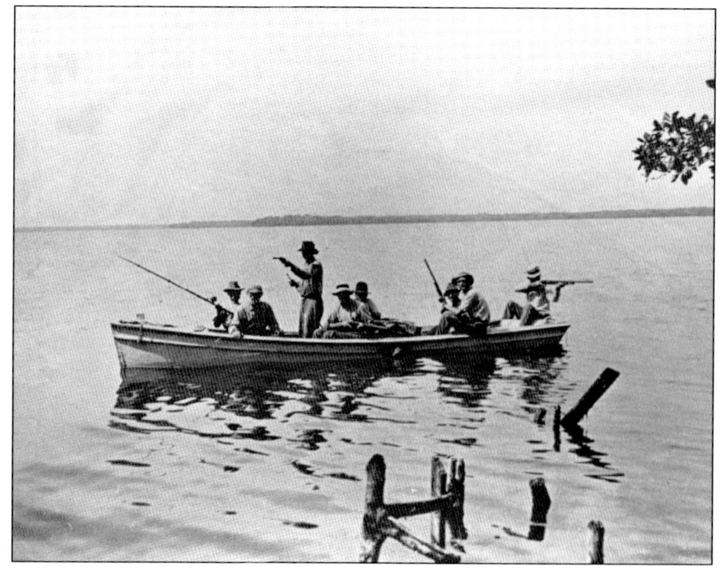

By the early 1900s, turtling and fishing, especially for mullet and permit, became economic mainstays. Visitors fished by rod and reel; locals netted fish off-loaded to ice-laden run boats heading to Key West. Rifle-armed local and visiting hunters penetrated the swamp ever more deeply, reducing game and plumes. Small-scale but well-timed winter agriculture, cane syrup, and whiskey were shipped to Key West or Fort Myers or were used locally. (OPN.)

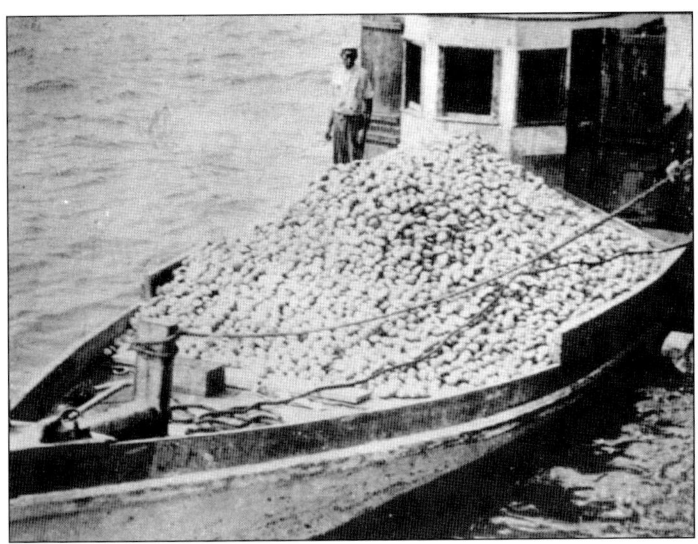

One commercial fishing industry surpassed the rest economically, until it destroyed the stocks that fed it. Starting in 1904, extensive clam beds off the Big Cypress estuaries were harvested by hand. In 1920, William Collier of Marco (town founder, successful farmer, and trading post keeper) invented a mechanized clam dredge that revolutionized the industry. Shown is a clam runboat. Clam works provided reliable employment. (CCM.)

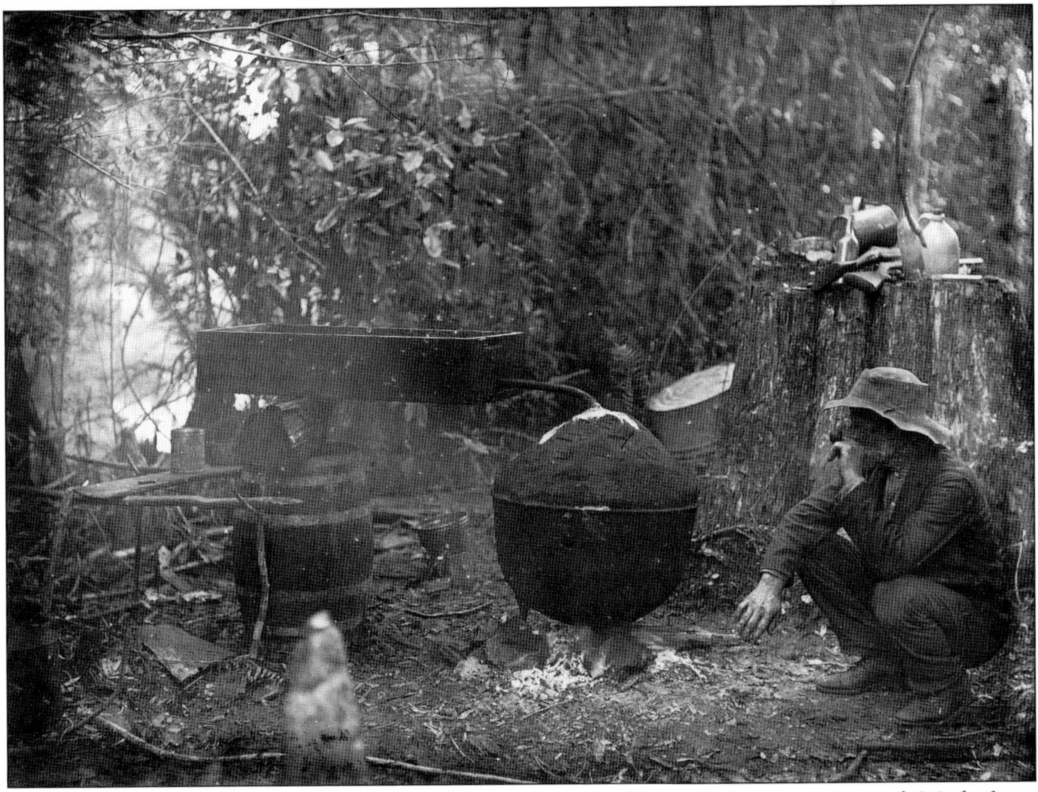

The commercial and community values of moonshine could hardly be overestimated. Made from sugarcane juice and trading post grain, moonshine production provided money, comfort, and problems. Both settlers and Seminoles distilled. Shown is a Big Cypress still in 1906. Prohibition made it more lucrative, although iffier, and increased smuggling opportunities, another historic economic mainstay of the Big Cypress, destined to meet its climax 50 years later. (AMNH.)

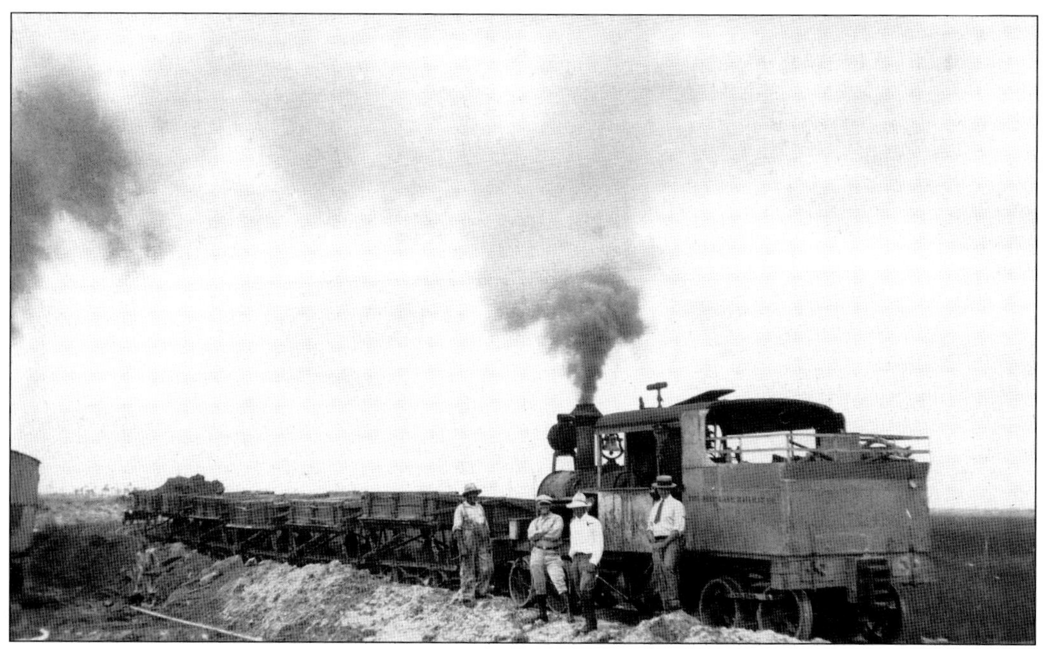

The pine and hammock soils of Deep Lake Strand were long appreciated. Destroying Holata Micco's garden there sparked the Third Seminole War in 1855. About 1901, the area was purchased by Walter G. Langford, Fort Myers rancher, banker, and Edgar Watson's son-in-law, and John Roach, Chicago streetcar company president and developer of Useppa Island resort. They cleared 300 acres to plant a Marsh seedless grapefruit grove. Oxcart transport to Fort Myers proved inadequate. In 1913, they built the 14-mile, narrow-gauge Deep Lake Railway (above). More of a surface tramline, it went south to the Deep Lake Terminal on Allen's River. The grove and its nationwide advertising proved commercial farming feasible in the Big Cypress Swamp, eventually attracting the interest of farmers and developers. Barron Collier bought the grove in 1921 and added a packinghouse (below) in 1929. (Both, CCM.)

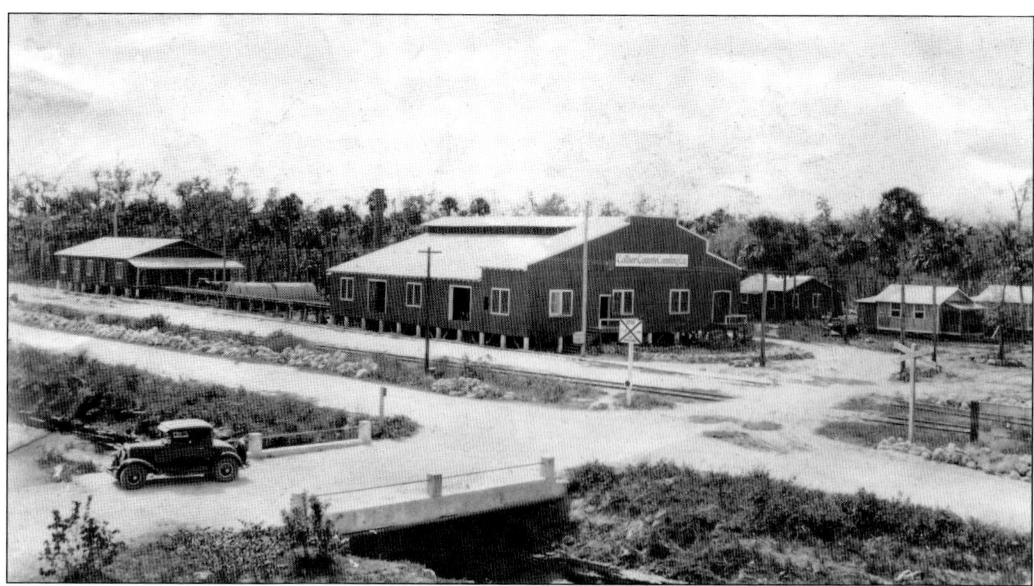

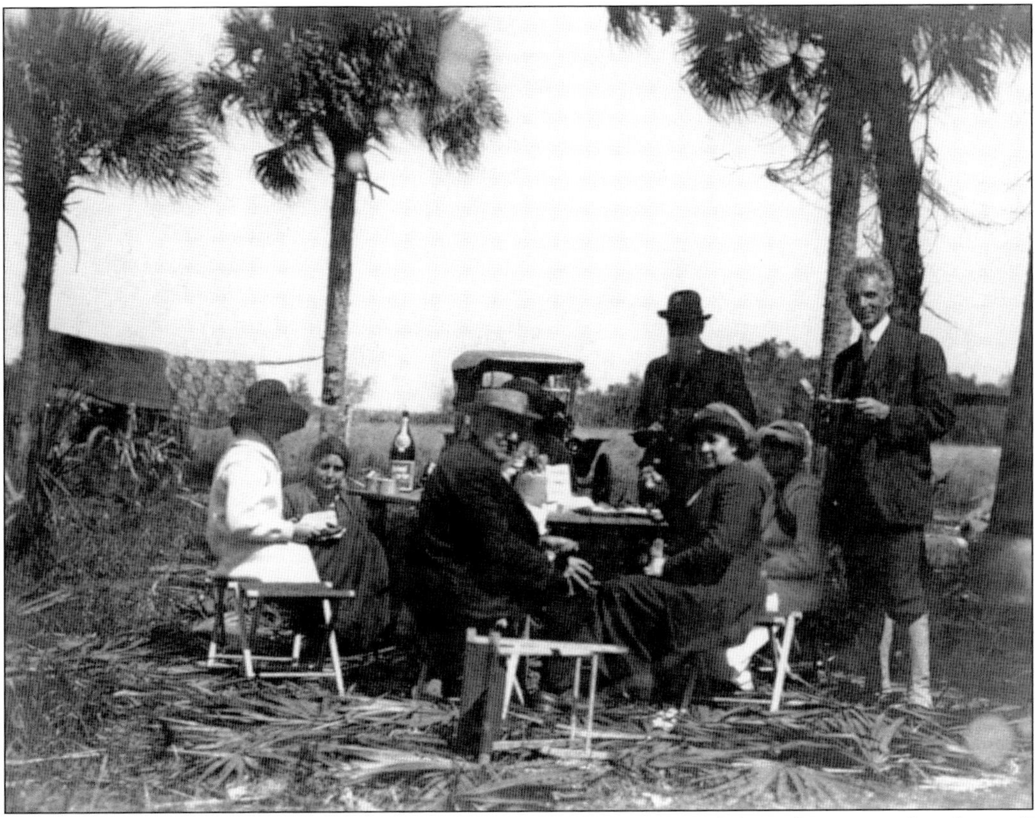

Big Cypress came to national attention in 1914 as the first of the celebrity "Four Vagabond Trips" by Thomas Edison, Henry Ford, nature writer William Burroughs, and their friends and families, which kick-started camping as an American pastime. With three armed local guides, they headed south from LaBelle through the flooded Cypress. The Big Cypress Swamp impressed Ford, although not the cranky Burroughs. They camped in torrential rains and went home early. (EFWE.)

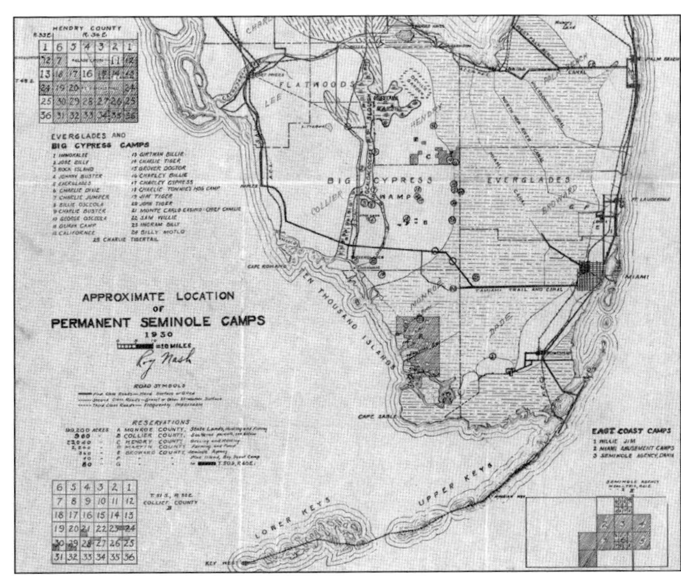

Seminole tree island–based communities continued through the Cypress (locations shown). In 1911, the state designated 100,000 acres in the southern Big Cypress as a reservation (also shown). Seminoles became increasingly frequent in towns, as workers, and at tourist stops. In 1904, in Miami, Thlocklo Tustenugee from Cow Creek created Tom Tiger's Camp, the first Seminole tourist camp, demonstrating a new economic opportunity. Others, such as Coppinger's Tropical Gardens, followed. (SLAF.)

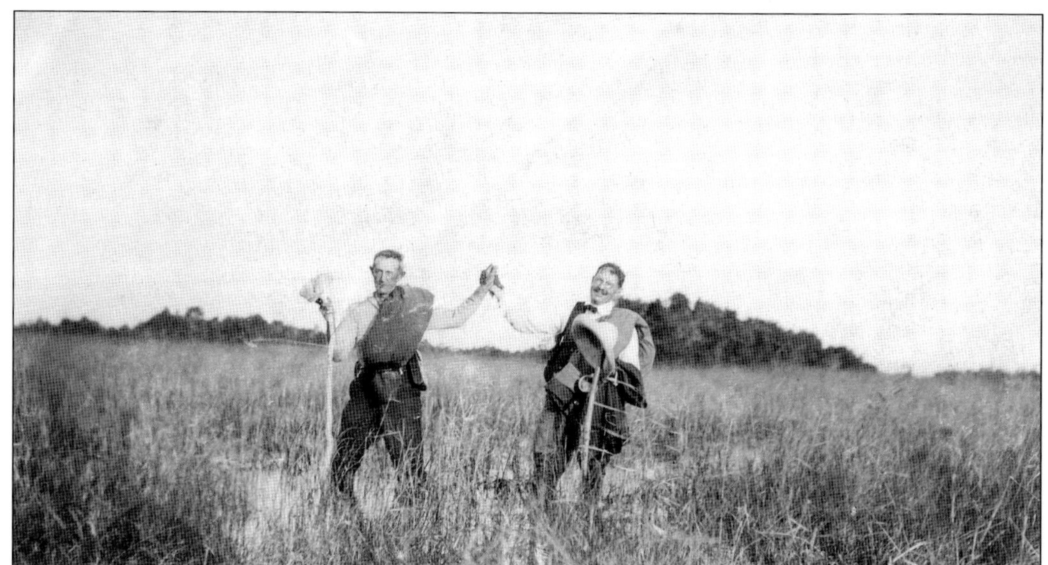

James Franklin Jaudon was a Miami merchant, volunteer soldier (and so was called "Captain"), tax assessor, farmer, vegetable wholesaler, and incurable developer. By 1915, Jaudon was a lead spokesperson for a cross-state road from Miami. In 1917, he formed the Chevelier Corporation that began purchasing and selling swamp and pineland in Monroe County. He is shown above (left) in 1917 with a sugarcane expert celebrating in the marshes. (HMM.)

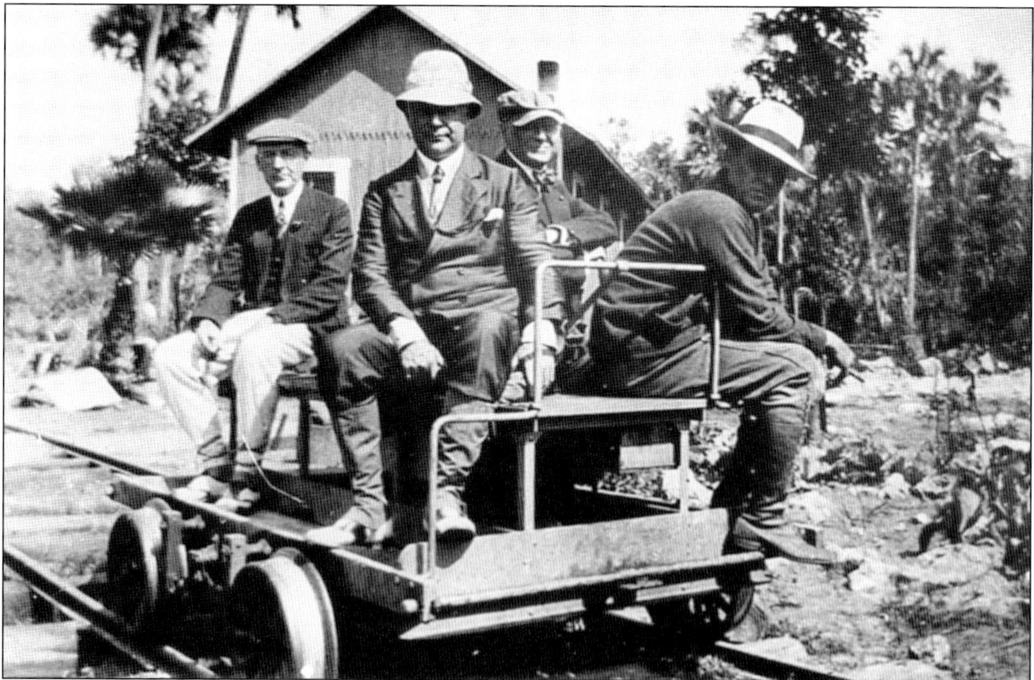

The 1920s history of the Big Cypress belongs to Barron Gift Collier. Wealthy from his streetcar-advertising franchise business, he bought John Roach's Useppa Island resort and then the Deep Lake citrus grove. This image shows Collier in a pith helmet at the grove. By 1924, he had accumulated a million acres, including most of the Big Cypress Swamp. He established headquarters at the isolated hamlet of Everglade (now Everglades City). (CCM.)

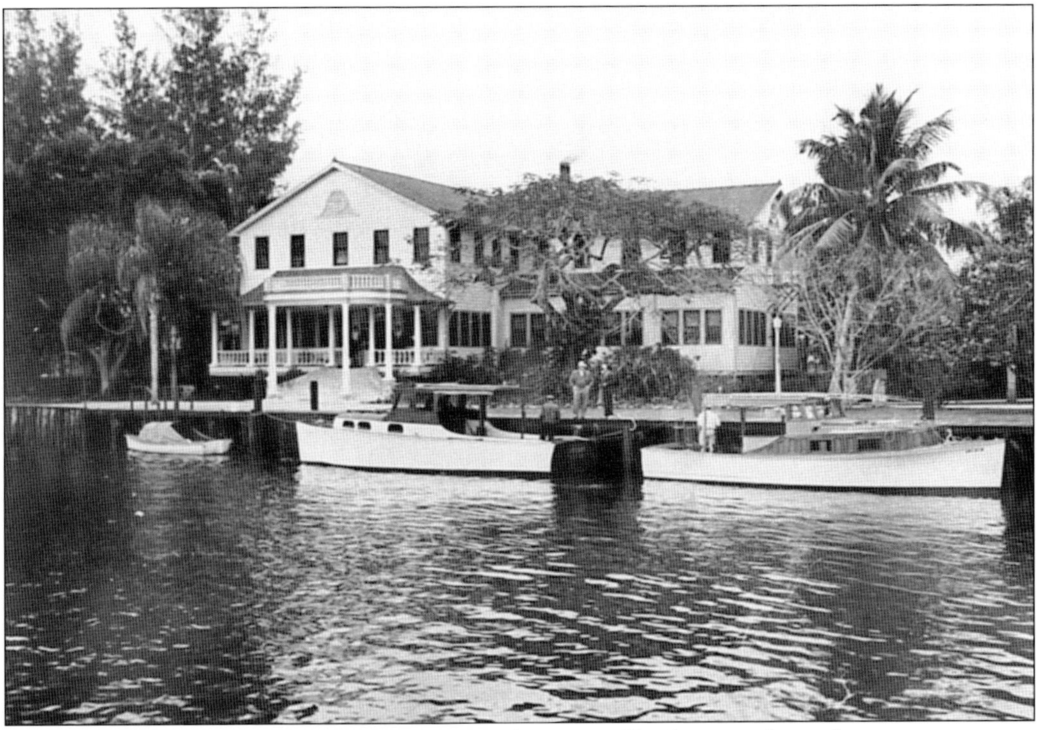

In 1922, Collier bought out George Storter Jr. and renovated his home and guesthouse into a private fishing resort, the Rod and Gun Club (above), which still exists. In 1923, Collier convinced the legislature to trisect Lee County, creating a new Collier County with what is now Everglades City as its county seat. The Bank of Everglades opened in a distinguished building, which is still there. In 1924, Collier started a public hotel and restaurant, the Everglades Inn, which also incorporated the Manhattan Mercantile Store (below). Allens River was dredged and renamed Barron River. Deep Lake landing became Port Dupont, which served as the construction center and living area for Black workers. From the port, a streetcar, the source of Collier's wealth, ran to town, and a canal was dredged northward through the mangroves to the higher ground. (Both, CCM.)

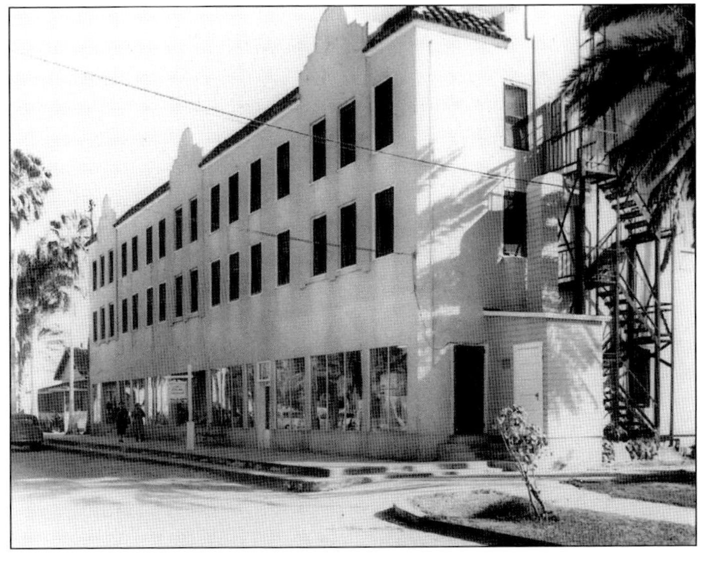

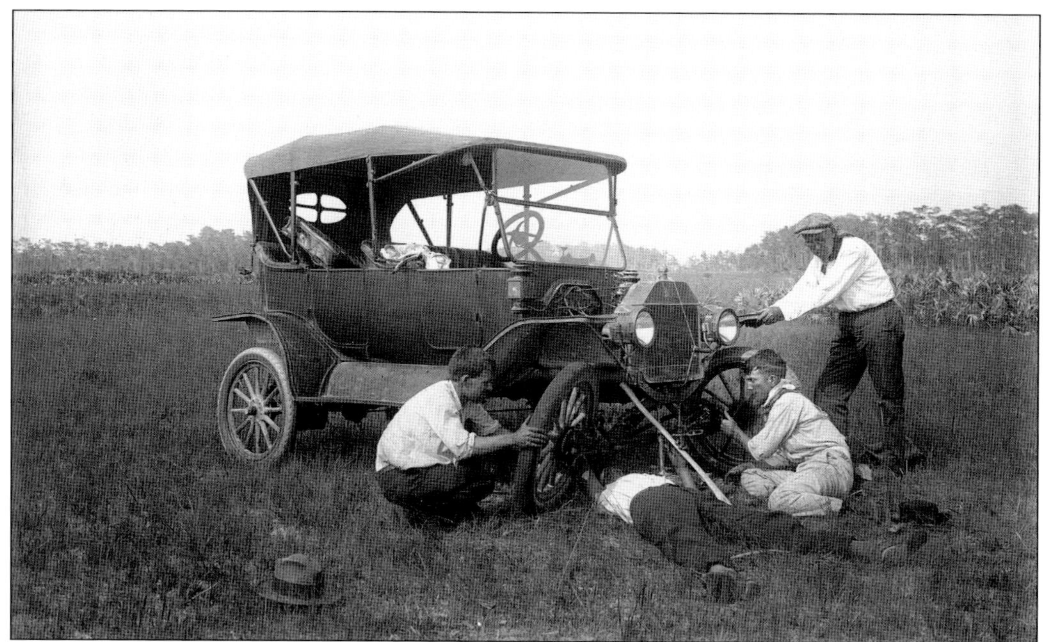

The desirability of a cross-state road was widely appreciated. This 1917 image from the Big Cypress shows botanist John Kunkel Small's car in a familiar situation. Official discussions for the road began around 1915. Jaudon successfully advocated for a straight west route from Miami. Despite technical and financial complexities, Dade County's leg across the Everglades progressed toward the Big Cypress and the county line. The state took over in 1925. (SLAF.)

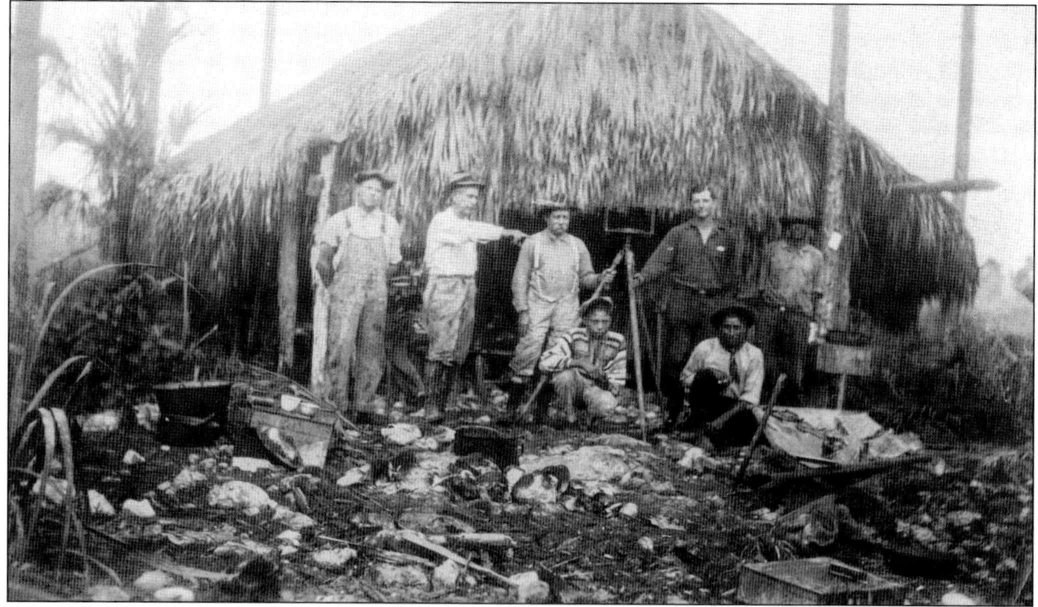

By 1919, Lee County's Tamiami Trail highway funds ran out, and Monroe County refused to participate. So, Jaudon offered to build a road straight to Chevelier Company lands. Jaudon's roadbuilding moved fast. He built through the high ground of his anticipated town of Pinecrest to as far as Roberts Lakes Strand. Shown is his Roberts construction and engineering camp in 1924. (HMM.)

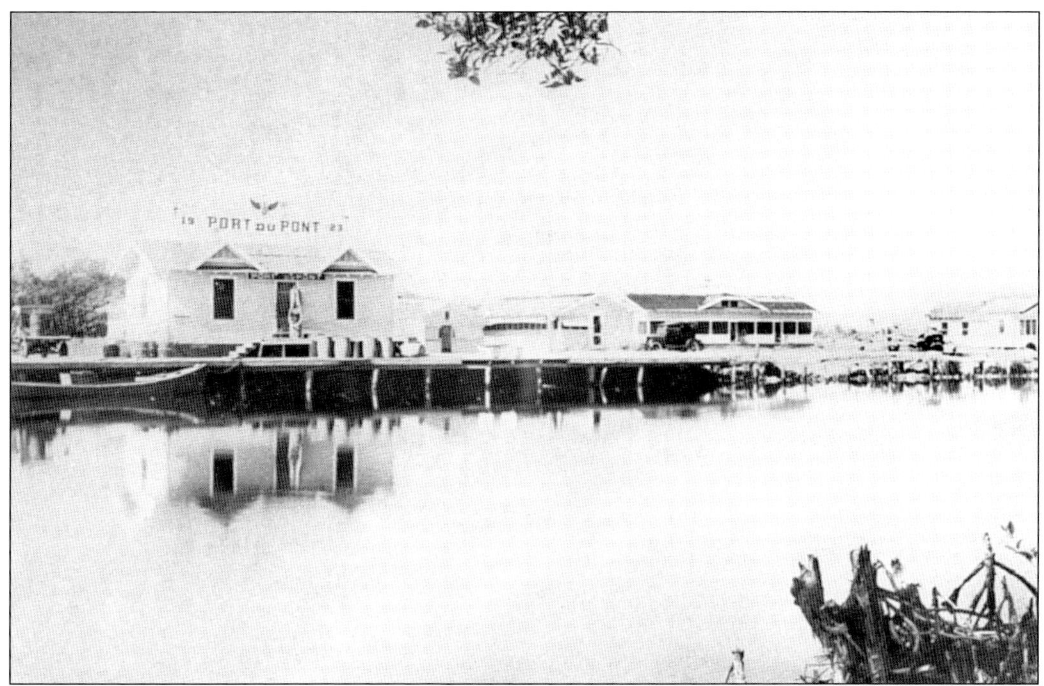

The route was altered because Barron Collier wanted it to. With his new county's bonding opportunities and directly managing the work, a Collier company took over the project, routing the road through his landholdings in what was now Collier County. Materials arrived by boat at Port Dupont (pictured) and were moved to a construction center created at Carnestown (named after his wife and a son). (CCM.)

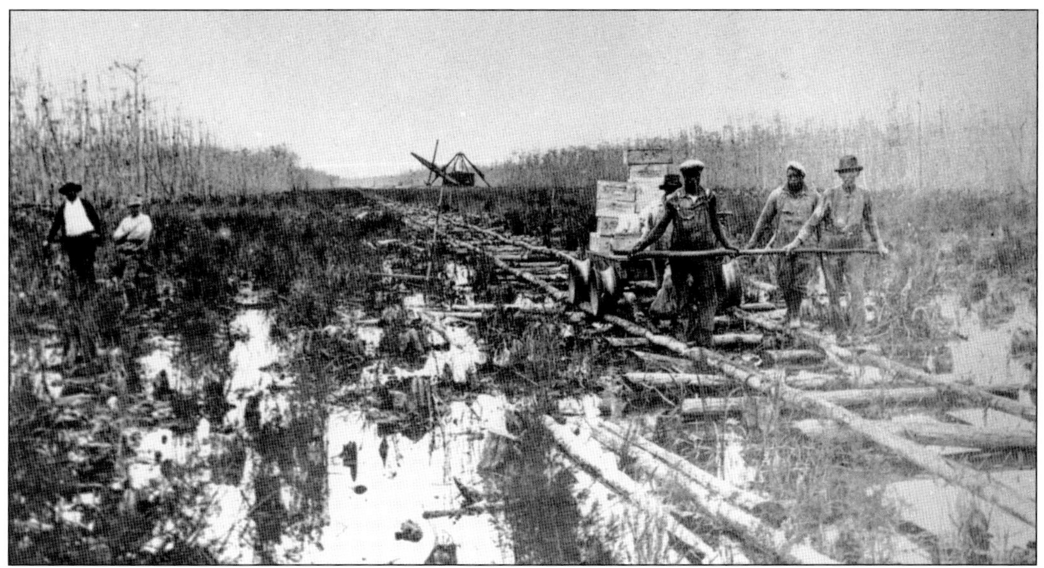

First, a path was cut by hand through cypress and pine trees by crews mostly of Blacks and Seminoles, making slow progress ahead of dredging and road construction. Track was laid on logs and brush beside the canal for ox or hand carts (pictured). Logistics were a challenge to get materials and equipment by boat to Everglades City, then moved from Port Dupont to Carnestown and distant worksites. (SLAF.)

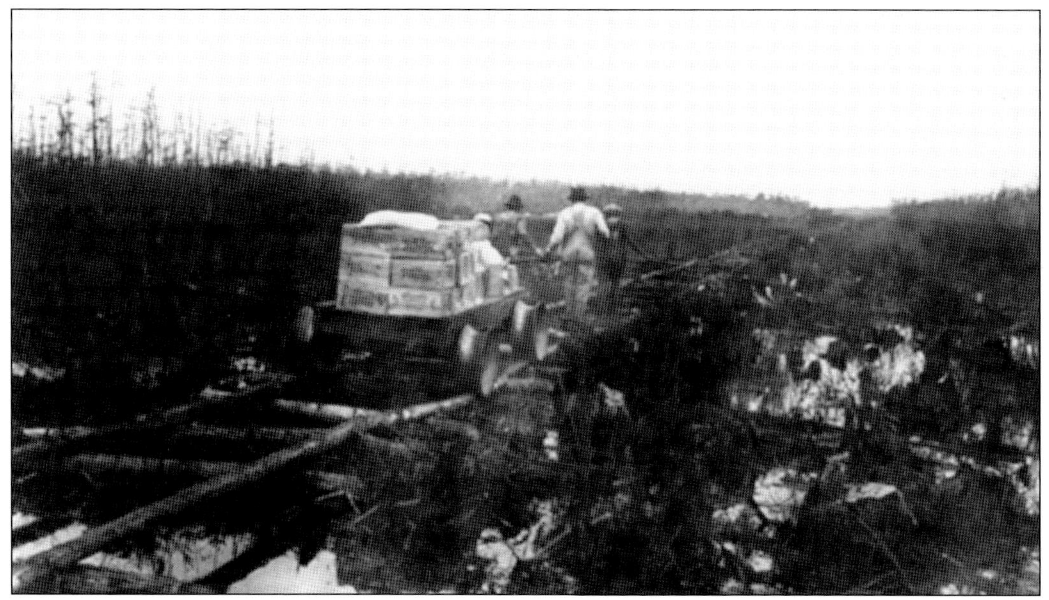

A crucial material transported—carefully—was dynamite (pictured), used to break up the rock. Initially, dynamite was put in natural cavities and hand-excavated holes, which was inefficient and dangerous. This was replaced by a rig that drilled hundreds of holes a day. It took over two million dynamite sticks. There was only one workman's death during the entire project, from typhoid fever caught in Miami. (CCM.)

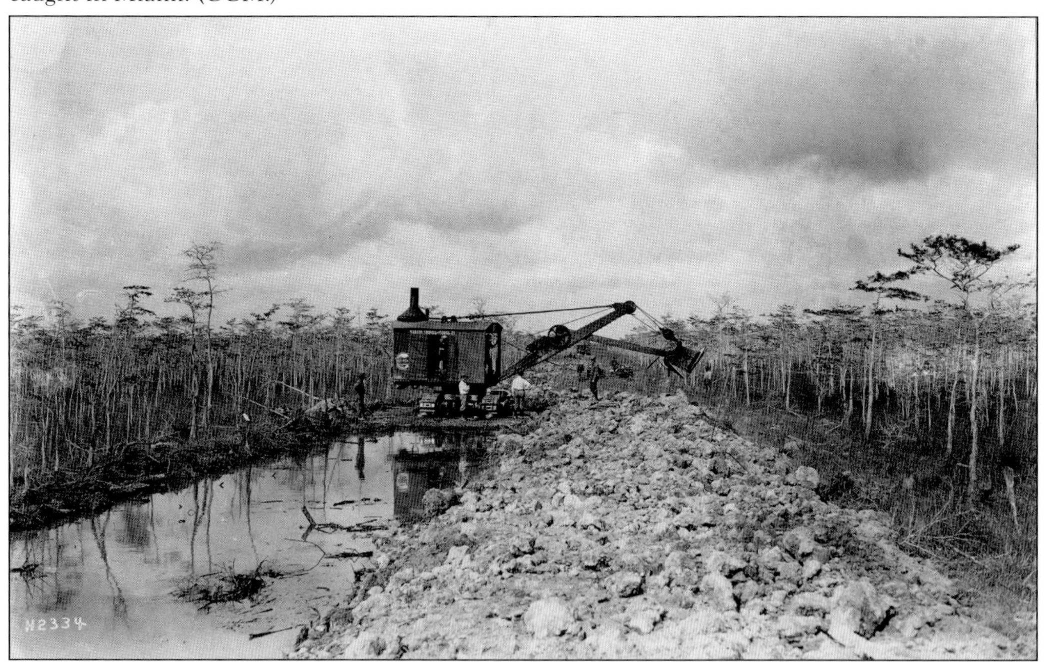

Steam shovels excavated the canal, scooping out limestone, piling it up to make a roadbed. Dredges floated on the canal or "walked" by intermittently being hopped forward, straddling the canal. Part of a Bay City walking dredge from the project may still be seen in Collier-Seminole State Park. From Carnestown, dredge crews struck out west, finding deep, unstable sand, and east, encountering hard limestone. (SLAF.)

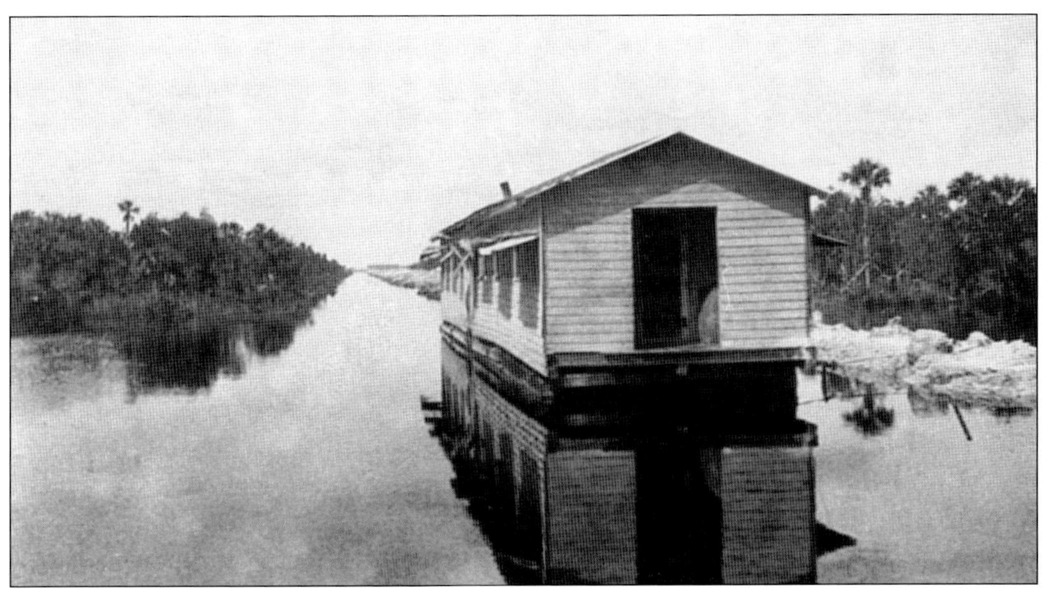

Trail building was a complicated undertaking requiring skilled staffing to be hired, trained, retained, and cared for deep in the wilderness, well away from base camp at Carnestown and even farther from civilization in Miami. Transport to anywhere was by boat from Everglades City. On-site housing was provided by mobile bunkhouses (above) pulled ahead by oxen on the new roadbed, making about 150 feet per day. Food and water were brought from Port Dupont, although local game was also procured. The dining hall moved with the bunkhouses. There are no recorded complaints about the food. The image below shows construction workers with food staff. By 1927, the construction crew numbered over 300 people. (Both, CCM.)

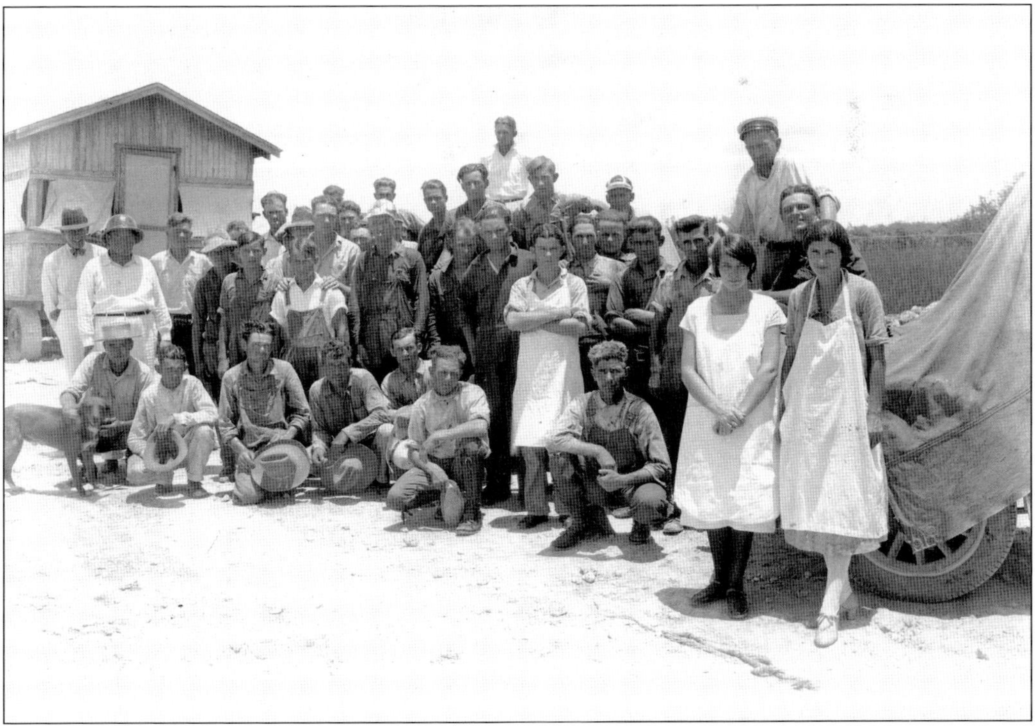

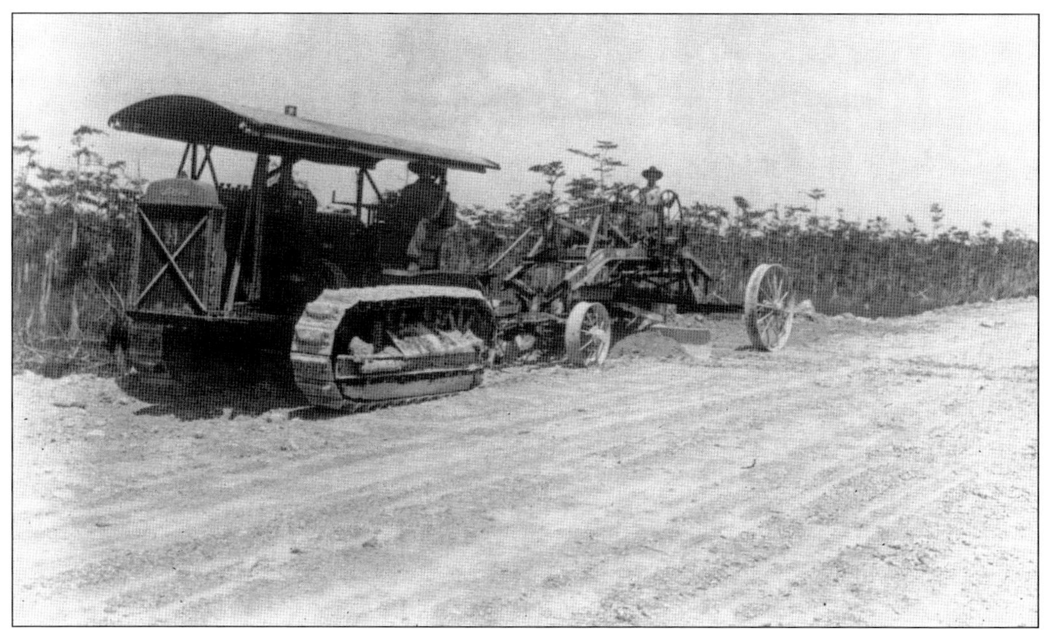

Creating a road out of a rock pile was not easy. Poorly defined specifications led to disputes between the contractor and the counties throughout the project; much of the Everglades' portion needed to be redone. Collier's people could be sure it was done right through the Cypress. The dredged rock was crushed, compacted, and graded (pictured). Learning from Dade County roadbuilding mistakes, multiple culverts allowed water flow. (SFCMC.)

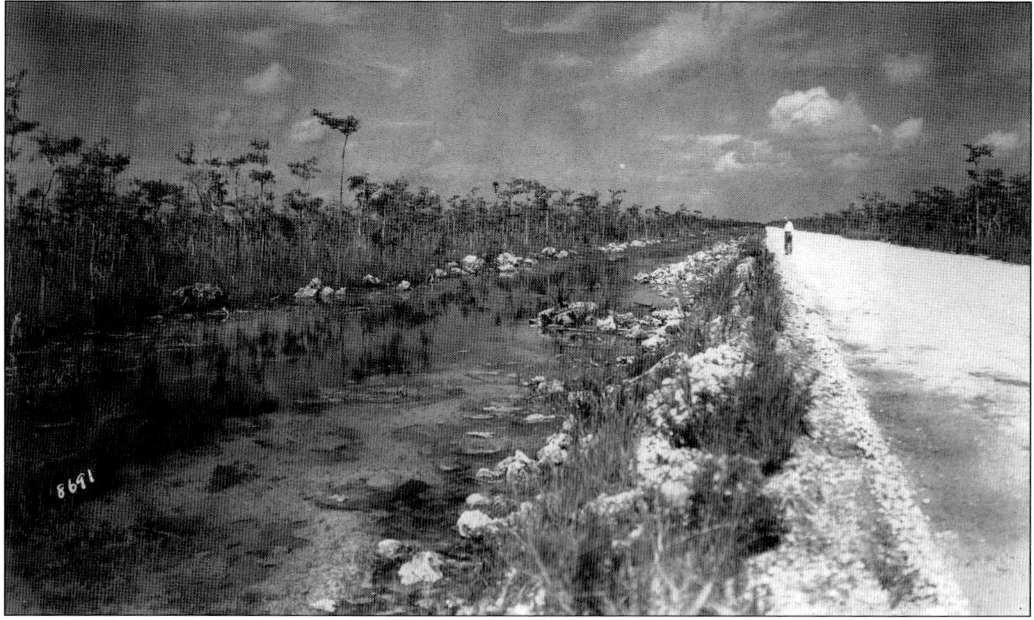

The final travelable roadbed was two cars wide, bordered by the canal dredged for fill. The Tamiami Canal was later fenced off by a hedge of Australian pine trees. Beyond was a seemingly endless cypress forest. When the state took over construction, Jaudon's road was connected at 40-Mile Bend in the east and at Monroe Junction. This image shows the Tamiami Trail between the two locations in 1929. (HMM.)

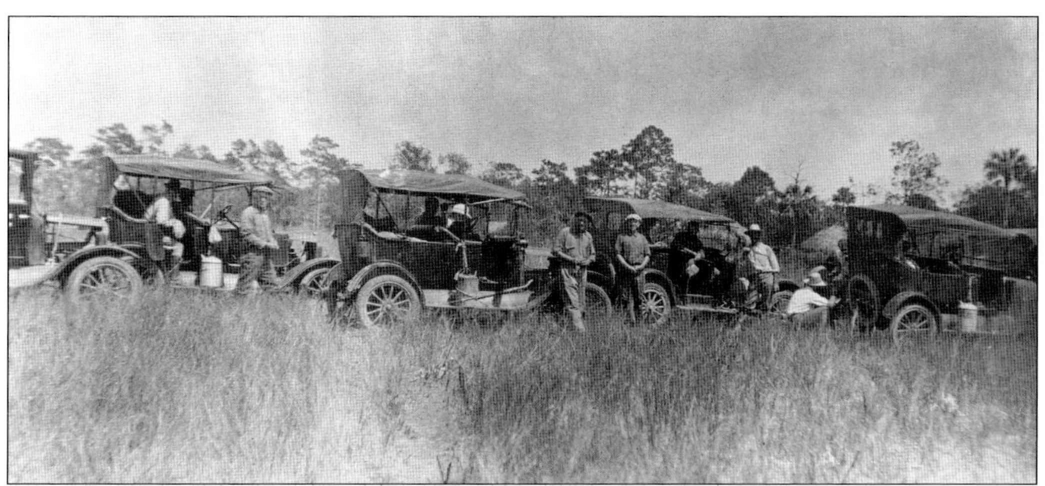

Publicity for the Tamiami Trail took on a life of its own, generating songs, poems, and notoriety, much of it orchestrated by Collier and Jaudon. Coincident with going to the legislature in 1923 to secure a new county, Collier organized the Tamiami Trail Association. Two weeks before the session, to great publicity, the association sent 23 men in 10 cars from Fort Myers to Miami (above and on the cover), mostly by road at the beginning and end, but needing to cross the unfinished Big Cypress gap. It took an accompanying tractor, spotter planes, resupplies from Collier, repeated rescues, and 19 days for surviving cars to begin appearing in Miami. To traverse the Big Cypress, none of the route followed the intended highway path. Nonetheless, the Tamiami Trail Blazer's trip was a publicity success for the trail, Henry Ford, press, and legislature (below). (Both, SLAF.)

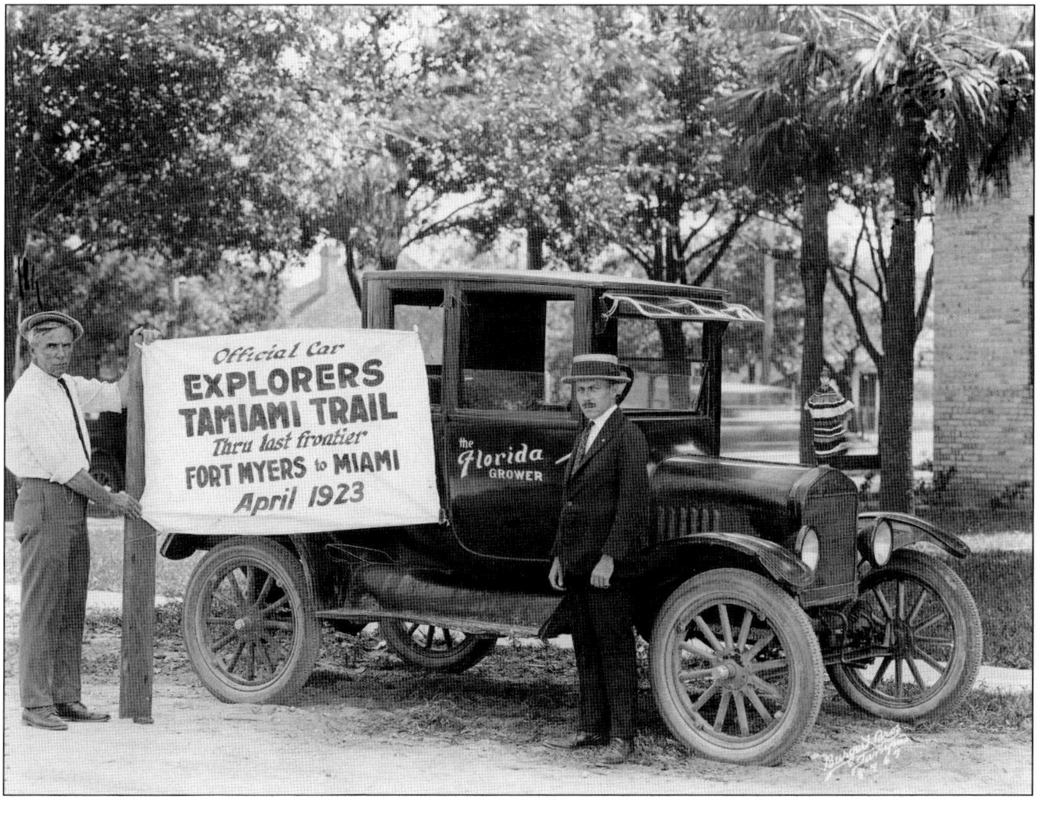

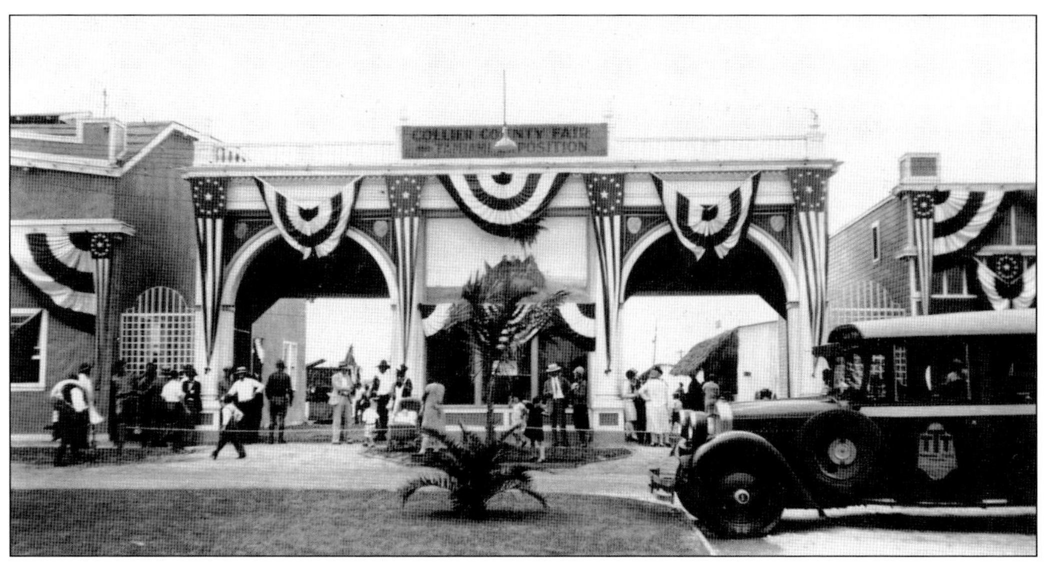

The Tamiami Trail officially opened on April 25, 1928, with a dedication in Everglades City, paid for by Barron Collier, at the first Collier County Fair and Tamiami Trail Exposition (above). Cars motorcaded from both directions (below). The celebration featured a band bus from Miami, county fair displays, a cowboy parade, a new-car show, barbecue, the ceremony in front of the city hall, and general milling about. The fair included Collier County's display of local produce and Seminole crafts exhibited at the 1924 New York World's Fair. Seminoles attended and built a demonstration village in the town. (Above, CCM; below, MDPLS.)

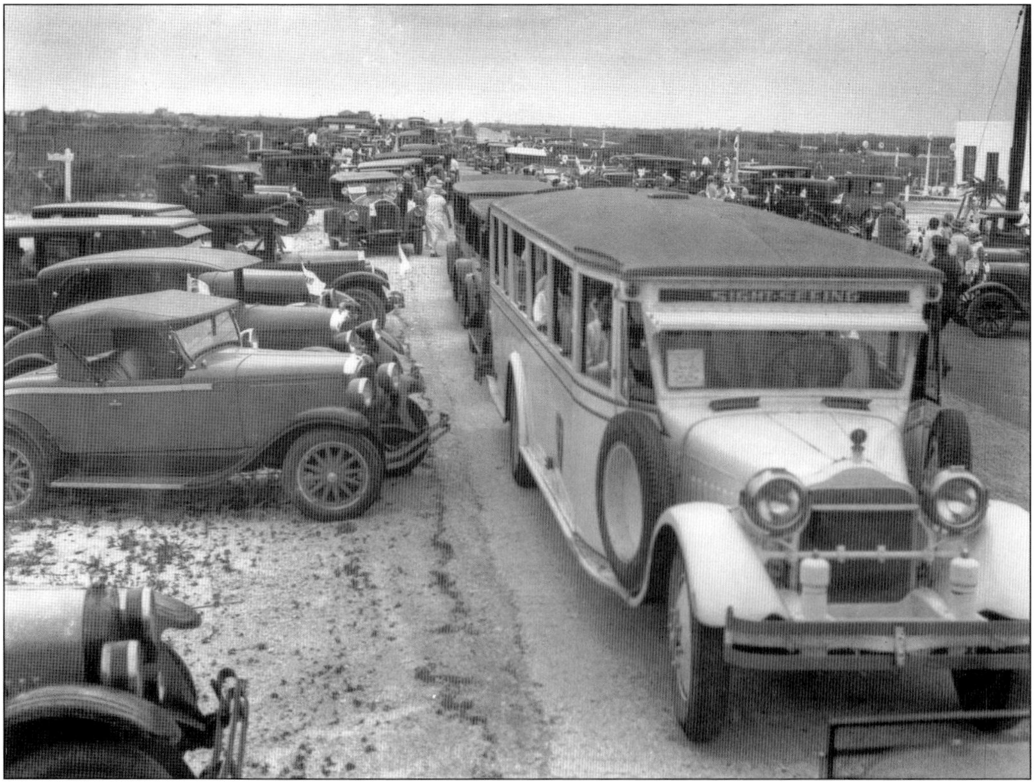

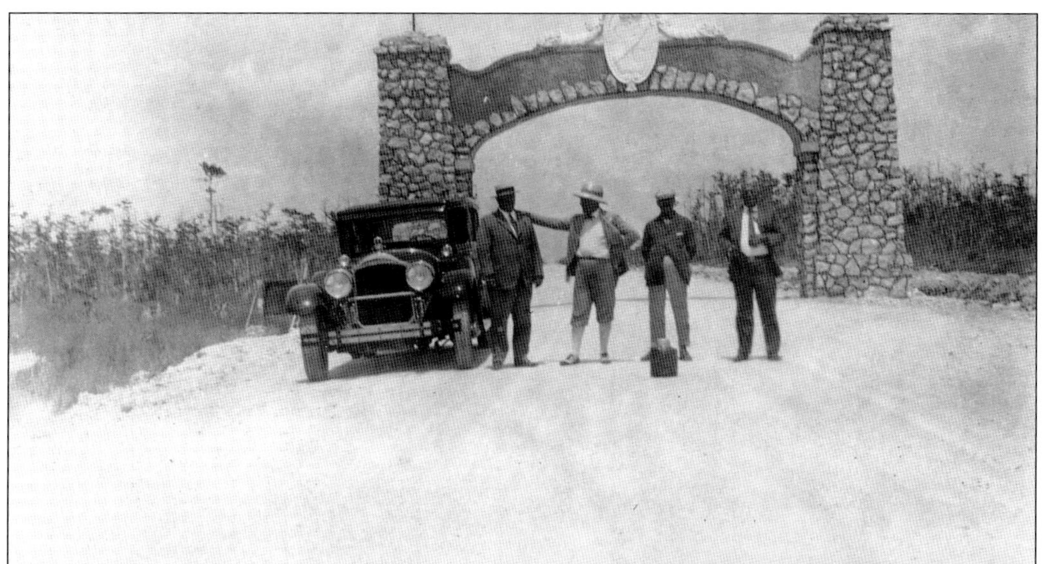

Collier wanted Tamiami Trail motorists to know when they passed into Collier County, so he built an arch over the road. It was located near 40-Mile Bend, where the three counties meet. The imposing arch stood for several decades until its removal in 1958, so the road could be widened. The Tamiami Trail arch remains a symbol of the road through the Big Cypress. (CCM.)

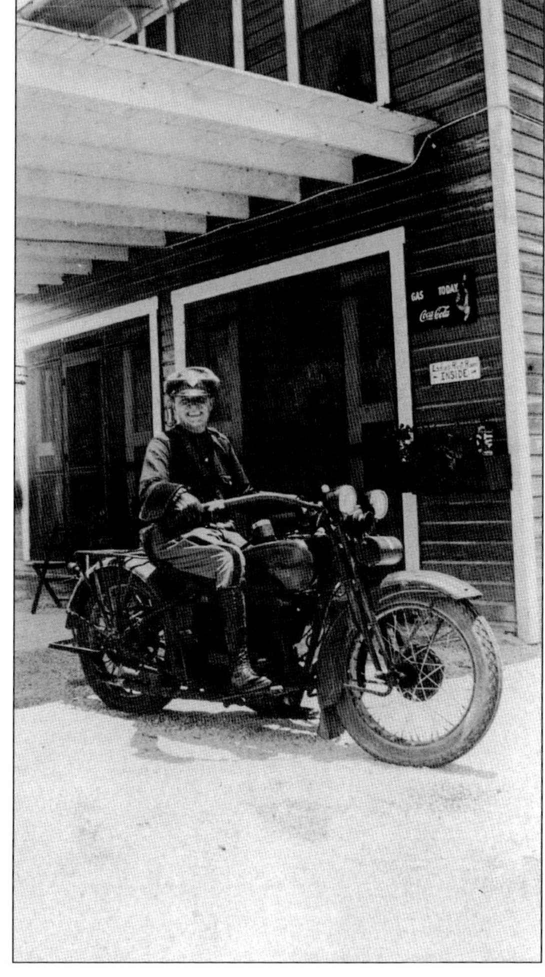

To care for mishap-stranded motorists along 50 miles of vacant, canal-edged highway through a same-looking swamp, Collier provided Harley-riding patrolmen. The Southwest Mounted Patrol was uniformed reminiscent of Canadian Mounties. Officially deputized, each patrolled a 10-mile stretch to help and to enforce the 45-mile-per-hour speed limit. The first patrolman from Monroe Station, William Erwin, was killed in a head-on collision in 1929. The patrol continued until 1934. (SLAF.)

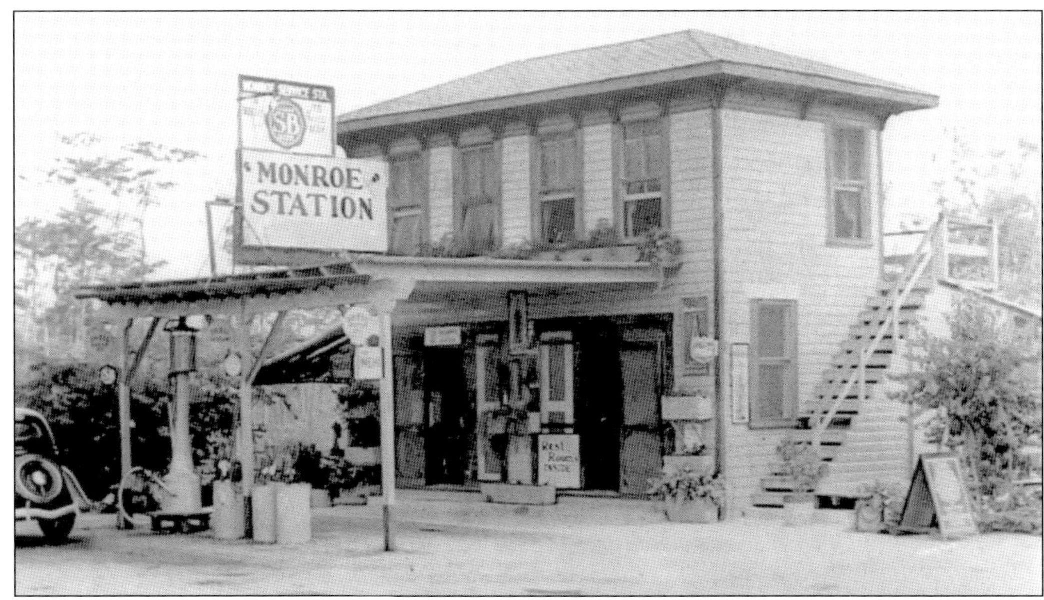

The patrolmen operated out of six service stations Collier built in 1928 at 10-mile intervals along the Big Cypress portion of the trail. Husband and wife teams managed the stations, with husbands patrolling. The couples provided fuel, vitally important restrooms, food, and sometimes lodgings. Collier held on to the stations until 1936, after which they operated independently. The above image is the original Monroe Station at Monroe Junction of the trail and Loop Road; the image below shows its later modification by private operators such as Dixie Webb and Big Joe Lord. Closed in 1987, it was listed in the National Register of Historic Places in 2000 but burned down in 2016. Festooned with business cards, the famous counter served memorable locally sourced menu items such as wild hog barbecue and southern caviar (boiled peanuts). The Lords made the most of their marketable name. (Above, SFCMC; below, MCPL.)

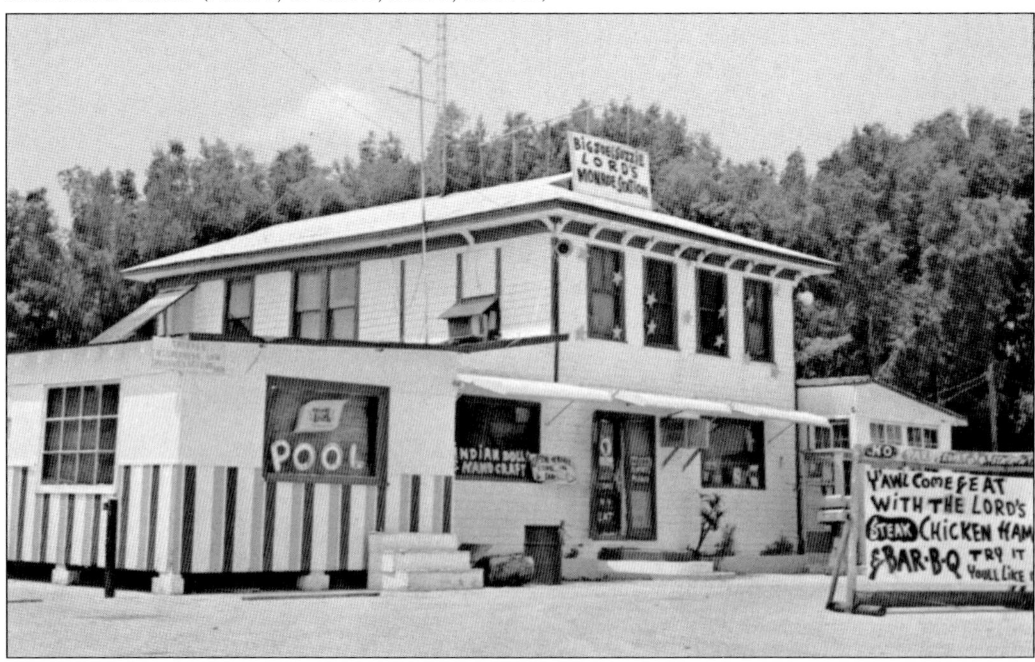

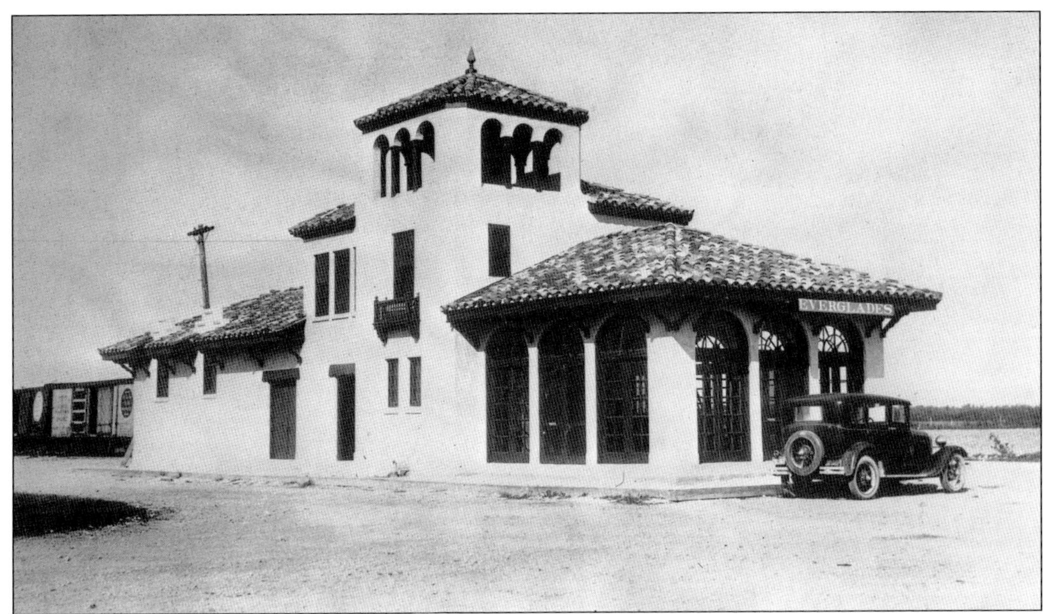

Along with the completion of the Tamiami Trail, Big Cypress was also connected northwards by road and train. Incorporating the Deep Lake Railway right-of-way, the Atlantic Coastline Railroad extended its line to a depot in Everglades City (pictured) with Carnestown as a freight station. The canal fill was also used to construct an adjacent road (State Road 29). Tamiami Trail sliced the Cypress east-west and the Immokalee Road north-south. (SLAF.)

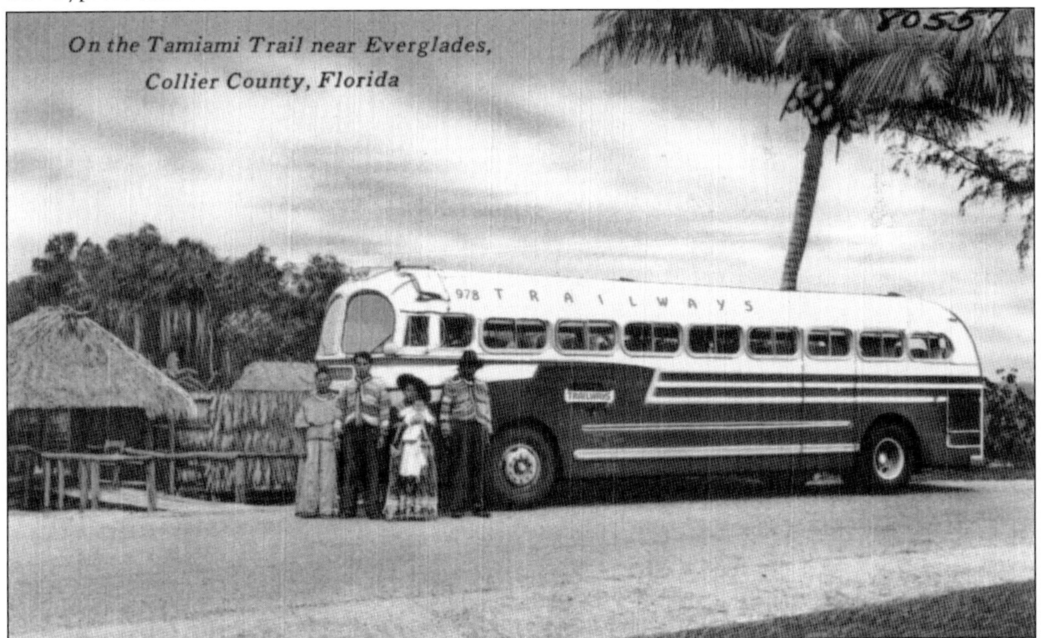

Private cars soon were traveling the Tamiami Trail across the Big Cypress between Miami, Naples, and Immokalee. Collier also provided freight transportation through his Tamiami Freightways and for people through his Tamiami Trail Tours bus company, to become Tamiami Trailways as a Trailways franchise. Buses ran from Tampa to Miami. They stopped at Everglades City, stations, and local villages—a service particularly useful for Seminoles living near the trail. (BPL.)

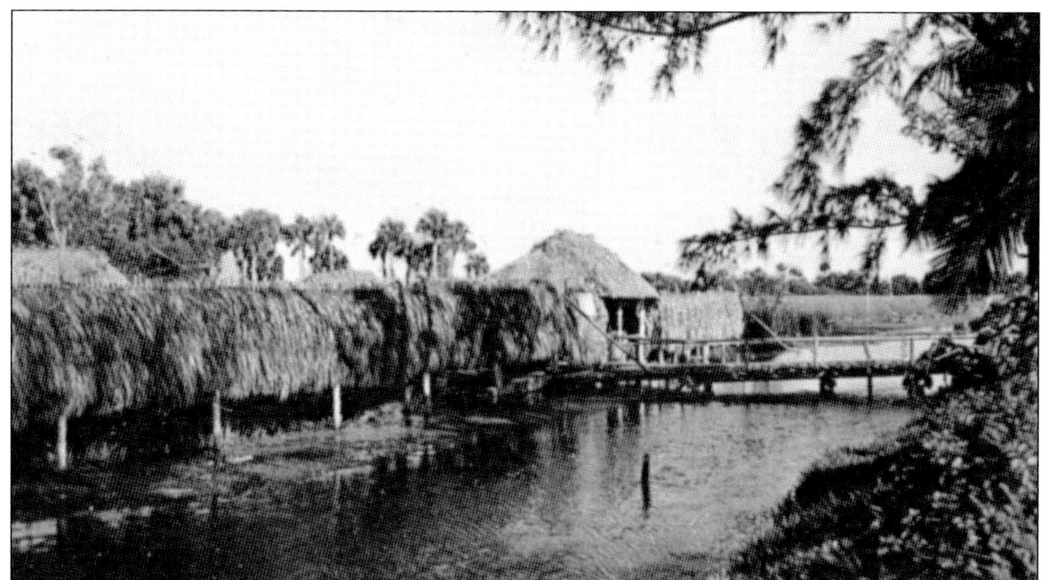

In the Big Cypress Swamp, dry ground was precious, especially for those living on minimally elevated tree islands. Tamiami Trail's elevation provided new high ground, enticing Big Cypress and Everglades Seminoles to move their family camps there. Having cut off historic canoe trails and altered hydrology, the trail and its canal provided more reliable communication, a homesite not periodically flooded, and canoe passages not periodically dried out. (SLAF.)

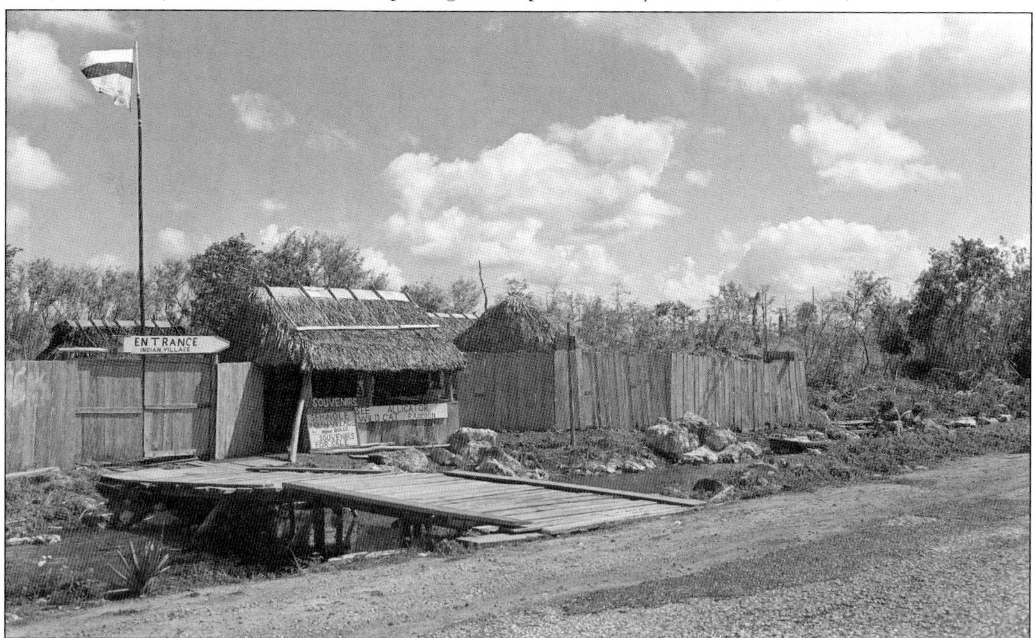

Living on the trail brought economic opportunity. The unconquered Seminoles were now famous worldwide. Miami's attractions, such as Willie Willie's Indian Village on Musa Isle, had proven the economic value of demonstrating Seminole culture, selling handicrafts, and wrestling alligators. Some trail families subsequently opened their homesites to passing motorists as Indian Villages. Travelers toured the compound, watched patchwork sewing, interacted with alligators, and bought souvenirs. (SLAF.)

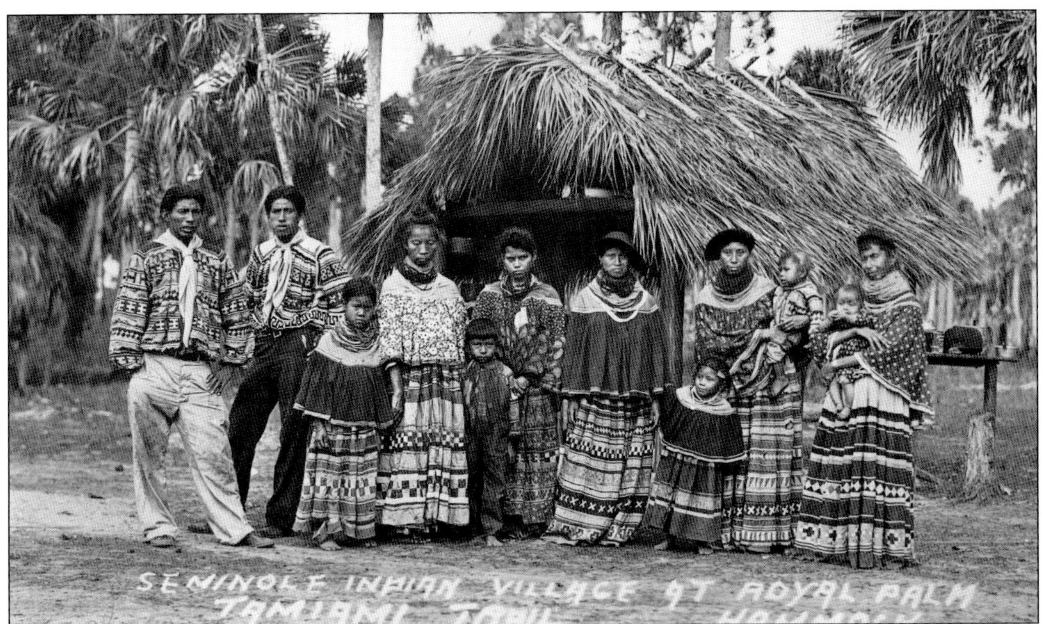

While participating in the new economy, many Big Cypress Seminoles chose to resist other outside cultural influences. The federal government opposed tourist Indian Villages, favoring reservations and New Deal social programs. Although reservation living eventually took hold on the East Coast and Brighton, the people of the southern Big Cypress more firmly maintained their independence. This image is at the village at Royal Palm Hammock (now Collier-Seminole State Park). (SLAF.)

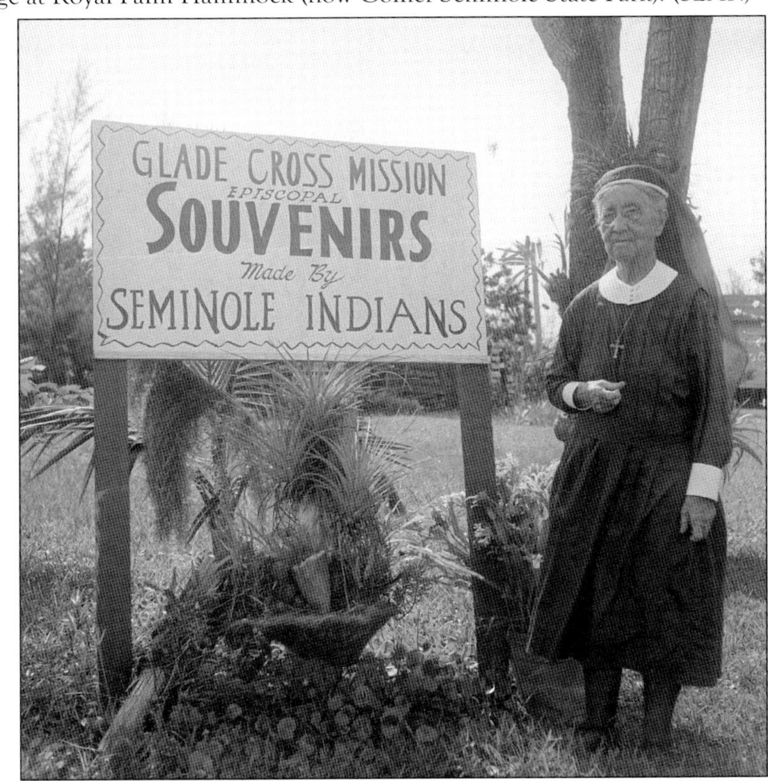

Christian missionaries attempted to influence the Big Cypress Seminoles from the time of the Glade Cross Mission at Godden's Landing, which started in 1908. In the 1930s, Deaconess Harriet Bedell began working with local Miccosukees, producing souvenirs, which she sold without markup and marketed widely for their economic benefit. Serving well into her 80s, until Hurricane Donna destroyed her buildings, she is considered an Episcopalian saint. (SLAF.)

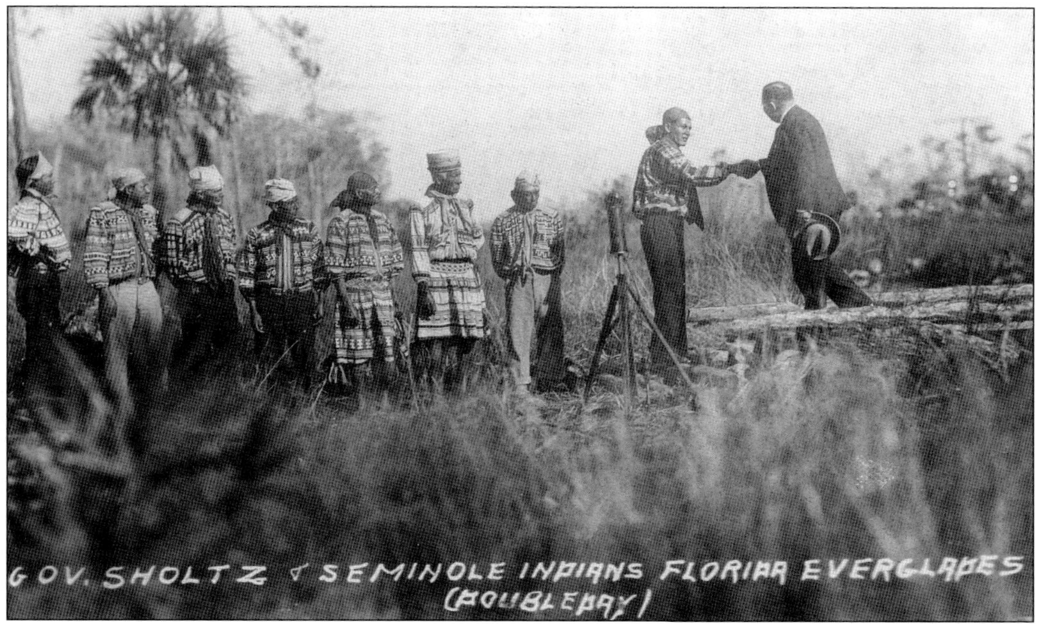

At the height of the Depression and New Deal in 1936, Florida governor David Sholtz requested a conference with Seminole and Collier government leaders. The governor asked Seminoles attending what the government could do to assist them. They answered that they would like to be left alone. A monument to commemorate the nonevent was erected in 1977. Its post remains at the entrance to Monument Campground; the original bronze marker was stolen. (SLAF.)

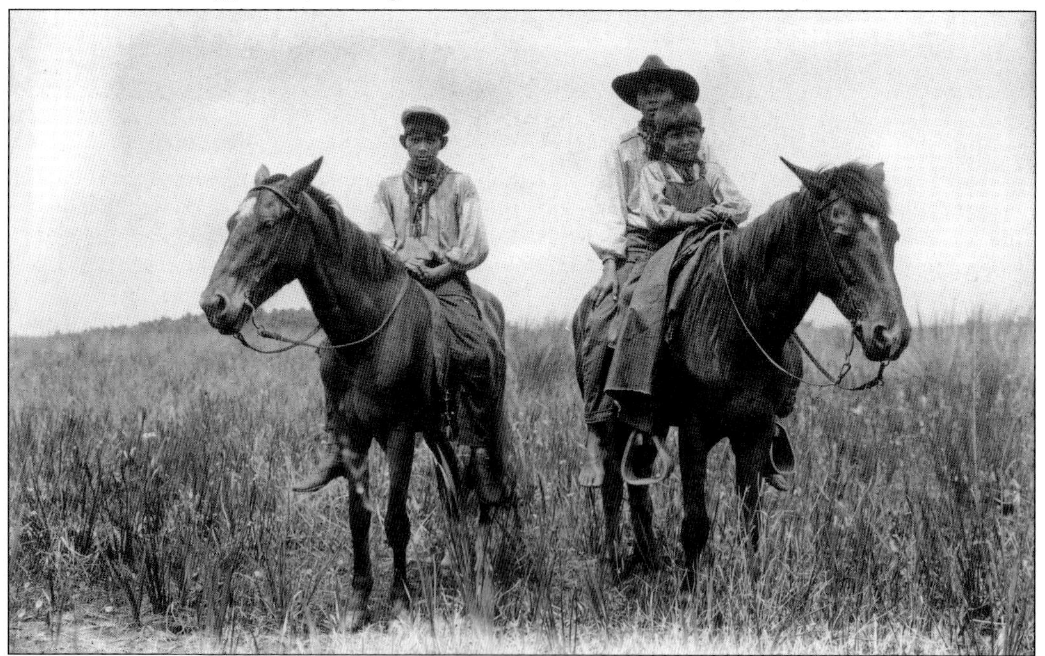

As early as the 1890s, ranching land at Gopher Ridge (to become Immokalee) was being purchased for an eventual Seminole reservation. The Big Cypress Reservation was formally created in 1911. Cowkeeper's (Ahaya's) legacy lived on as Seminoles were able to return to cattle ranching independently after decades serving as cowmen for others. This image is from 1924. (SLAF.)

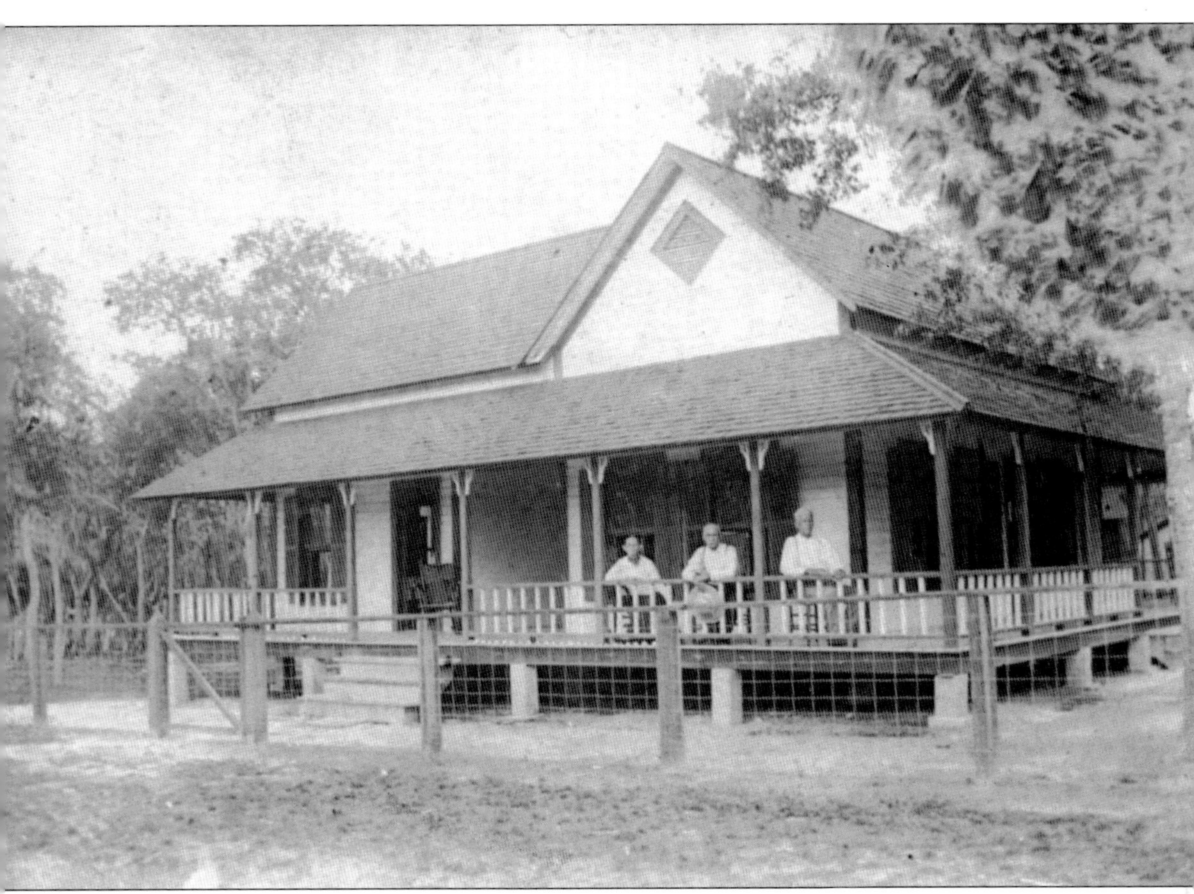

Big Cypress's far-inland settlements were Immokalee and Corkscrew. From the 1870s, Immokalee became a center for open-range cattle operations. Small, skinny, locally adapted cracker cattle, tended by cowmen, including Seminoles, and suitable only for sale in Cuba, free-ranged southward into the Cypress. In 1914, Bob Roberts arrived, accumulating over 100,000 acres of ranchland and was joined by other ranching families such as Lykes and Summerlin. The Roberts' 1926 ranchstead (shown in 1904) is now a museum in the National Register of Historic Places. The Cuban trade for Florida's scrawny cattle dried up in the 1920s. Other breeds were introduced that were not immune to the local cattle tick. By 1928, when Immokalee was connected to the world by road and train, citrus and winter vegetable farming complemented ranching. In the late 1930s, open grazing ended, and the Department of Agriculture established the last stand of its Tick Eradication Program in the Big Cypress, requiring regular arsenic dipping of cattle while paid hunters slaughtered 10,000 Cypress and Everglades deer. The Seminoles refused the killing on their land, sparking national-level conflict. (CCM.)

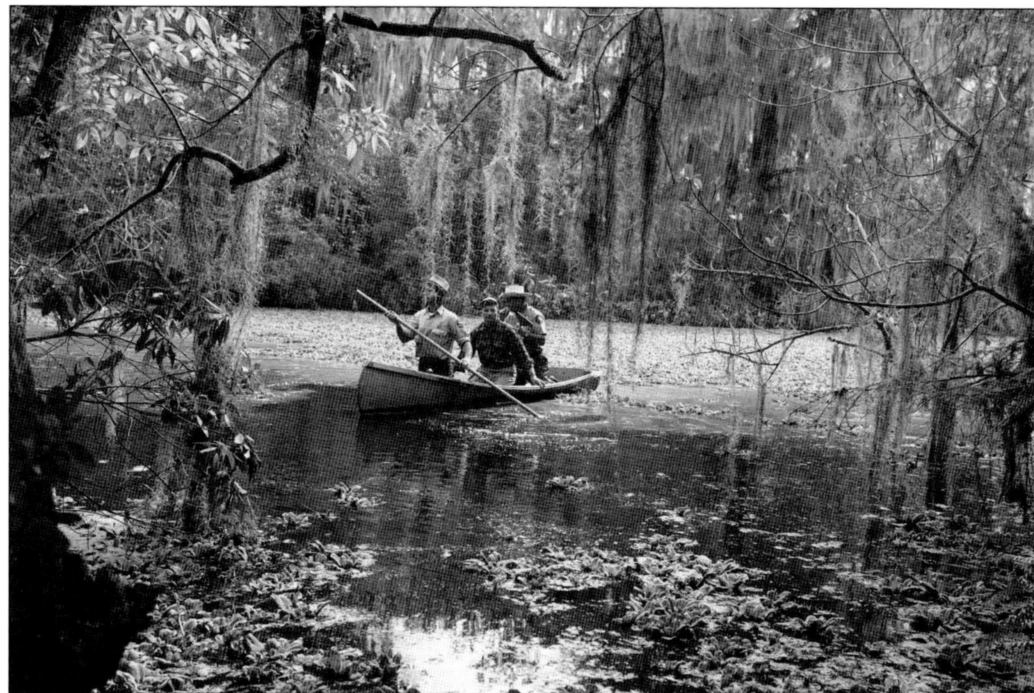

At the southern Corkscrew Strand, Corkscrew Island also provided high ground for settlement, particularly plume-hunting camps. Starting in 1911, Jehu Whidden expanded into ranching and farming. In 1912, Corkscrew became one of the first rookeries patrolled by wardens. To protect the swamp from lumbering, over 5,000 acres were acquired to establish Corkscrew Swamp Sanctuary in 1954. This image shows warden Hank Bennet (front), Andy Harrold (center), and Audubon naturalist Robert Allen (rear). (SLAF.)

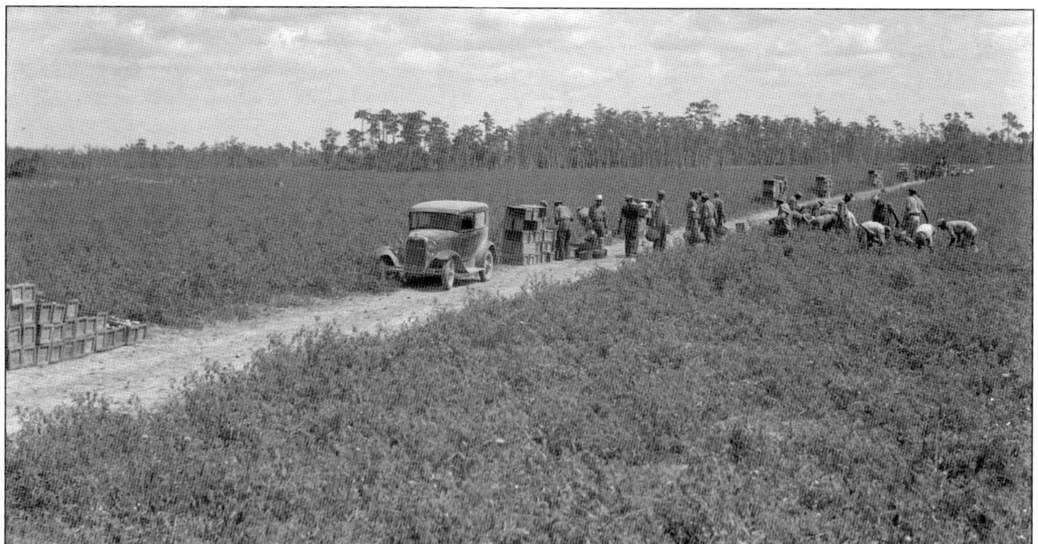

Copeland, on Immokalee Road a couple of miles north of the trail, started as a tomato farming area (pictured) in the 1930s. Founded by Alfred Webb, J.B. Winford, and the Janes brothers, the town had housing, a packing plant, a juke joint for the Blacks, Janes Restaurant for the Whites, and Janes general store. As farm fields gave out in the 1940s, lumbering revived the town. (MDPLS.)

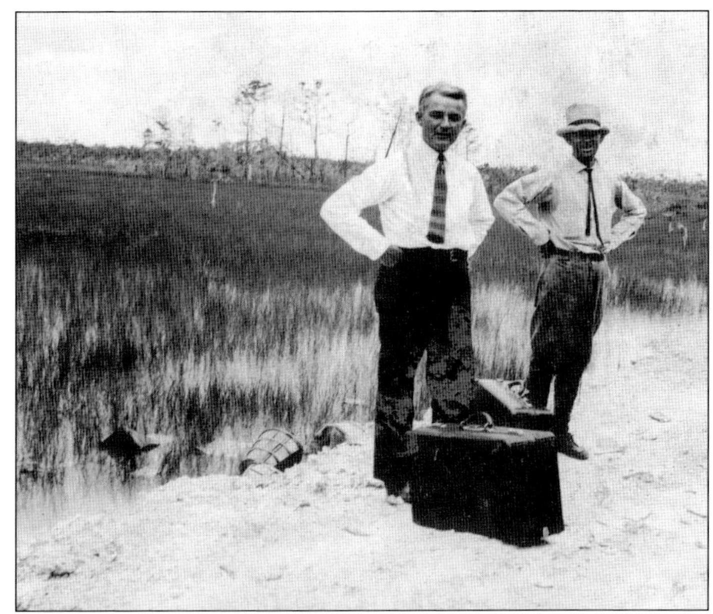

The town's namesake was D. Graham Copeland, who started a farming enterprise there. He was chief engineer for Barron Collier's Alexander, Ramsay & Kerr construction company, a longtime county commissioner, a state representative, and the first historian of the area. Collier was not a hands-on manager; much of the success of the various Collier enterprises was owed to Copeland. This 1928 image shows Copeland (left) and his Tamiami Trail supervisor, Pop Neal. (CCM.)

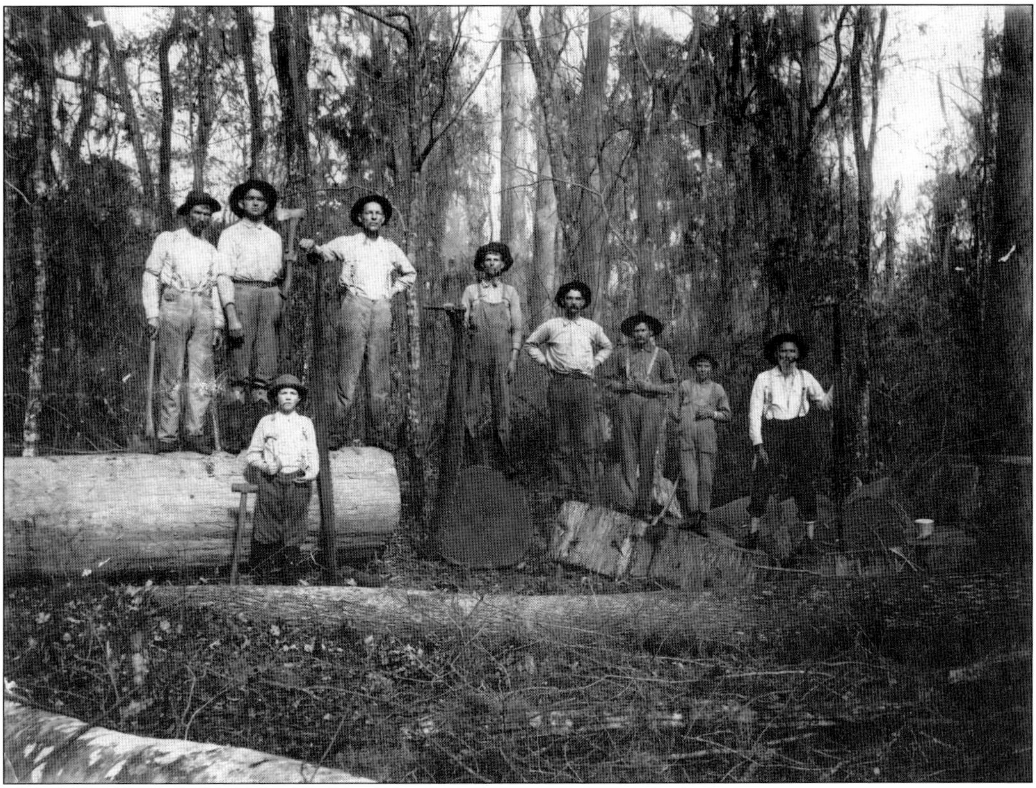

Logging of readily accessible lumber for local use began by 1900. This 1910 image shows George Storter's men hand-cutting lumber for his mill. Collier had a mill at Port Dupont. Others included Maxcey Mill at Turner River; Reynolds Sawmill, west of Monroe Station; Williams Sawmill, south of the trail; and more along Loop Road. Trains provided transport; World War II created insatiable demand. Through the 1950s, Big Cypress was logged ruthlessly. (CCM.)

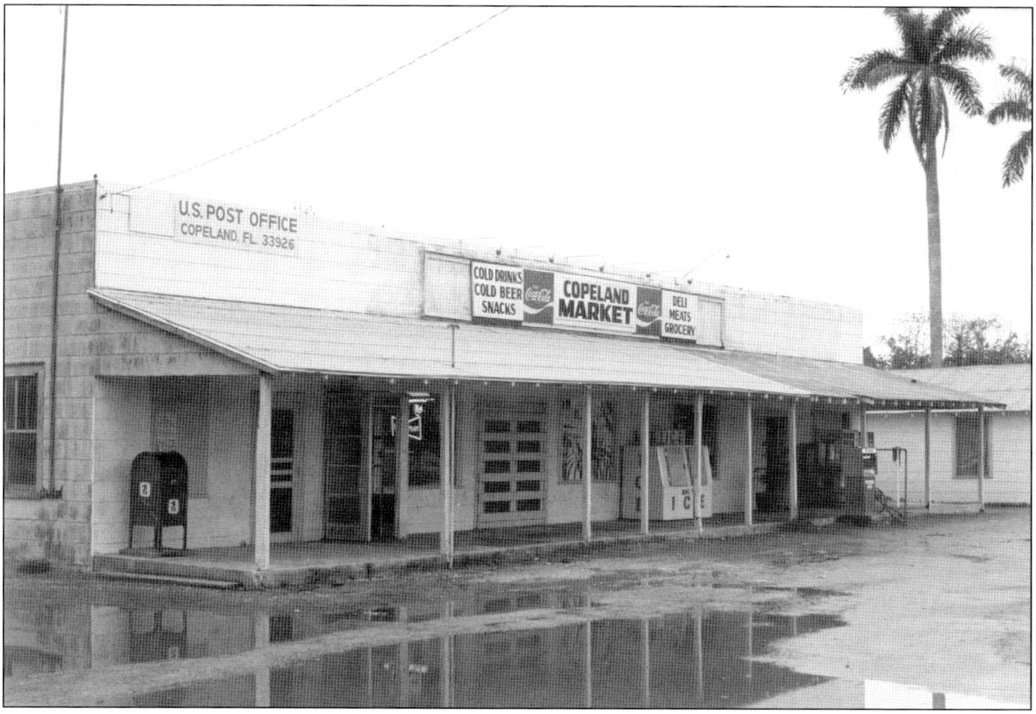

In 1943, the Lee Cypress Lumber Company established its logging operation alongside the town of Copeland, which prospered into the late 1950s; Copeland Market is shown. The company was headquartered in Perry, Florida, 400 miles north; J.R. Terrill superintended over 300 employees. Whites, Blacks, and Seminoles lived in segregated areas. Homes were made of leftover cypress slabs. Janes Scenic Drive now follows the main railroad line through Fakahatchee. (CCM.)

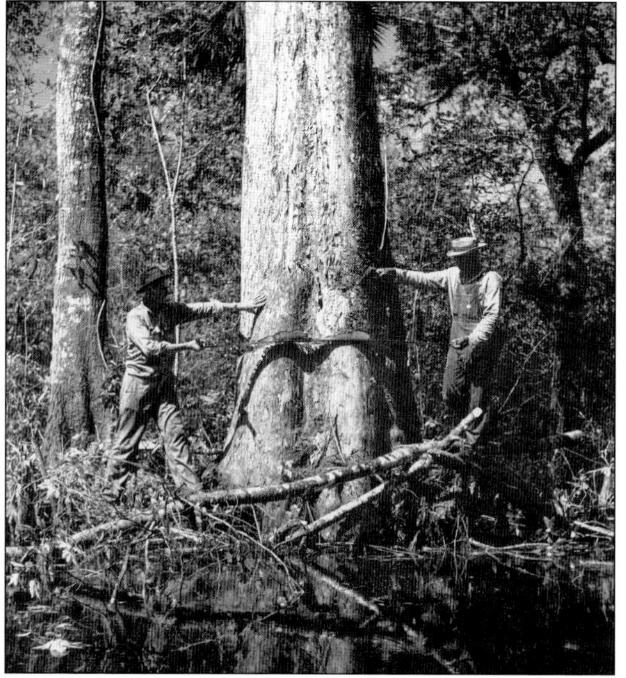

An advance party chose trees to be cut, ignoring those that were small, crooked, or hollow. Trees were girdled to dry and shrink, a step later hastened by kiln drying. The men used meticulously sharpened, two-person, crosscut saws, where necessary, standing on makeshift elevations to get above the buttress (pictured). Once felled, the top and branches were removed and lower trunk cut into 20-to 30-foot lengths. By the early 1950s, chainsaws increased production manyfold. (SLAF.)

To get to the trees, a line was cleared, a grade or trestle created, and a railroad track laid down, mostly by Black workers. These lines radiated off the main Copeland track, creating a 190-mile network of arcing tramroads through the swamp, remaining recognizable today. The train transported crews to the end of the line, who then walked to the worksite, working dark to dark. (SLAF.)

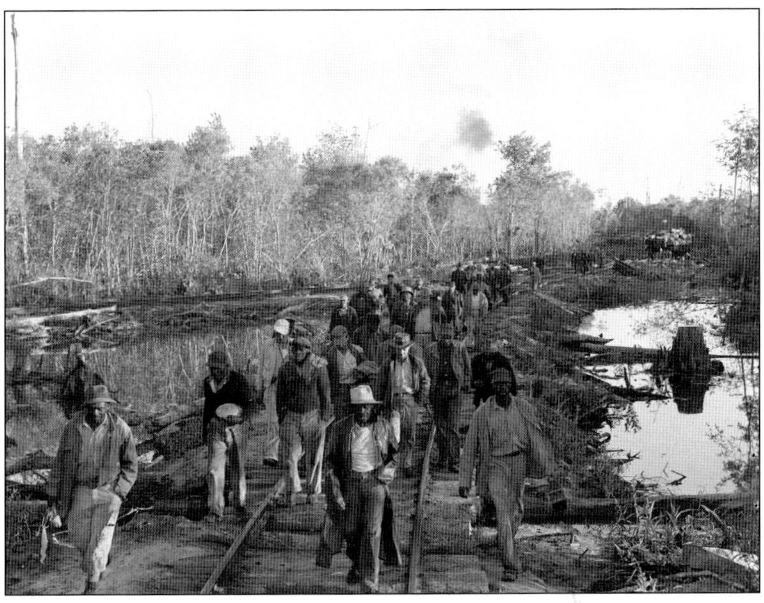

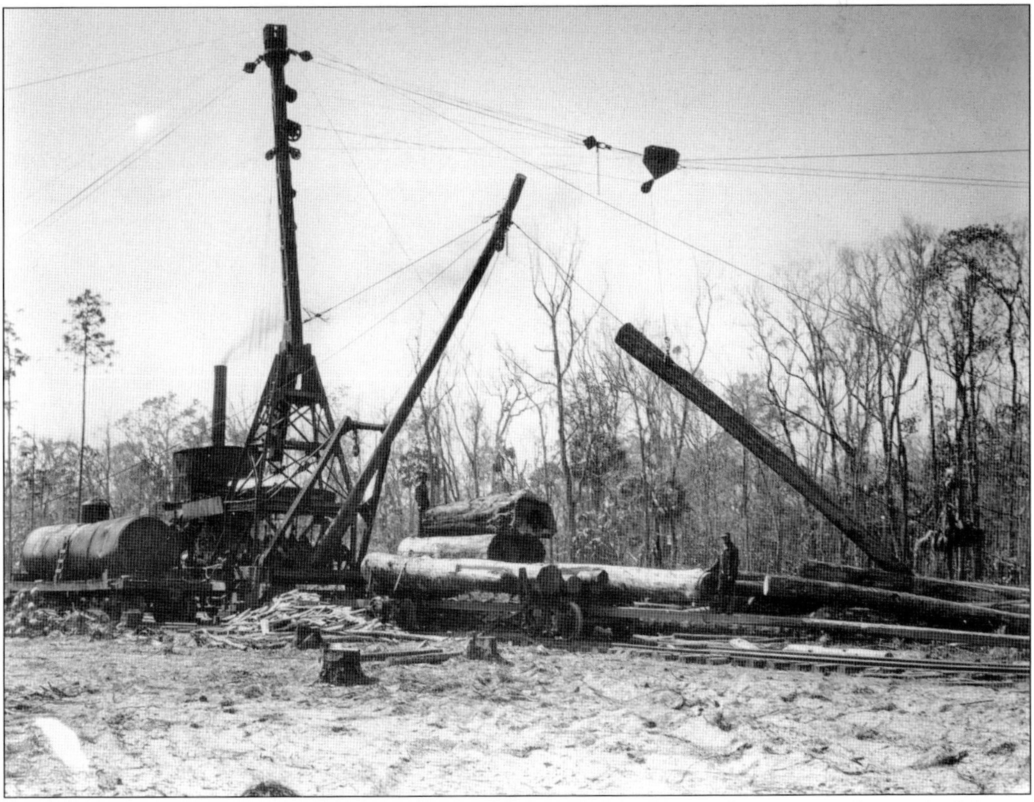

Logs were carried on overhead skidders or snaked out of the swamp by oxen, mules, or bulldozers to an overhead cableway or crane that placed logs on railroad cars. Old steam engines were used long after they were retired elsewhere because they could pull large loads, slowly, fueled by locally sourced pine logs. The train returned to Copeland in the evening. If it came back sooner, someone had been hurt. (SLAF.)

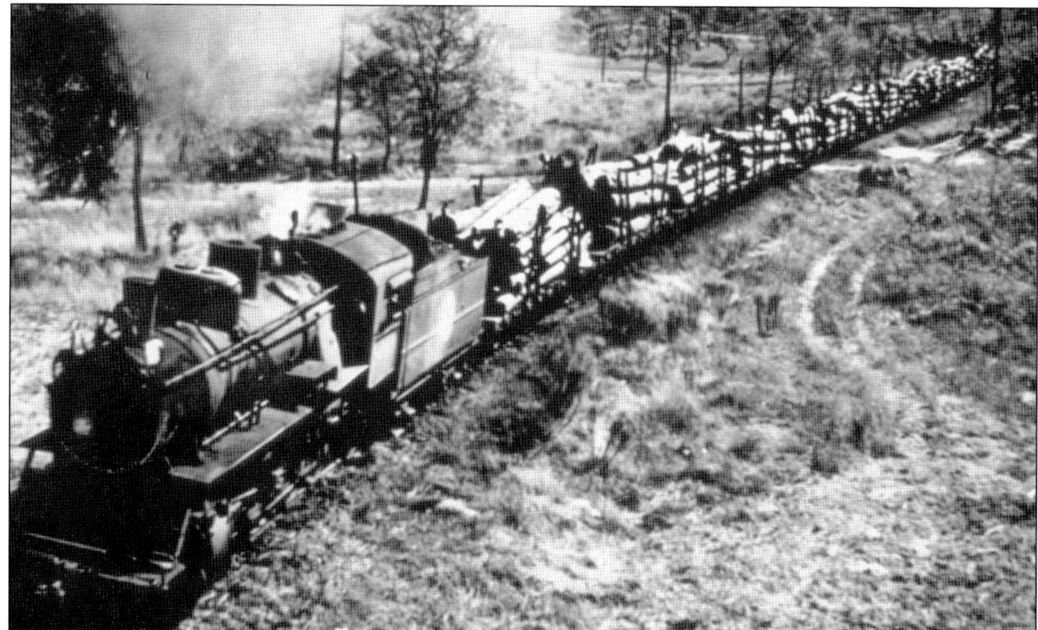

Whistles and the trains' comings and goings marked the day. Lumbermen's and steelmen's families worked as cooks and at part-time jobs. All were paid in private coinage spendable for such things as cabin rent or at Winford Janes's store. Into the 1950s, 360 million board feet of cypress shipped by train to the company mill in Perry mostly from Fakahatchee and Picayune Strands. When the timber was depleted, the company moved on. (SFCMC.)

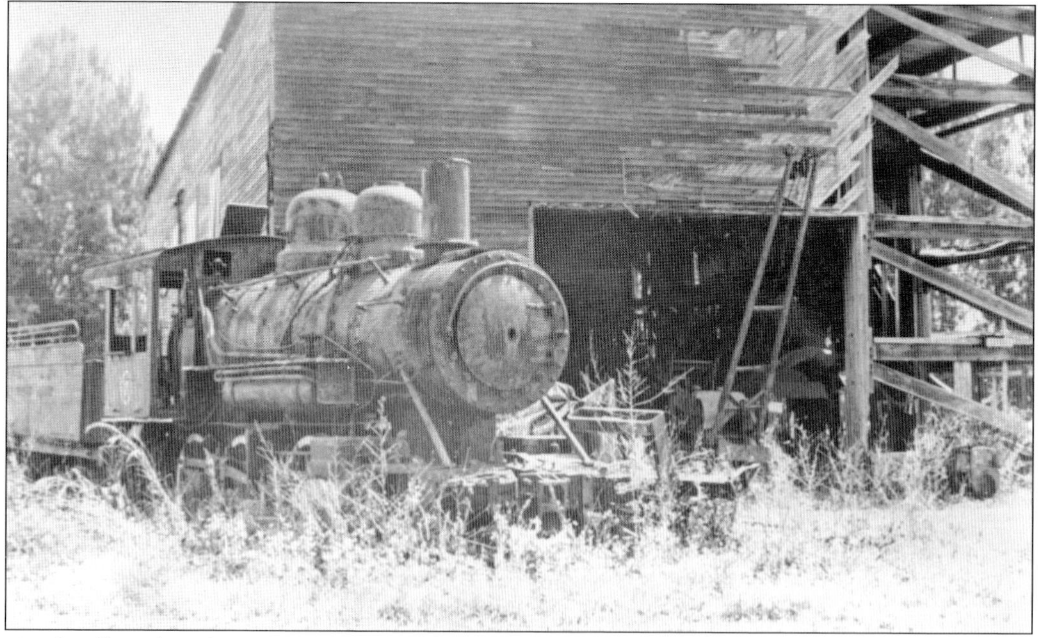

Nearly all workers left when the company pulled out, abandoning the camp, houses, mill, and locomotives (shown). Lumbering opened the forest canopy to invasive species, seed trees were not purposely reserved, and treetops and branches were left as slash. Pole cutters followed removing over-looked small trees. Leftover tramlines and ditches altered water flow. (CCM.)

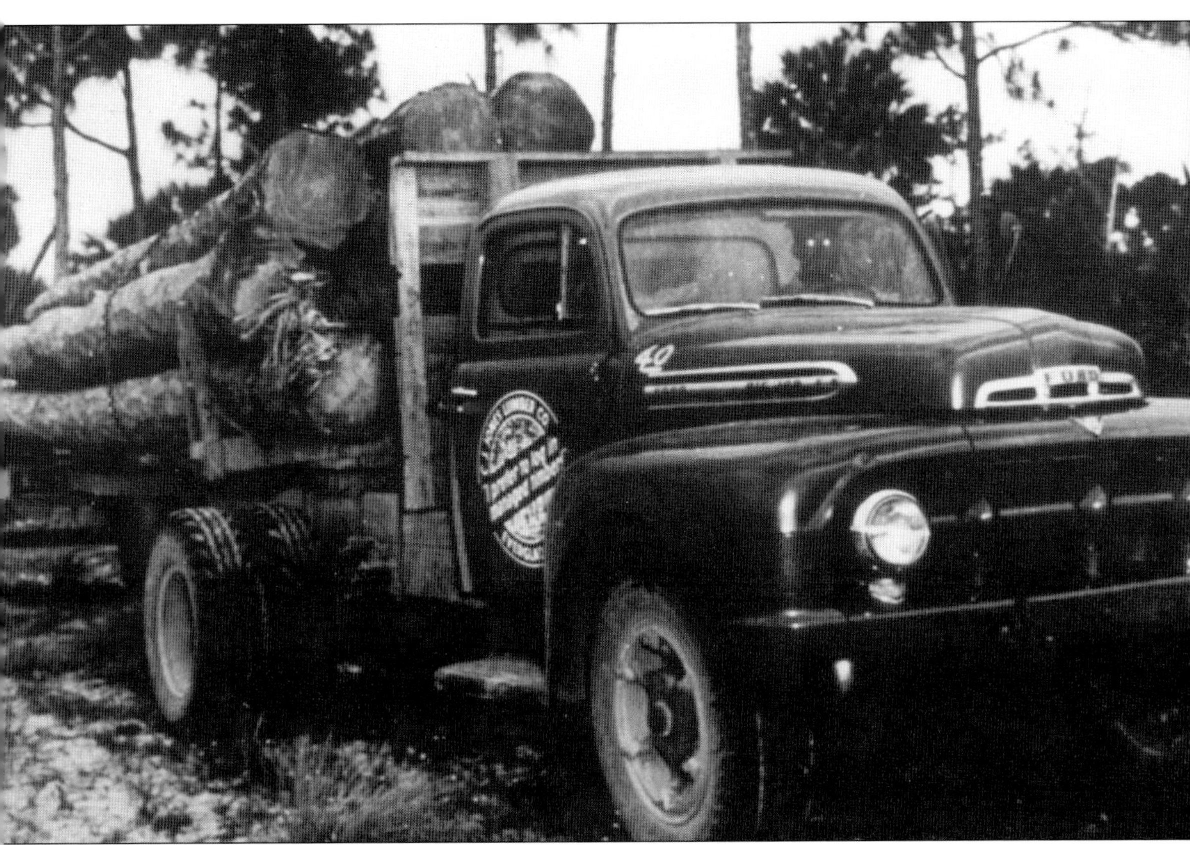

Pine was also in demand, especially the slow-growing, dense, South Florida variety. Cypress and pine saws were not interchangeable, so mills specialized. C.J. Jones started at Reynolds Mill, and in 1940, his C.J. Jones Lumber Company established the town of Jerome, Jones's middle name, four miles north of Copeland. The town grew to over 100 workers and 40 homes separated by the railroad track, Whites on one side, Blacks on the other. The company had moved to Florida after depleting pine yards farther north, so most of the workers came from other southern states. The company lumbered pine and other softwoods starting in the Deep Lake area, but eventually movable railroad tracks extended over 200 miles throughout the swamp, reaching to its eastern border. All work was done on site: milling, loading, hauling, local sales, and creosoting, which contaminated the soil. Processing 100,000 board feet of lumber a day, Jerome became the largest steam-powered lumber mill in the south. Having exhausted the lumber pines, the mill closed in 1955 and burned down the next year. (SFCMC.)

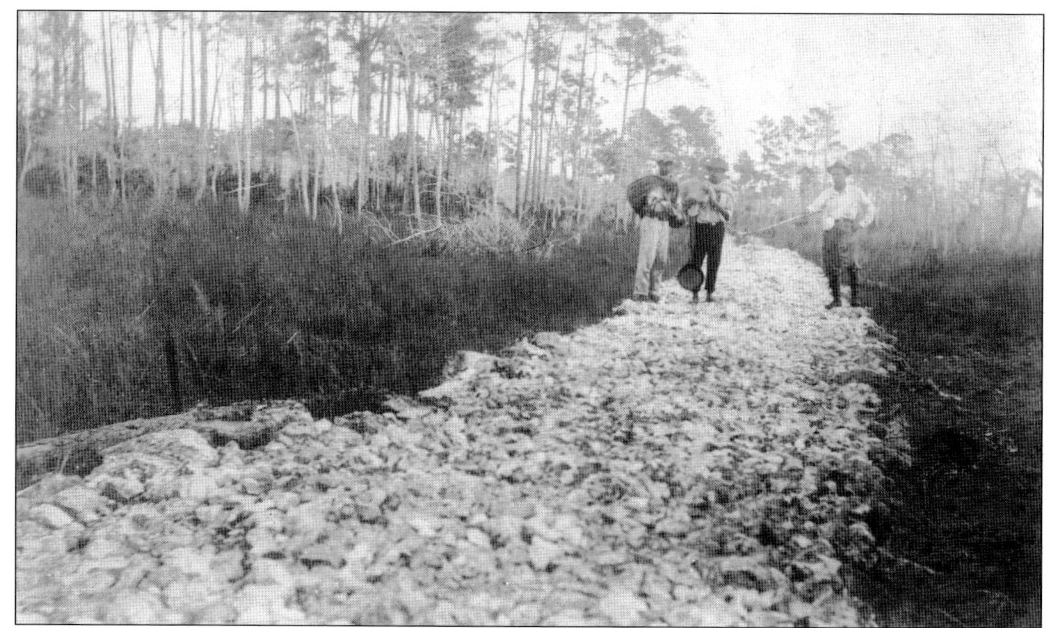

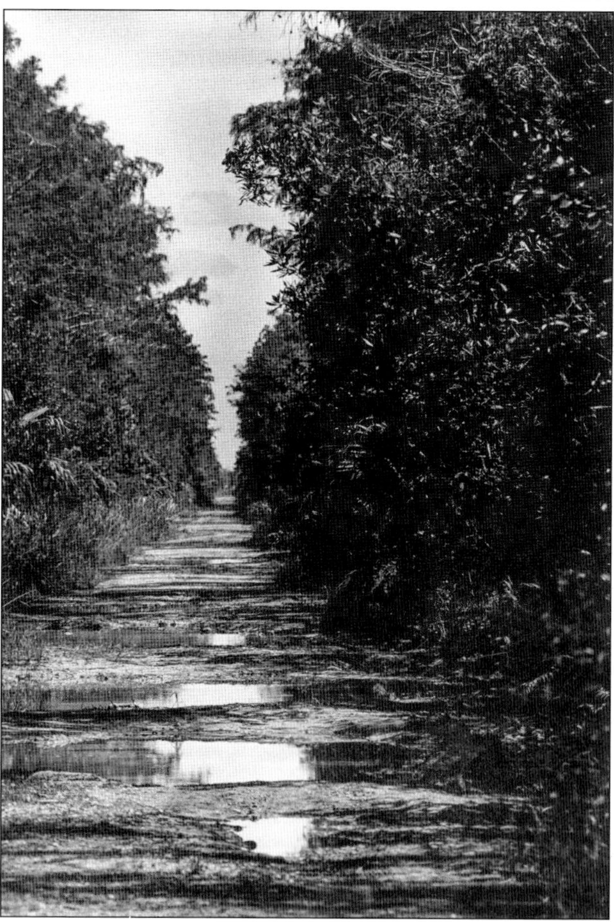

J.F. Jaudon's road (above) also enticed the setting up of lumber mills and accompanying settlements. He laid out the road through pine and cypress forests. When connected to the Tamiami Trail, it became Loop Road (left). He had his surveyors do an appraisal of the standing timber, which he advertised as giving value to the properties. He also advertised that he planned to build a railroad to transport the lumber. Pine and cypress were harvested around Pinecrest, at Lostmans' Pines, Gator Hook, Gum Slough, Roberts Lakes Strand, and Rodgers River Strand. Stumps nearly five feet in diameter remain, as do tramline crossties, to be seen along Gator Hook trail. (Above, HMM; left, UM.)

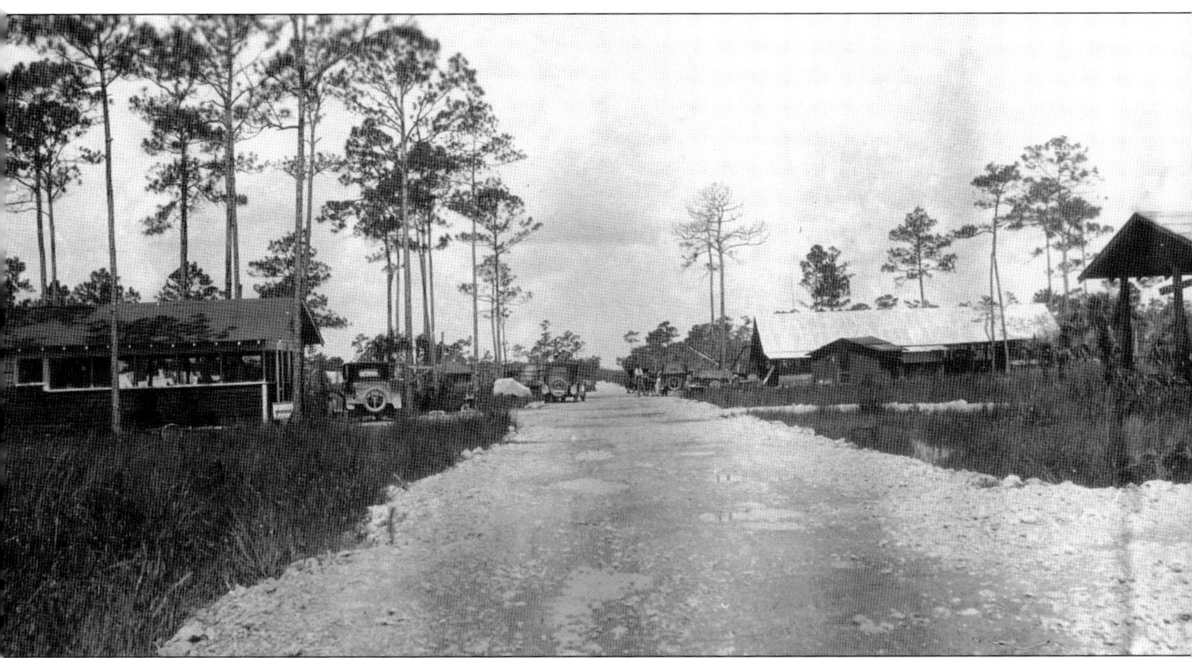

Jaudon marketed his $20-per-acre properties every way he could. He brought prospects to Pinecrest, to the end of his road, and onward by canoe or by boat from Everglades City to his planned town of Chevalier on Chevelier Bay. Marjorie Stoneman Douglas invested in a plot. Jaudon sold his interests in Pinecrest, which was platted into 54 city blocks with his intended Tamiami Trail as the main street. Pinecrest grew with the lumbering at Williams sawmill. By the 1930s, it had 200 people, homes, worker bunkhouses, school, library, general store, and gas station. Over 175 miles from its county seat and law enforcement in Key West, it attracted folks pleased with such a situation. During Prohibition, the Big Cypress Lodge, titled to Al Capone's cousin and run by Jack Miller, was built conveniently just outside the Dade County line. Its steps remain. Financial manipulations faltered, lumber gave out, mills closed, and the Depression and hurricanes hit. By early 1940s, the town declined. People remaining had chosen to get away, from whatever, and tended to avoid minding each other's business. (MCPL.)

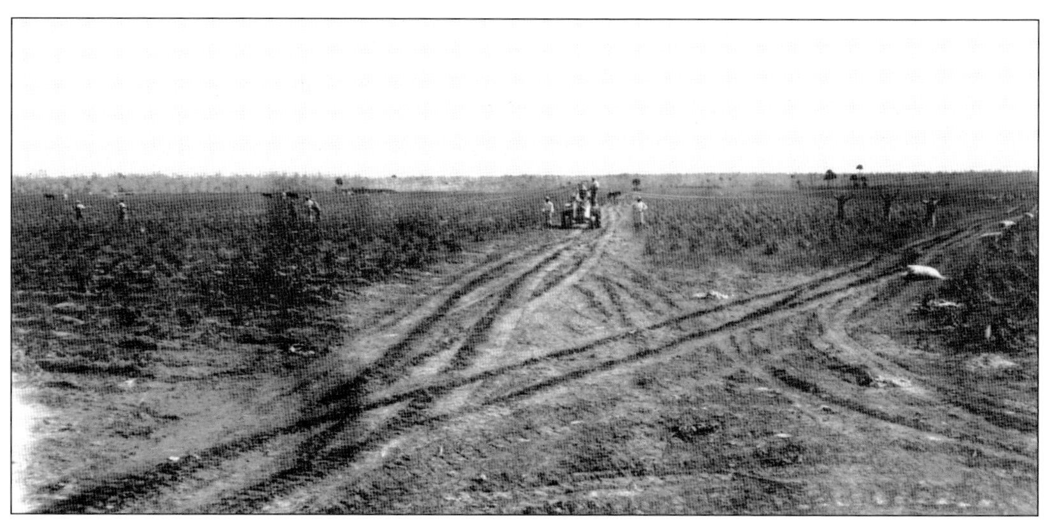

In 1930, James Jaudon shifted attention from his failing Loop Road and Chevalier Corporation ventures to the now-completed Tamiami Trail, where he began buying investment land. He also returned to farming with H.W. Bird; their farm was Birdon (a composite of their names). Their main street remains. Buying land from Jaudon, J.B. Janes moved his tomato operation from Copeland and Edgar C. Gaunt moved his operations from Miami to farm the seasonally flooded, muddy prairies. The J.T. Gaunt Company became the largest enterprise, acquiring over 3,000 acres that were farmed seasonally around the winter dry period (above). In the early season, while the soil was still saturated, mules with 10-inch mud-plate shoes were used to plow furrows, making elevated ridges where the tomatoes were planted and fertilized by compost imported from Georgia. Later in the season, large-wheeled tractors could be used (below). (Both, CCM.)

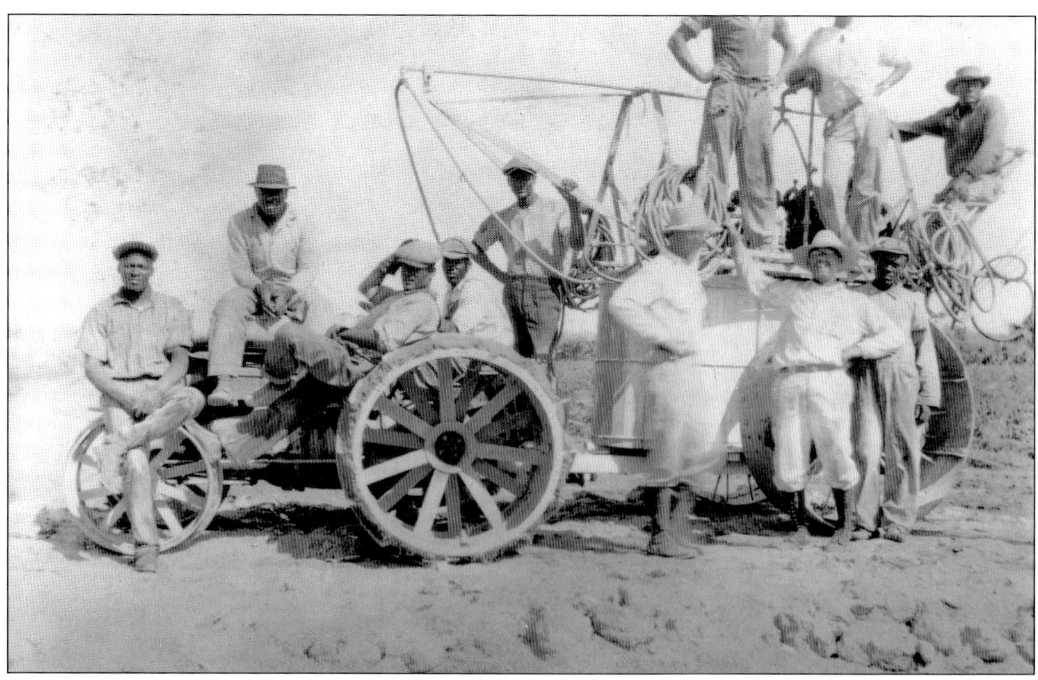

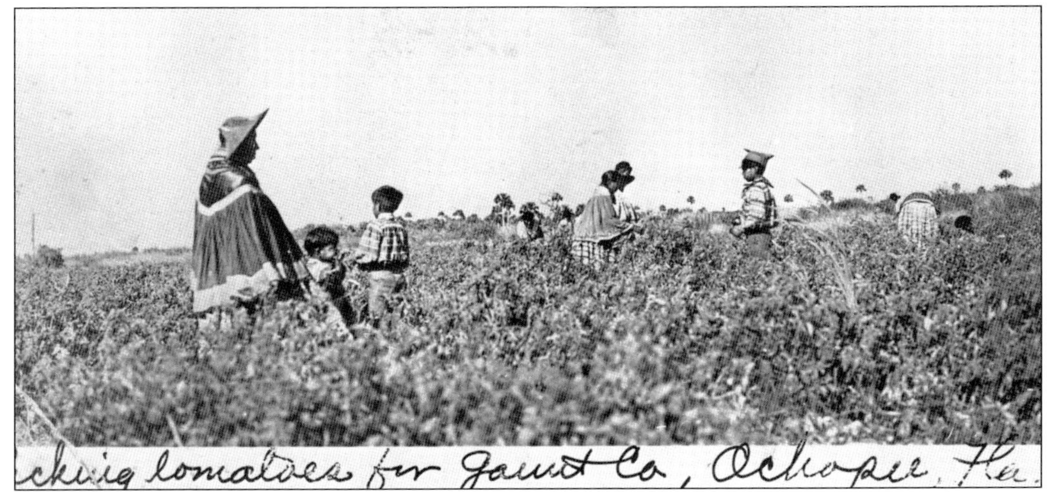

Tomatoes were picked by hand by temporary crews, including Seminoles, hopefully before the next rainy season reflooded the fields. They were hauled to the packinghouse and shipped out of Carnestown by railroad. Ochopee became a primary national producer of winter tomatoes. Eventually employing nearly 1,000 people seasonally, Gaunt's had a reputation for fair treatment, paying in dollars and not company tokens, as was the case at the lumber mills. (SLAF.)

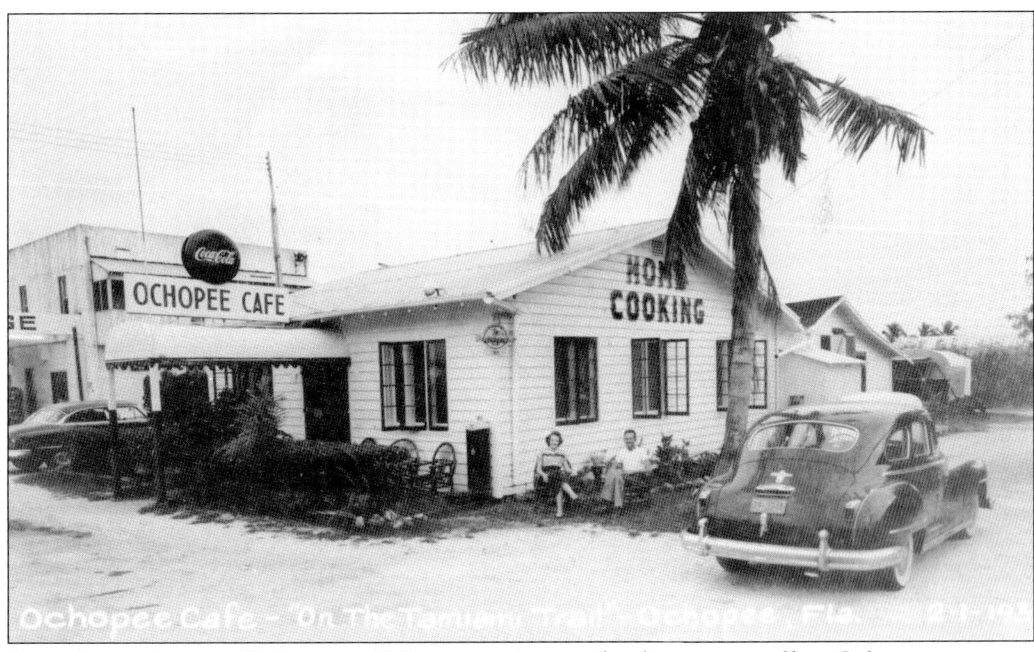

Gaunt's town became Ochopee in 1932, a name invented to have a post office. Ochopee was never totally a company town. Over time, various plots were sold off to others. The town included multiple residences, cottages, offices, warehouses, the packinghouse, stores, the Ochopee Café (pictured), Griff's garage, a power plant, a general store with the post office, and a three-story boardinghouse. Boardwalks were needed in the wet season. (KH.)

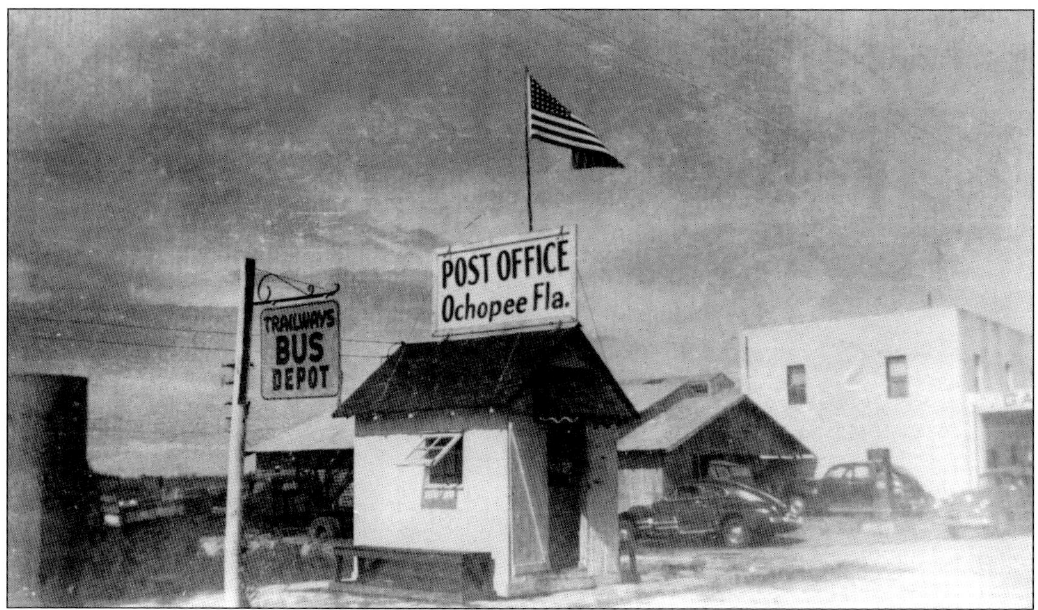

In time, flooding and failing fertility made farming increasingly difficult in the coastal prairies. In the 1950s, the Gaunt company moved to higher, sandier ground at Immokalee, leaving behind the photogenic smallest post office, housed "temporarily" by postmaster Sidney Brown in a pipe-storage shed after the Ochopee general store and its post office burned in 1953. The tiny tourist-attracting building persists. (KH.)

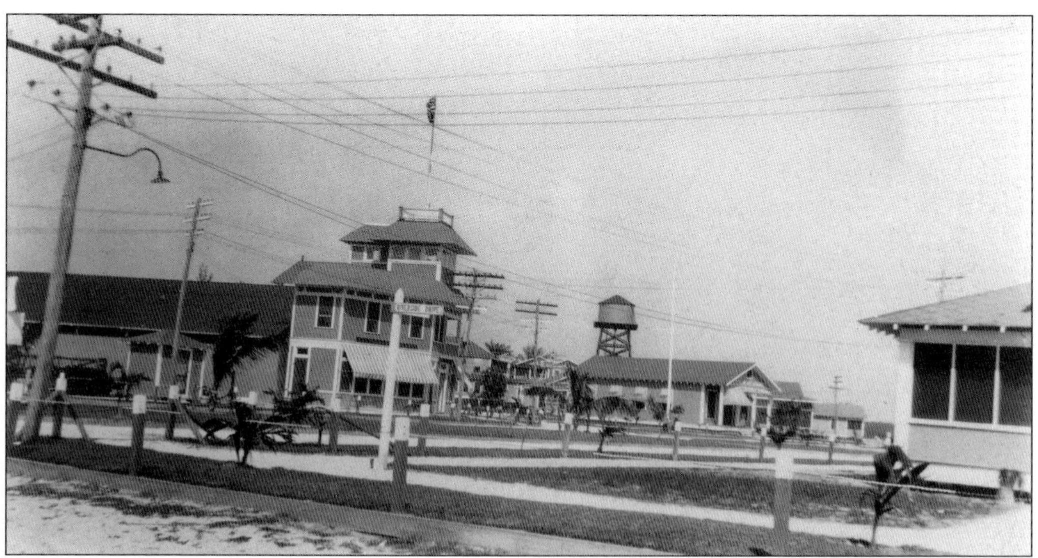

Barron Collier developed his town. It had residences, his companies' offices, a bank, a hotel, stores, a streetcar, and more. This typical view from Riverside Drive in the 1920s shows, from left to right, the post office, water tower, the first Bank of Everglades building, and the mayor's home. Daniel McLeod was the Collier-endorsed mayor of this company town for 36 years. (SLAF.)

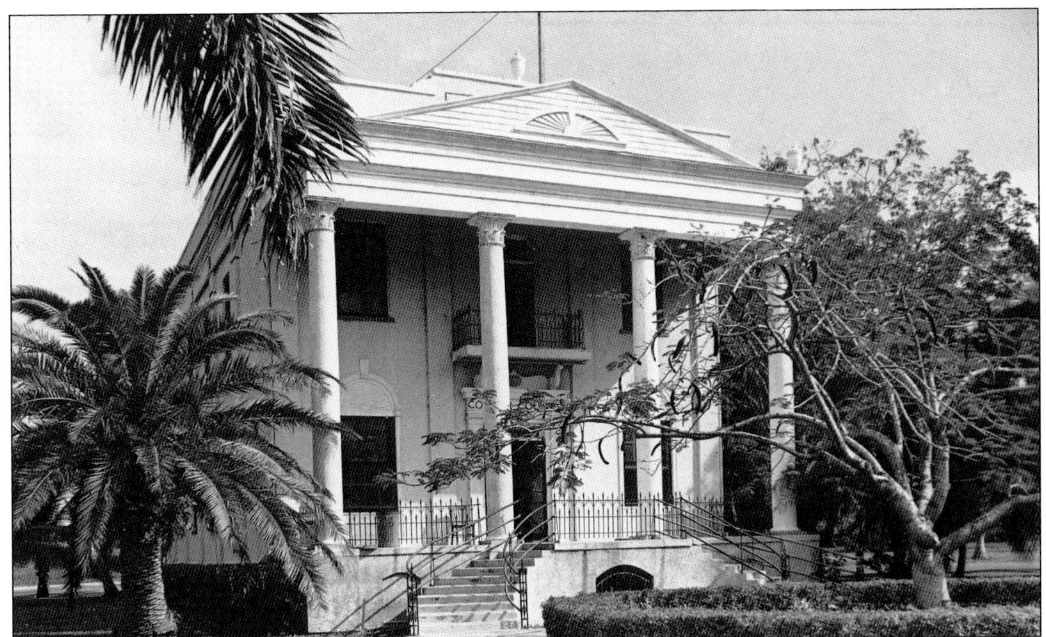

The distinguished Classic Revival courthouse was built in 1926 to serve the brand-new Collier County. This image is after a 1940s renovation of the portico. Following Hurricane Donna, the county seat was moved to East Naples in 1962, after which the building became the city hall. It is in the National Register of Historic Places. In 1965, the town was officially renamed Everglades City. (SLAF.)

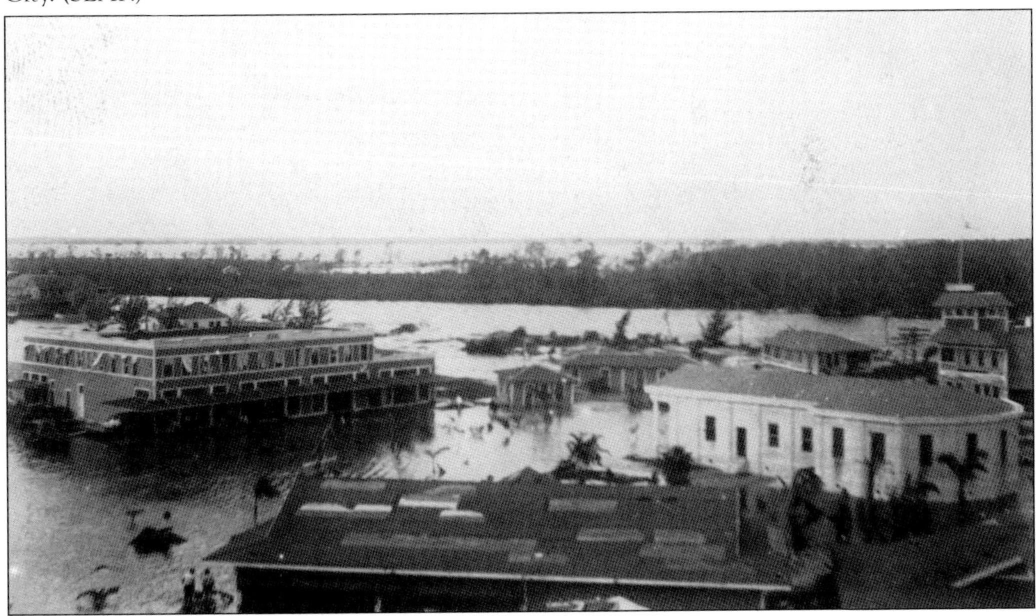

Hurricanes have not been kind to southwest Florida. Over 60 storms have hit Everglades City in 153 years of record. The 1910 storm, with exceptional flooding, played a role in the famous mob killing of Edgar Watson at Chokoloskee. This image shows the 1926 hurricane that devastated Everglades City. The mid-October 1947 hurricane caused massive flooding, leading to the imposition of flood control measures. Hurricane Donna in 1960 caused widespread damage. (SLAF.)

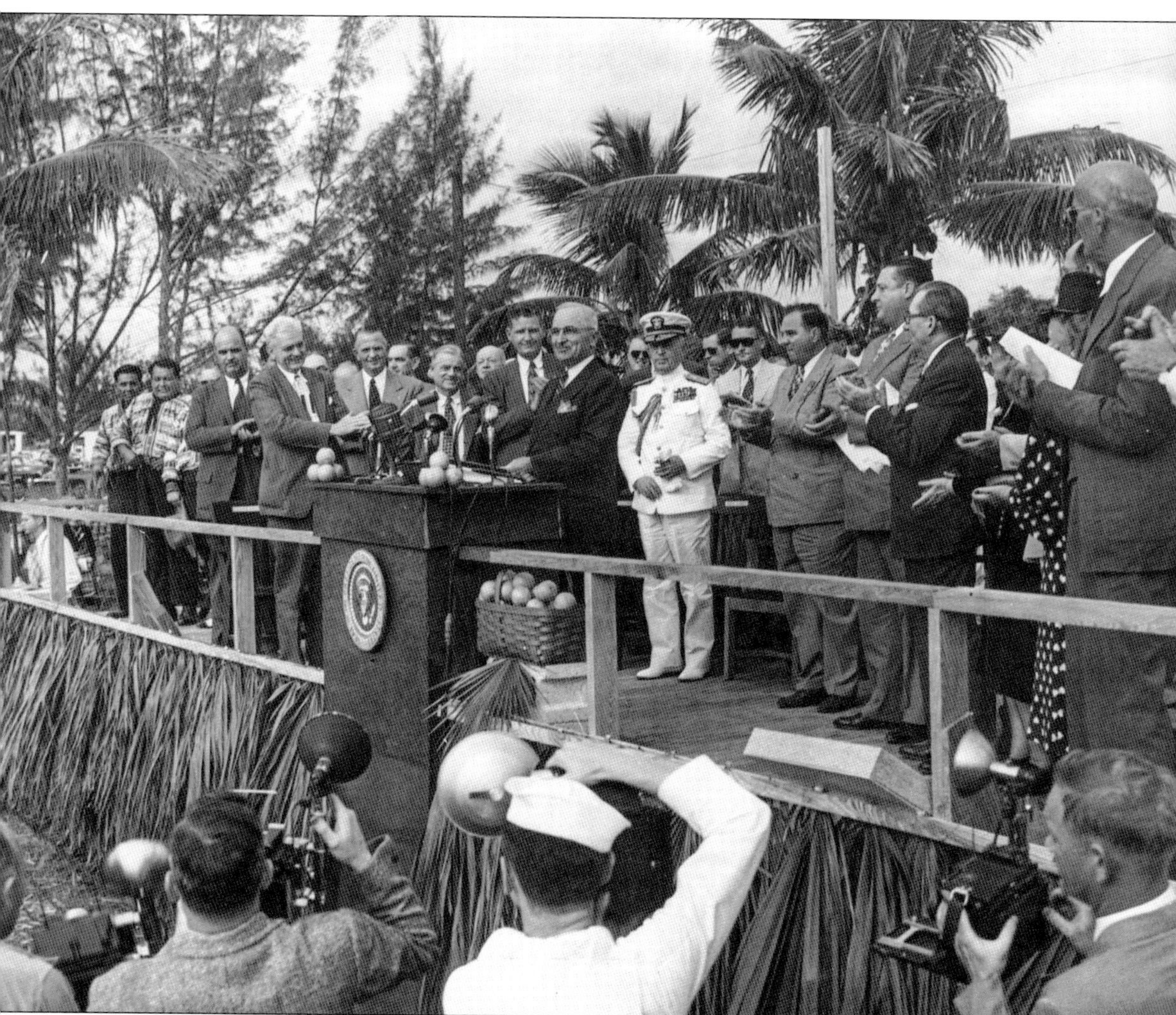

Everglades City hosted Pres. Harry S. Truman's dedication of Everglades National Park in 1947, ironically a ceremony held not in the actual Everglades wetlands but in the Big Cypress Swamp. Stopping by the Rod and Gun Club on his way to Key West, Truman's speech suggested the region's natural subtleties: "Here are no lofty peaks seeking the sky, no mighty glaciers or rushing streams wearing away the uplifted land." Rather, here was a land of quiet waters. The park's establishment was a turning point in the region's environmental and social history, changing how land and waters were accessed and used and how old and new fish and wildlife protections were implemented. Much of the southern Big Cypress Swamp was included in proposed boundaries for the park, but inclusion was opposed by Barron Collier who said he could smell oil under the surface. With much effort and expense, these ecologically valuable lands and water were eventually set aside as Big Cypress National Preserve and other protected lands. (OPN.)

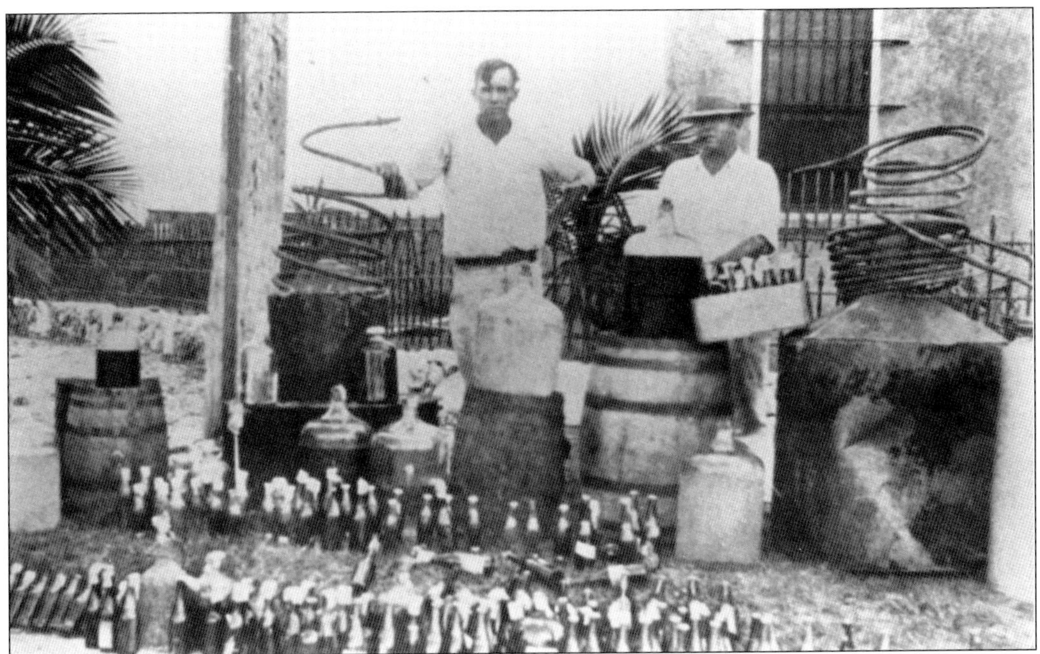

Two mainstays of the local economy expanded in the 1920s and 1930s, moonshining and smuggling. Never a "dry" culture, citizens generally were supportive of profit-making alcohol ventures. Stills were secreted in mangroves and the cypress swamp. Raids tended to be mostly for show. This late-1920s image (above) shows evidence displayed for newspapers by the long-serving sheriff, Lewis J. Thorp. After Prohibition, moonshining persisted meeting local demand, illustrated in this 1939 handbill (right). Policing smuggling was more risky. In 1925, Deputy J.H. Fox and family disappeared just before testifying against local smugglers, and in 1935, deputy W.E. Hutto was gunned down in Everglades City. Local boatsmen unloaded offshore ships; some liquor departed by road, some went to Carnestown to be repacked in produce crates and loaded on the train beneath real tomatoes. It is hard to imagine Collier interests being unaware. (Above, CCM; right, HMM.)

WANTED

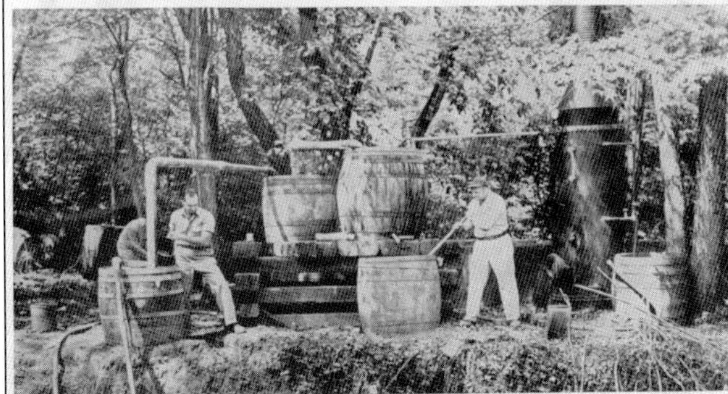

information from **YOU** the taxpayer on the locations of

BOOTLEG STILLS

Moonshine stills in your locality like that pictured above, are robbing you of many thousands of dollars in Federal and State liquor taxes. Help your Government by reporting them, by mail or phone, to

ALCOHOL AND TOBACCO TAX DIVISION, INTERNAL REVENUE SERVICE

P.O.Box 381,
Miami, Florida

All communications held strictly confidential

Form 1793 (8-54)

U.S. TREASURY DEPARTMENT, INTERNAL REVENUE SERVICE

16—70765-1 GPO

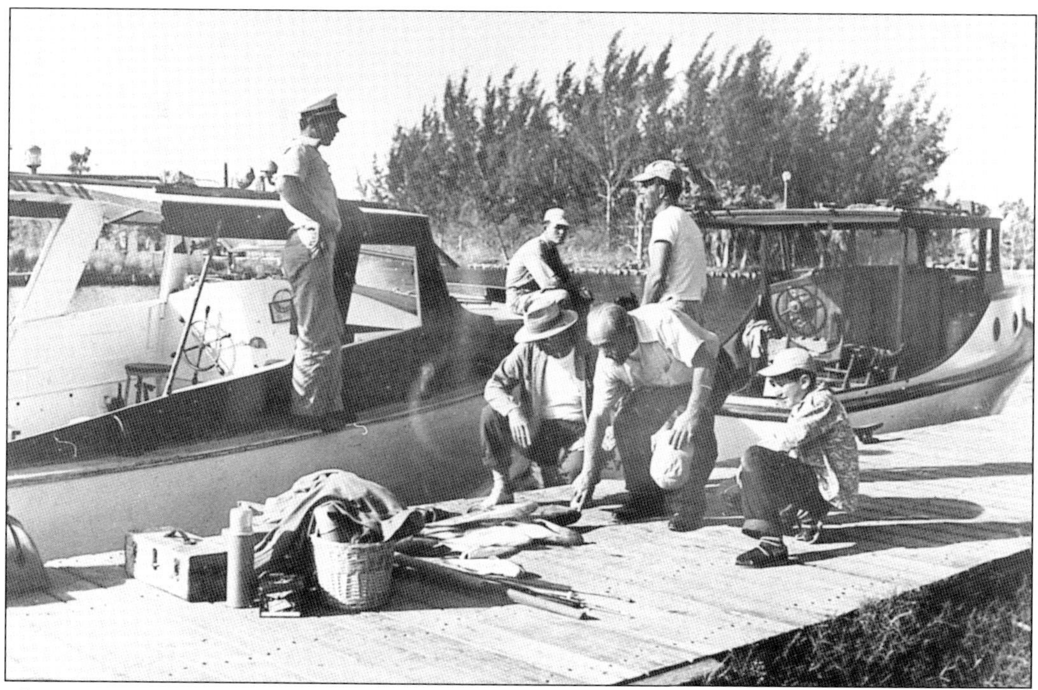

The unregulated pioneer hunter/fisher lifestyle of sailboats, canoes, skiffs, and open access gave way to powerboats, private land, government-managed parks, and game and fish regulations. Some took to commercial fishing and guiding (pictured). Some took to smuggling and what became poaching of deer and alligators (by then an endangered species). Peg Brown is considered an icon among Big Cypress alligator poachers. Traditions began coalescing into a "gladesmen" swamp heritage. (CCM.)

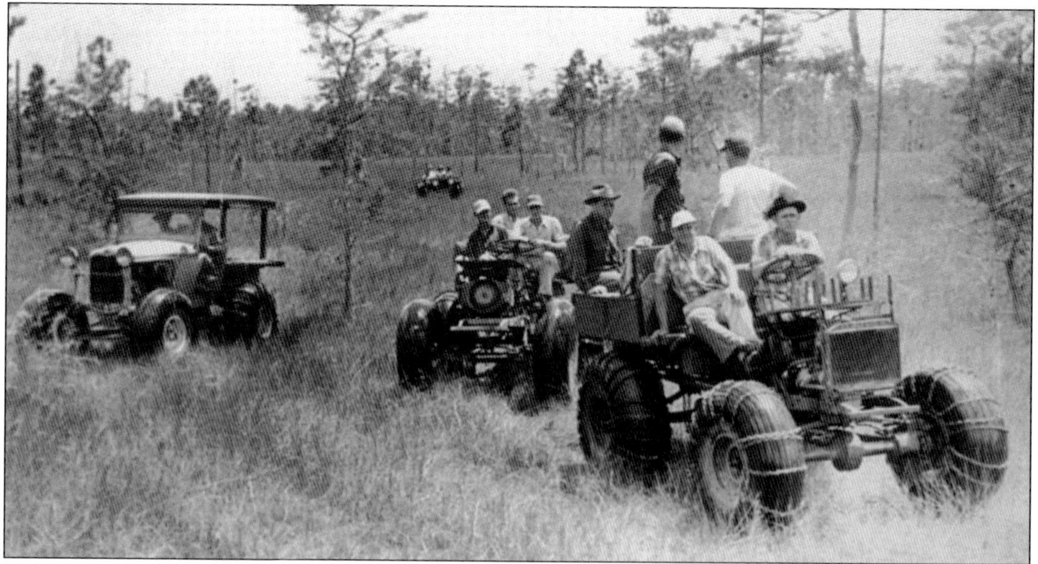

Inspired by California dune buggies, Ed Frank is credited with introducing swamp buggies in the 1910s. Frequently starting with Model As and spare parts, early swamp buggies were unique creations (and uniquely named), high enough to clear stumps, and sufficiently powered to plow through mud or over small trees. After World War II, aircraft tires and jeeps appeared. To test them, swamp buggy races began in 1949. (CCM.)

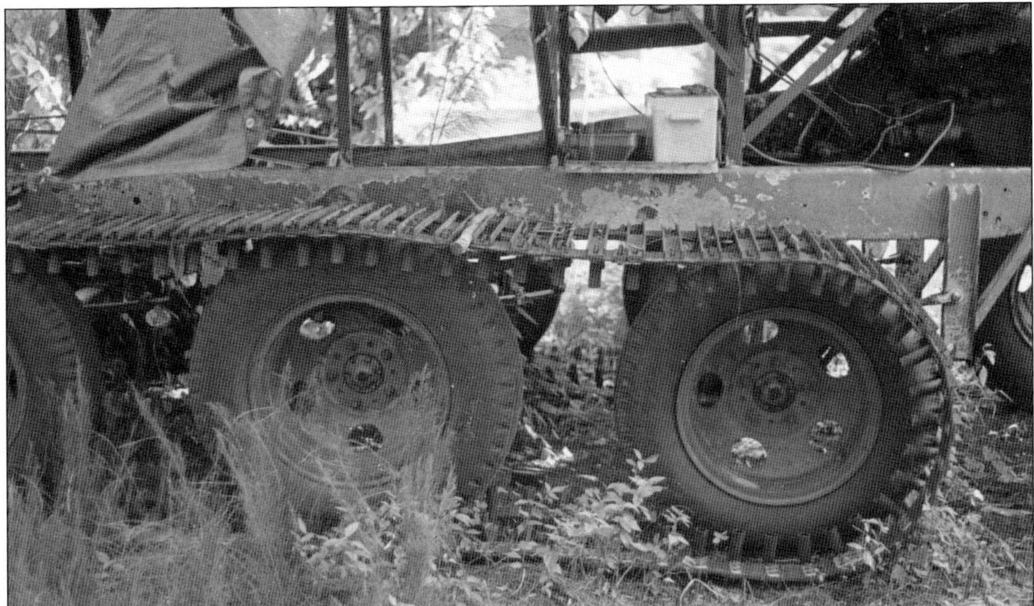

A further elaboration, pioneered by Frank Denninger, used continuous caterpillar treads evolving into full-track and half-track buggies, or "weasels," capable of crushing their way through most of the swamp. Buggies of all manner of designs opened the swamp, allowing motorized penetration farther and easier than ever before, to hunt deer and hog, to fish canals, to explore, to go to a camp, or just to ride. (SLAF.)

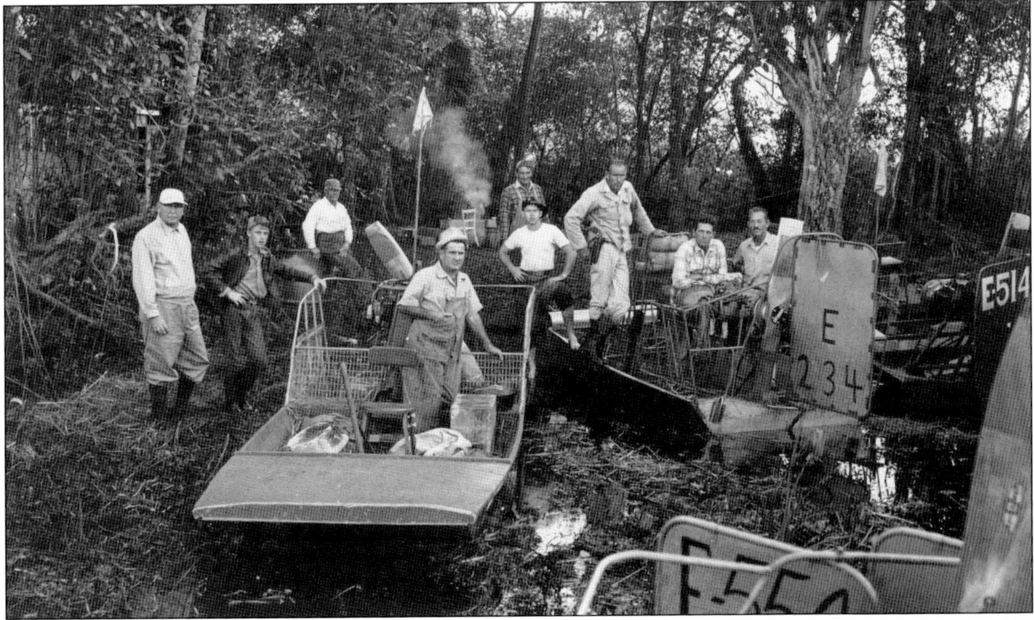

Airboats used airplane propellers to push a flatboat hull over the water, damp grass, or even dry land. The earliest were as narrow as the glades skiffs they replaced. Aviator Glenn Curtiss was among the first to use one locally. In 1933, Johnny Lamb of Chokoloskee built a 75-horsepower "whooshmobile." Horsepower increased as airplane engines became available after World War II. Franny Taylor produced commercially built Taylor-Made hulls. (SLAF.)

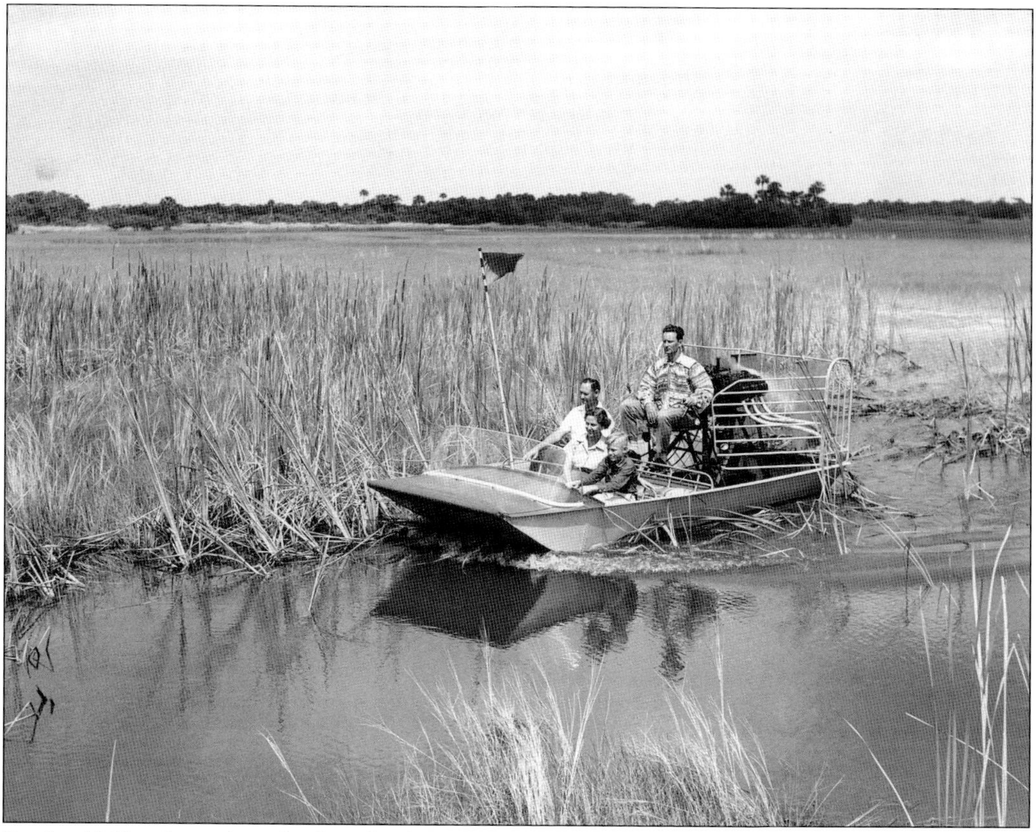

By the 1950s, the airboat had evolved into a powerful machine, although still without brakes. Raymond Wooten fitted Cadillac engines with airplane props and opened Wooten's Airboat Rides. To accommodate his tourist rides, especially in the dry season, he acquired 400 acres off Tamiami Trail and excavated landings and trails. Similar attractions developed all along the Tamiami Trail, including those run by Trail Seminoles. (SLAF.)

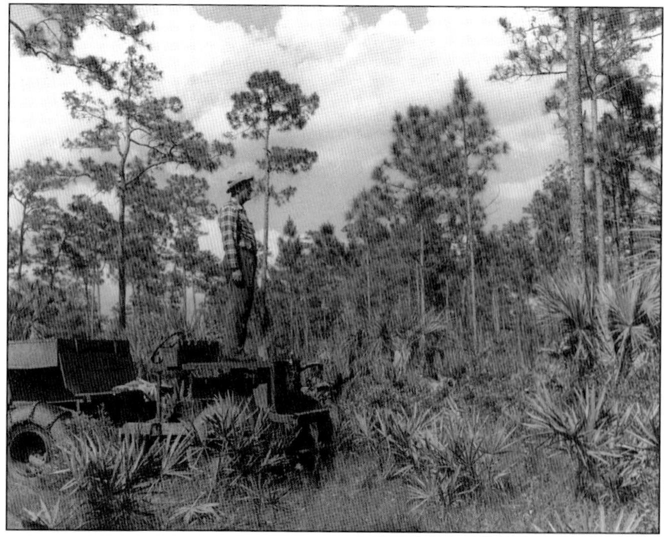

Buggy and airboat owners supported protecting South Florida wetlands and their preferred uses. The Everglades Conservation and Sportsman Club was organized in 1950. Pictured is founder Cal Stone surveying his Big Cypress property. The Halftrack Club of Dade County was founded in 1960 by Frank Denninger; the Airboat Association of Florida was founded in 1951 by airboat builder Franny Taylor. In 1989, the Everglades and Francis S. Taylor Wildlife Management Area was named for him. (CCM.)

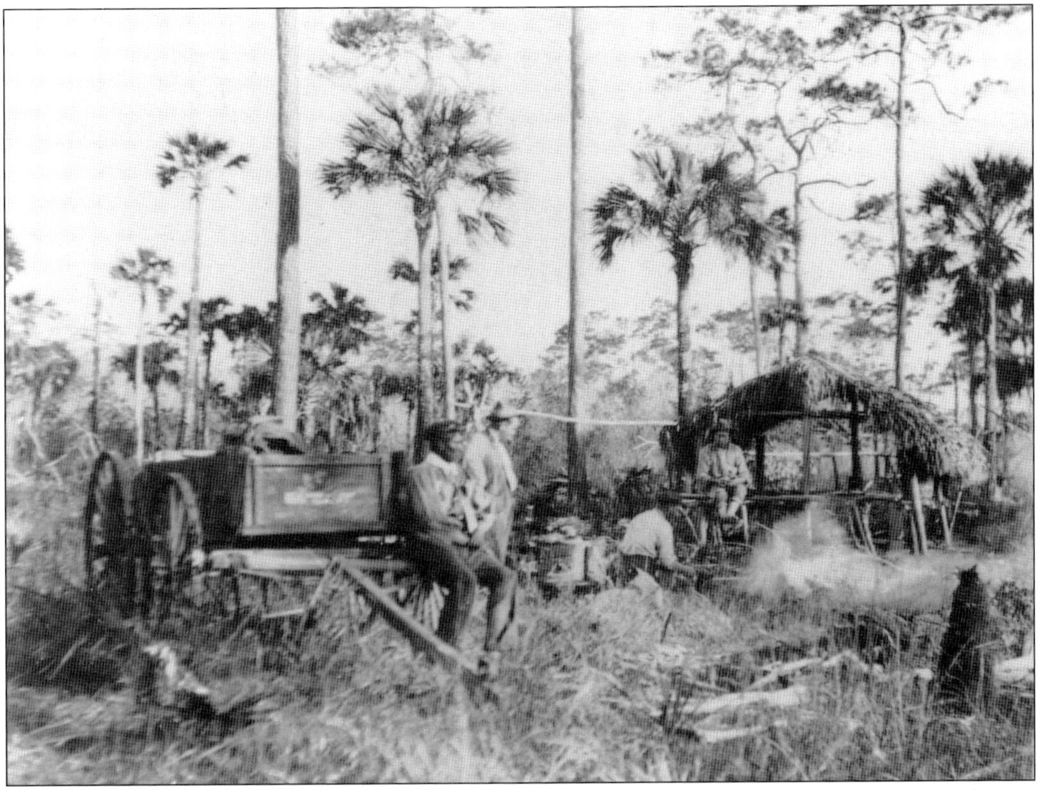

When gladesmen had to walk and pole skiffs, excursions for hunting, poaching, or exploring lasted days. As did Seminoles before them, they set up camps on tree islands using tents or palm-thatched huts (pictured). Swamp buggies and airboats allowed more frequent, faster, and more deeply penetrating trips. Cabins became more elaborate with materials hauled in, more permanent, and more personally claimed, although few were on occupant-owned land, which was mostly unsurveyed. (CCM.)

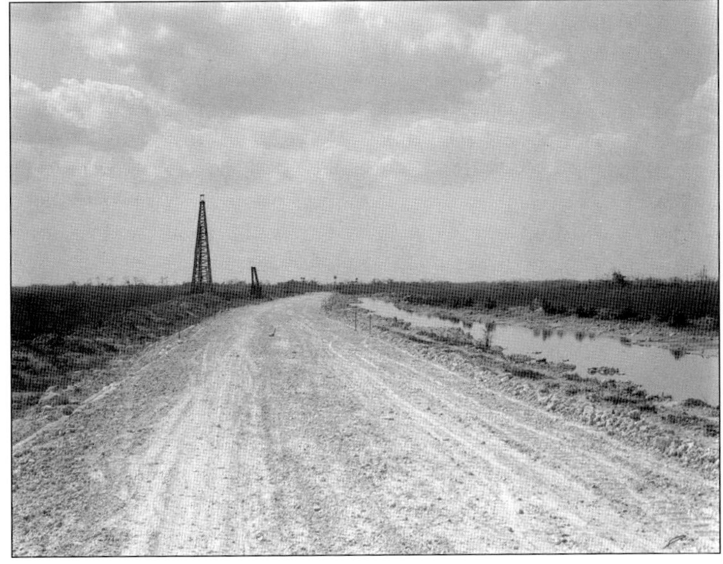

Barron Collier's unwavering ambition was to find oil in the Big Cypress. In the 1920s, test wells followed the new Tamiami Trail, shown at what would become Monroe Junction. In the 1930s, Collier contracted with the Gulf Oil Company, which explored unsuccessfully from giant swamp buggies. Humble Oil (later ExxonMobil) finally discovered the Sunniland Field in 1943. By 1954, the oil field produced 500,000 barrels of oil per year. (MDPLS.)

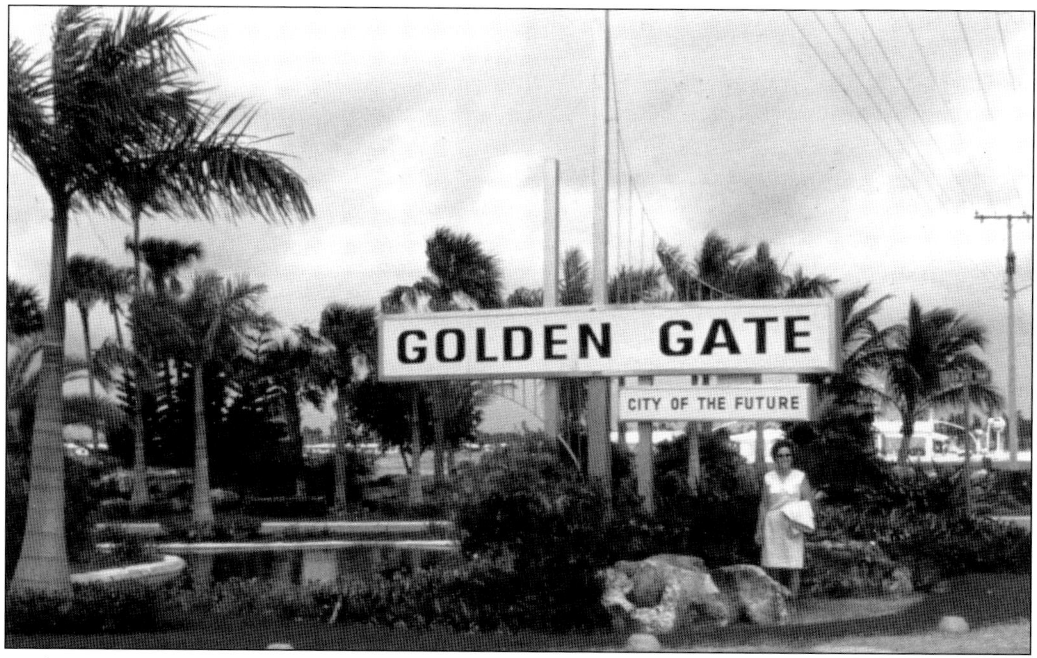

Real estate development came to Big Cypress big-time in the 1950s. Gulf American Land Corporation bought 175 square miles at $100 per acre and quickly drained it, dropping water levels two feet. The company built 183 miles of roadbed without any infrastructure. Lots were marketed nationwide for $30 down, $30 a month. Prospects were flown into the company's on-site hotel. By 1967, over 17,000 lots were sold, mostly sight unseen. (CCM.)

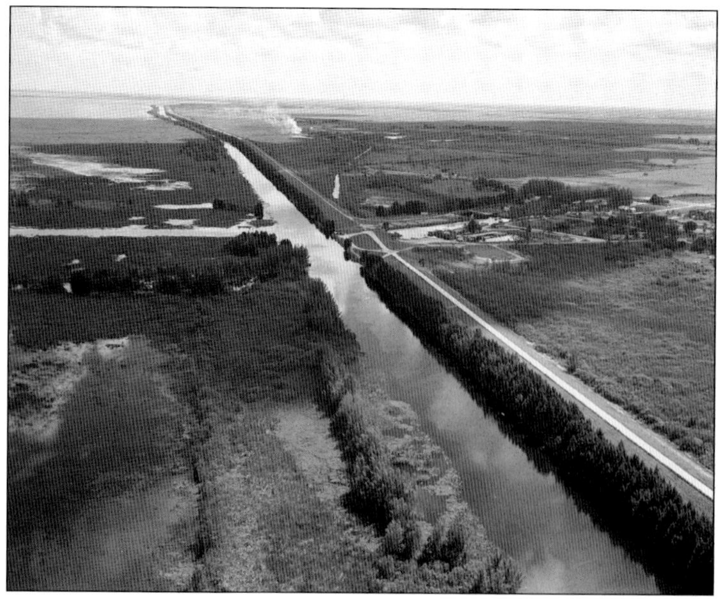

After the floods of 1947 hurricanes, the federal government authorized the US Army Corps of Engineers to control flooding in South Florida, and the state created a flood control agency, starting decades of landscape-scale plumbing—building levees, digging canals, and installing pump stations. The project initially focused on the Everglades east of the Big Cypress, isolating the developing Atlantic coast and providing agricultural land south of Lake Okeechobee. (SLAF.)

Four

Preserving the Swamp
The 1960s, an Airport, and a Preserve

The Big Cypress Swamp of the 1960s was becoming a far different place from the pristine wilderness encountered by Calusas, Seminoles, soldiers, pioneer settlers, or even the early developers. Having taken all the trees they could, lumber companies had departed; their company towns waned. Ochopee declined after Gaunt moved his farm to higher ground inland. Everglades City, no longer a developer's dream or county seat, marked time as a fishing town. Pinecrest persisted, attracting diverse humanity. Tourism increased, enticed by sport fishing, airboat rides, alligator wrestling, and Everglades National Park's western gateway. By the 1960s, the Seminole and Miccosukee tribes had achieved legal recognition. Canals and levees of water management reached the Cypress. Swamp buggies, recreationists, and hundreds of camps proliferated. Golden Gate continued to sell nearly raw swampland. The health of wildlife populations became a concern.

Into this world, Dade and Collier Counties, with limited public notice but decades of behind-the-scenes planning, inserted into the Big Cypress a massive airport. The conservation community was stunned and became engaged, as did water managers, the federal government, Miccosukees and Seminoles, and, belatedly, Gov. Claude Kirk. Friends of the Everglades and the Everglades Coalition were founded in opposition. Studies showed that accompanying development would threaten Everglades National Park. Full jetport development was halted. In 1971, Pres. Richard Nixon proposed that the Big Cypress become a national freshwater reserve, and in 1974, Pres. Gerald Ford signed the bill creating Big Cypress National Preserve. It was not a normal assignment for the National Park Service. This was not a national park but a new concept supporting multiple activities ranging from ORVs to oil wells and traditional uses by Miccosukees and Seminoles, while also protecting the swamp ecosystem, hydrology, rare plants, and endangered wildlife—a tall order.

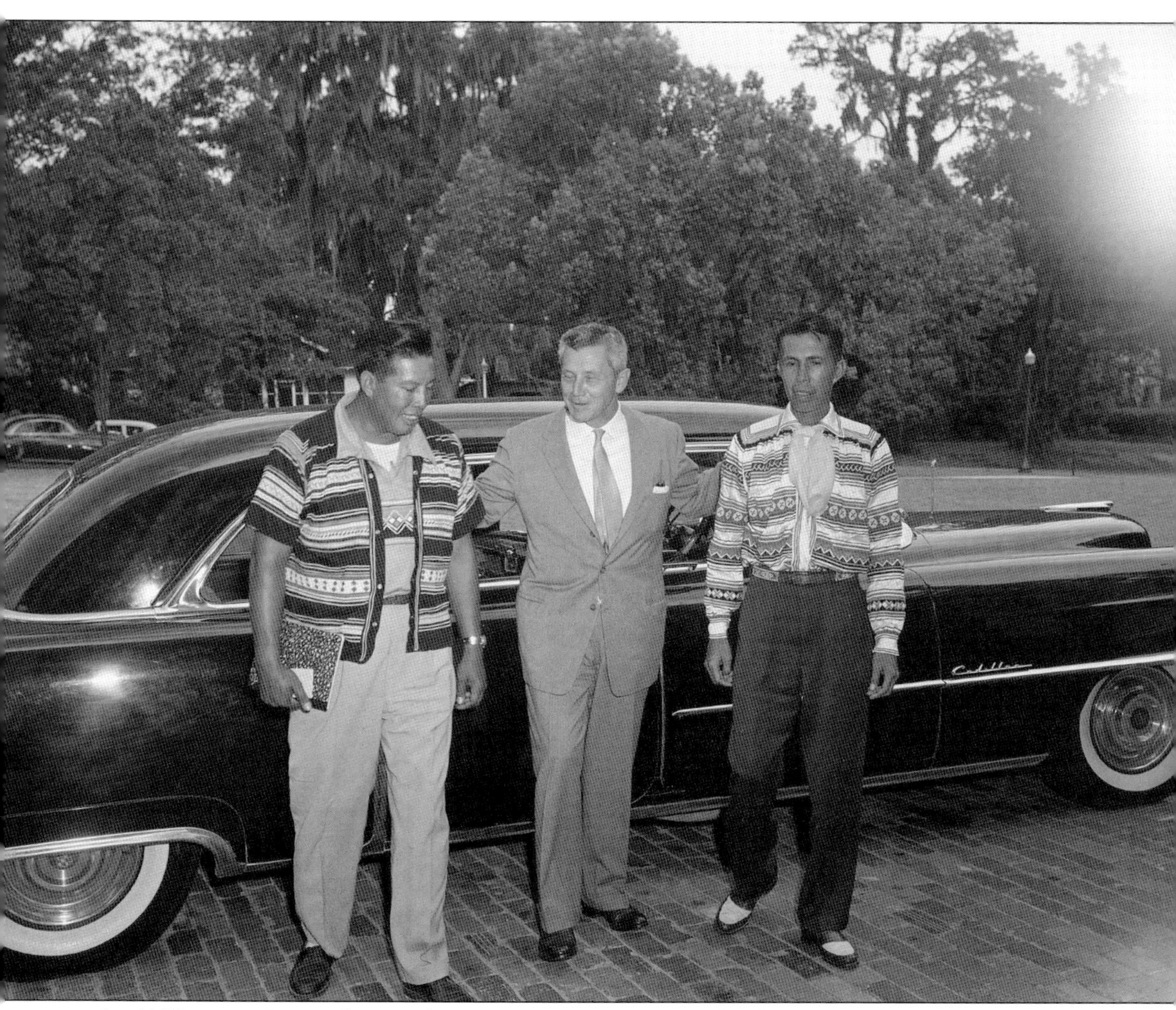

In 1950, some Seminoles sought reparations from the federal government for the loss of over 30 million acres of treaty-guaranteed Florida lands. Others wanted their land returned. The lawsuit, federal Indian termination policy, and tribal recognition issues meant dealing with the government. In 1951, Mike Osceola (left) and Buffalo Tiger (right) met with Gov. LeRoy Collins (center) to assure continuation of their traditional uses in the Big Cypress. In 1954, a Miccosukee delegation handed Pres. Dwight Eisenhower a Buckskin Declaration affirming that Trail Indians wanted nothing from the government other than to be left alone. The Seminole Tribe of Florida was organized in 1957 with the first chairpersons Billy Osceola and Betty Mae Tiger Jumper; James Billie was elected in 1979. Following international recognition by Cuba, the Miccosukee Tribe of Indians of Florida was recognized by the US government in 1962. William Buffalo Tiger was a long-serving chairman. The Big Cypress Swamp remained home to people affiliated with the Miccosukee and Seminole tribes and also unaffiliated Independents. In 1964, Big Cypress reservations were finalized: Big Cypress Swamp Seminole Reservation and Miccosukees' Alligator Alley and Tamiami Trail Reservations. (SLAF.)

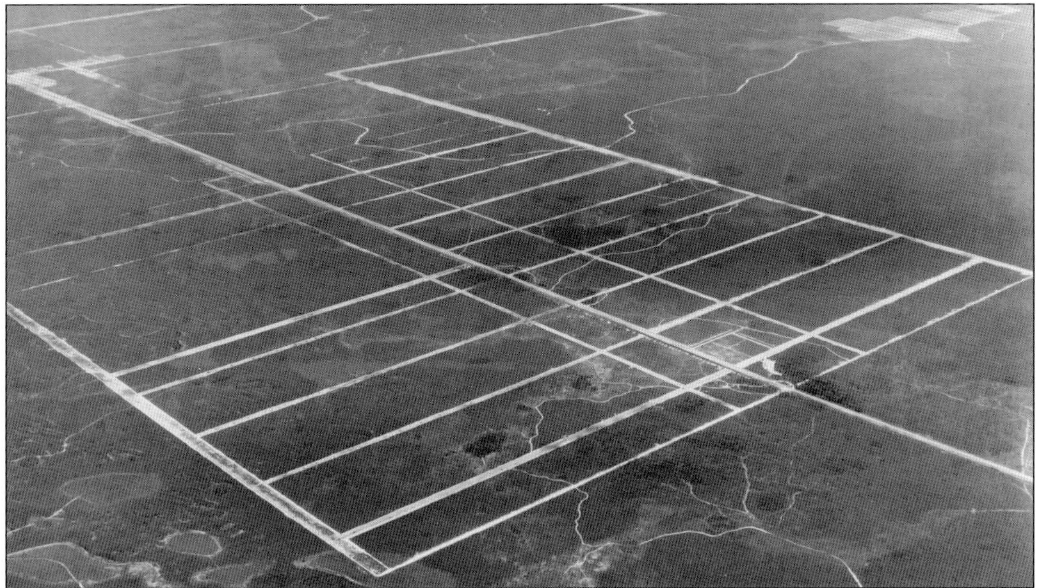

By the 1960s, Gulf American Corporation's Big Cypress land operations came under government scrutiny. In 1967, stock trading was halted, and the state suspended Golden Gate Estates sales. This aerial view shows the road network in 1963. The General Acceptance Corporation took over but filed for bankruptcy in 1975. Tens of thousands of lots had been sold. Roads continued to block waterflow; its canals continued to drain the swamp. (CCM.)

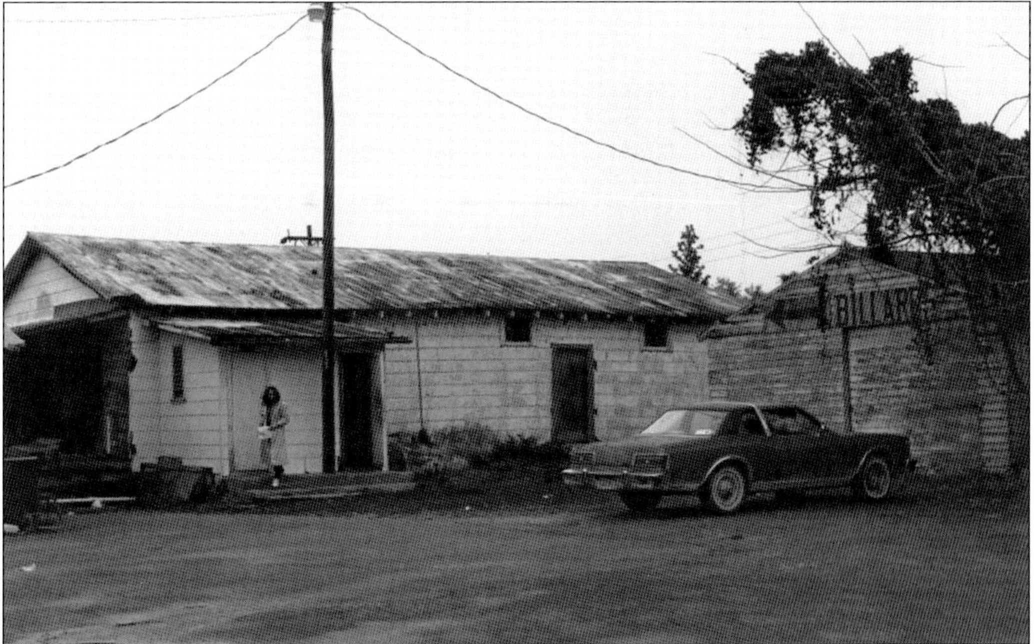

After the Lee Cypress Lumber Company departed, its adjacent town of Copeland declined (commissary building shown) but persisted when individuals were given the option to buy their lots. After its mill closed, Jerome shrank to a few homes, contending with creosote-polluted water. By the mid-1960s, about 50 families remained in Ochopee, as did basic businesses, such as Ma Watson's General Store, service stations, and the mini post office. (CCM.)

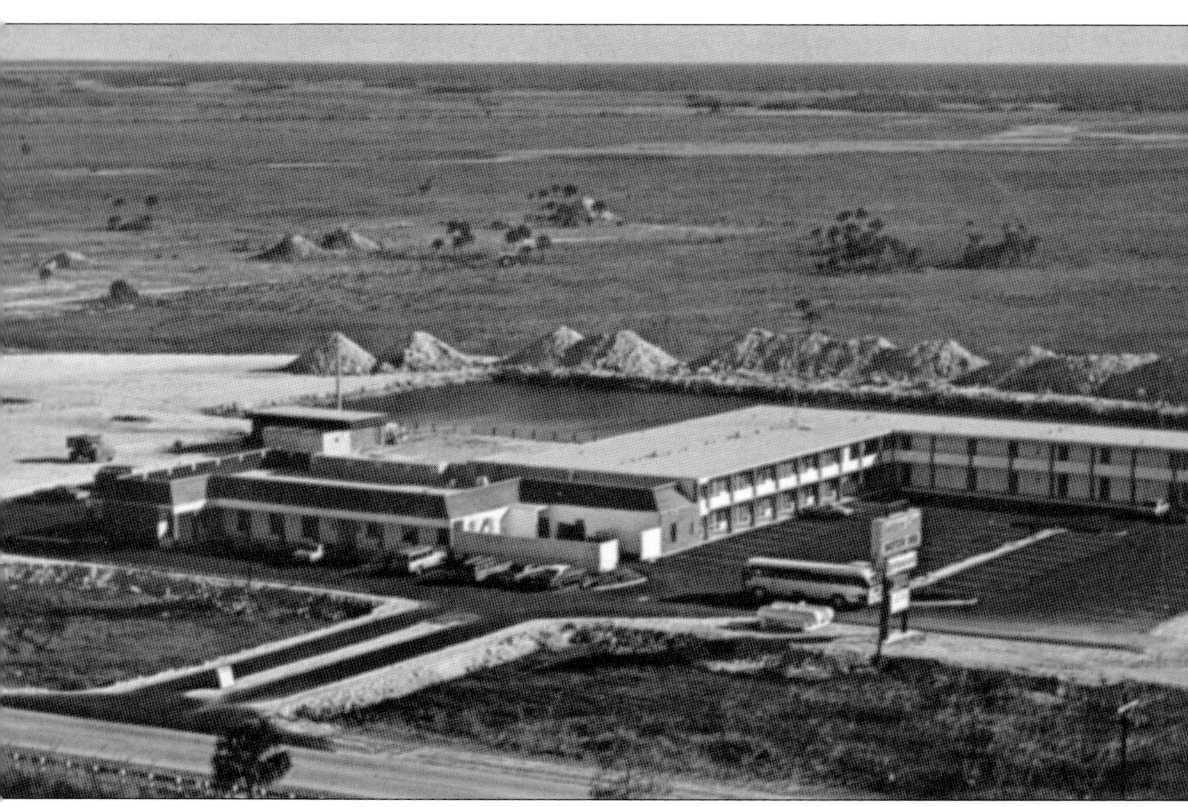

New development also emerged nearby Ochopee or tried to. Forrest Hammon's Ochopee Rock Company excavated limestone and provided significant local employment for a time, digging, blasting, and trucking rock (rock piles visible in image). His Ochopee quarry's canals persist, such as along Dona Drive, named for Hammon's wife. He also tried a residential development, Kentuckyana. In the 1960s, Ken Weimer, former tomato farmer and owner of the Ochopee Water Company, tried his developer hand with Everglades Shores, now part of the National Preserves' headquarters area. Adjacent, the Golden Lion Motor Inn opened in 1970 on land bought from Weimer (pictured). The Whichello family conceived, built, and ran the motel. It became popular for Ochopee residents and transients, including Miamians watching Dolphin football just outside the regional television blackout boundary. The community gathered in the restaurant, bar, and pool, which was open to residents. Local stories of airboats in the pool and annoying movie-star guests persist. As Ochopee declined in population and infrastructure over the next decade, so did its businesses. (KH.)

In the 1960s, car and trailer camping became popular. In 1971, Jack Shealy Sr. began developing Trail Lakes Campground along Tamiami Trail. It had trailer and tent sites and an isolated location. Over time, it expanded to include other tourist-oriented attractions and adventure tours. Looking for a way to entice passing visitors, Shealy envisioned a bigfoot-type swamp creature. The first Skunk Ape Festival was held in 1976. (MMP.)

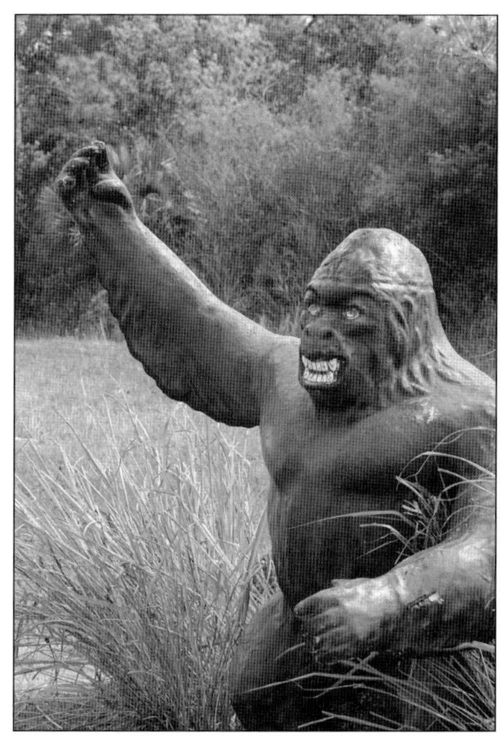

In 1960, Everglades City lost half its buildings to Hurricane Donna. Water flooded the distinguished county courthouse; two years later, the county seat moved to East Naples. The town was never the same. The Collier companies were split up with the passing of Barron Jr. in 1976. Commercial fishing and sportfish guiding continued as economic mainstays, and tourists launched to visit the Ten Thousand Islands in Everglades National Park. (SLAF.)

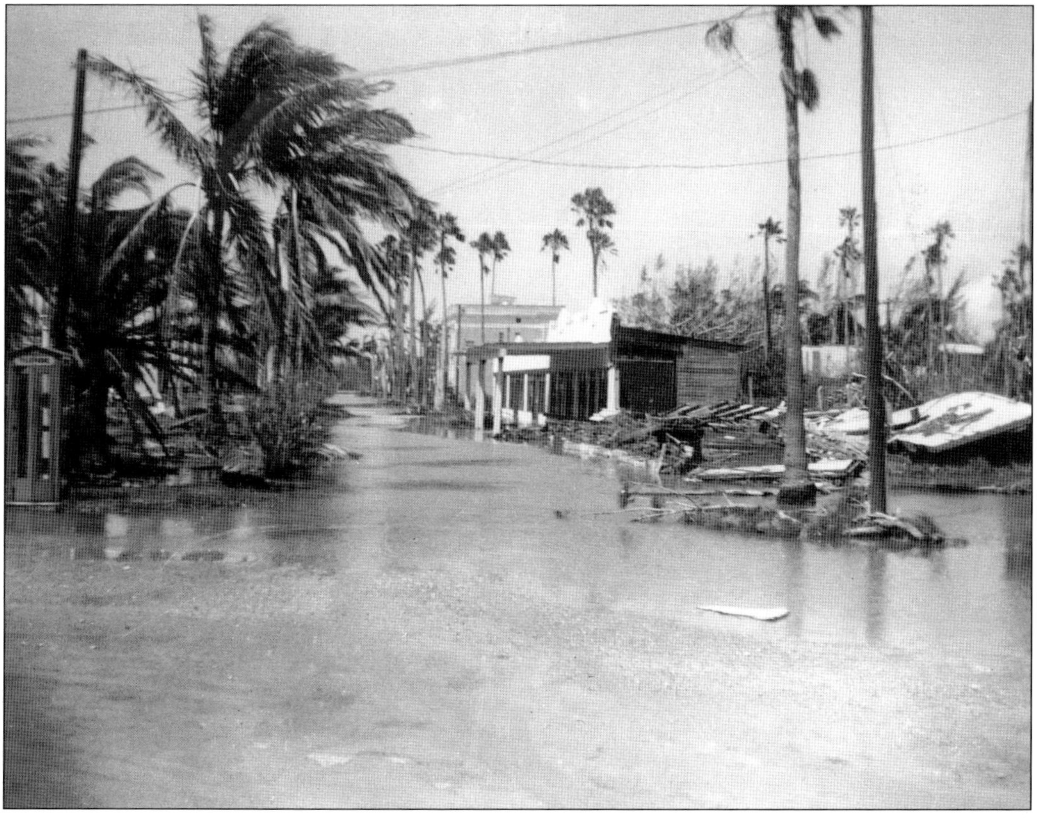

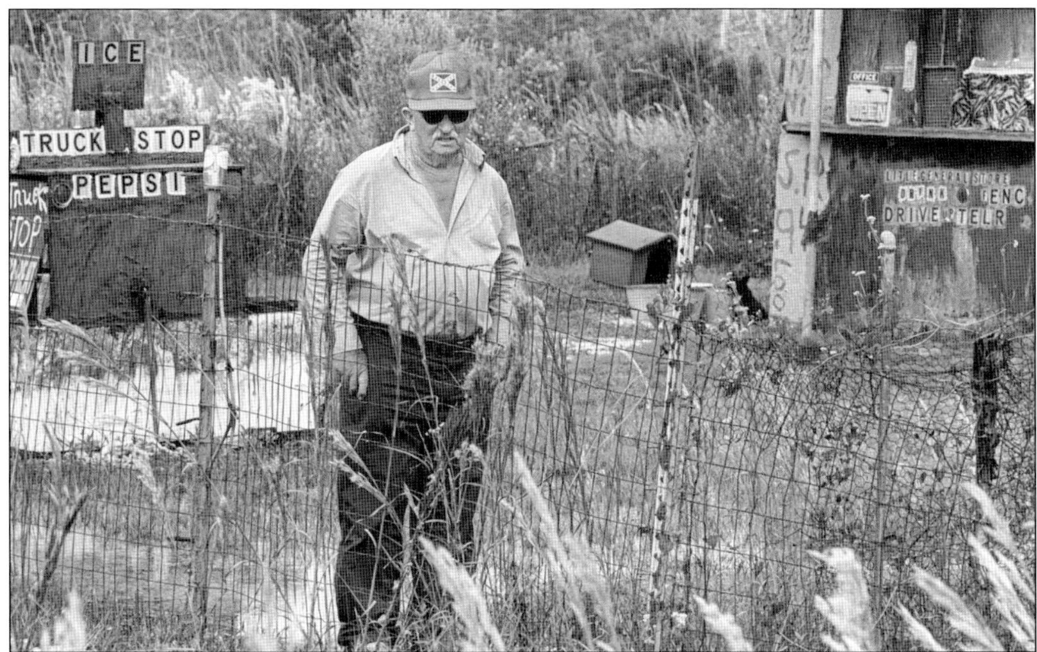

In the 1960s, Pinecrest had regained several hundred very diverse residents supplemented by transients, weekenders, and passersby. By the early 1970s, there were three bar-restaurants (Pinecrest Lodge, Gator Hook Lodge, and Sullivan's) and a chicken-egg farm. It also had its service station, junkyard, Hughes sandwich shop, and residences ranging from houses to shacks to incapacitated school buses. The Pinecrest Lodge's restaurant fed the community. (UM.)

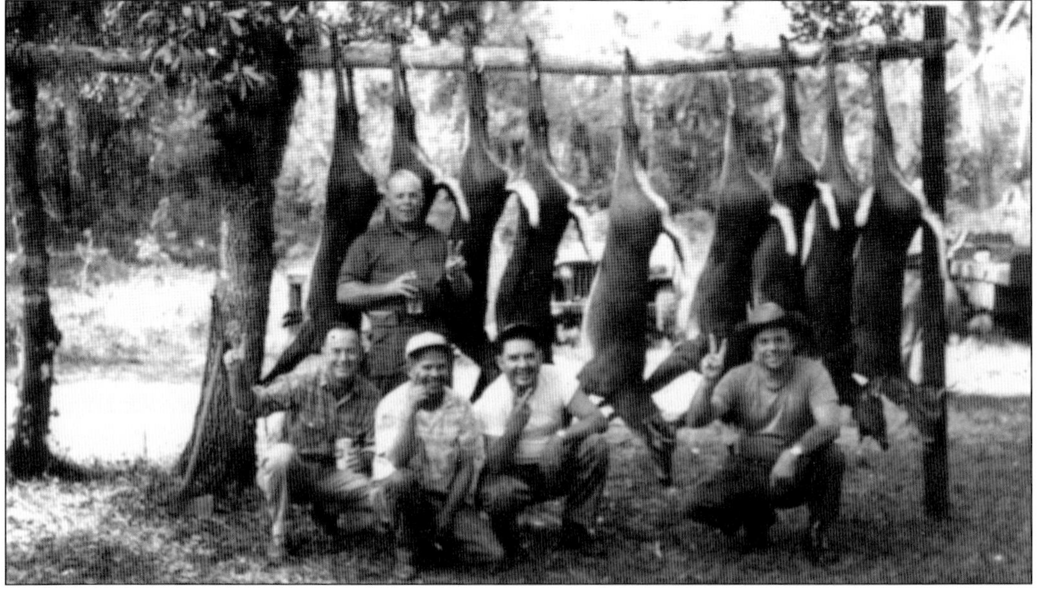

Pinecrest was a gunning, gigging, and hunting sort of place, harvesting pig frogs, a dietary mainstay; alligators, an endangered species by 1967; and wild hogs, turkey, and, of course, deer (pictured here around 1960). In addition to gator hides and frog legs, turtles, catfish, orchids, tree snails, and snakes could be sold. Park boundaries, hunting seasons and limits, and nighttime hunting restrictions were considered suggestions. (CCM.)

The Knight family founded the most famous Pinecrest establishment, Gator Hook Lodge, in 1958. Starting as a grocery in a frame building hauled from town, it morphed into Gator Hook Lodge, a bar run for years by retired Sweetwater police chief Jack Knight. Operating until 1997, fact and fiction are hard to distinguish as Gator Hook tales were featured in novels by Peter Matthiessen, Randy Wayne White, and Tim Dorsey. (SFCMC.)

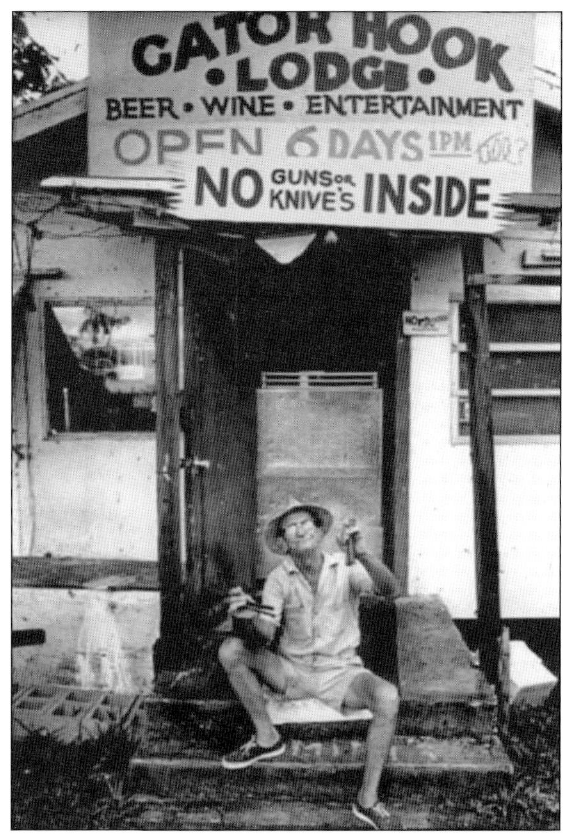

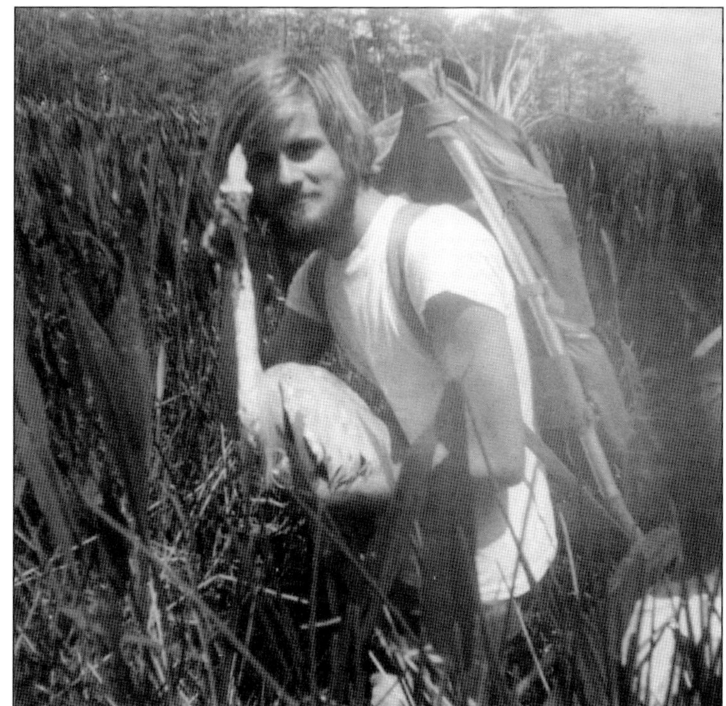

As depicted in Peter Matthiessen's *Shadow Country*, Pinecrest was a place for both gator poachers and college professors. University of Miami, owning 6,000 acres of discarded oil-exploration property, set up a research trailer on an abandoned well pad, now a preserve camping site. In the late 1960s, James Kushlan, an author of this book (shown with an injured heron), studied wildlife with the help and hindrance of residents, such as Gator Bill Schoelerman. (KH.)

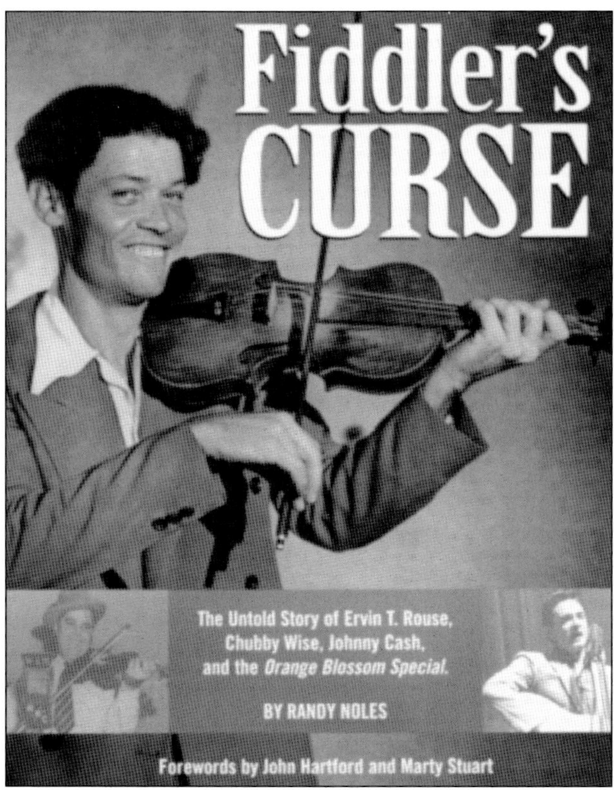

One of the more famous of Pinecrest's many part-time residents was Ervin T. Rouse. Credited with writing the song "Orange Blossom Special," he lived off royalties secured for him by Johnny Cash, who popularized the song. *Fiddler's Curse* by Randy Noles (Centerstream Publishing) tells his story. Escaping to a Pinecrest cabin, Rouse was a frequent drinker and fiddler at Gator Hook. His 1976 depiction in *National Geographic* brought Pinecrest fame. (CP.)

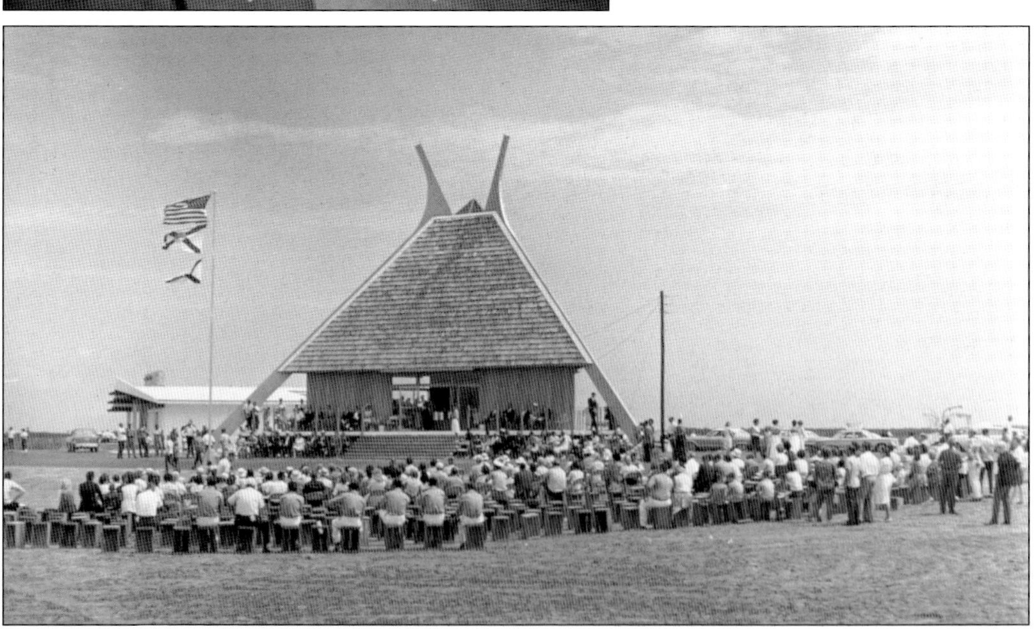

The once bustling Collier construction and train depot site of Carnestown, at the intersection of Tamiami Trail and Immokalee Road, declined in concert with Collier's construction projects and freight from farms, groves, and mills. In 1966, it became Collier County's first welcome center. This image shows its dedication. The center's distinctive teepee building was a popular stopping spot, attracting motorists until 2017, when a hurricane shuttered it. (CCM.)

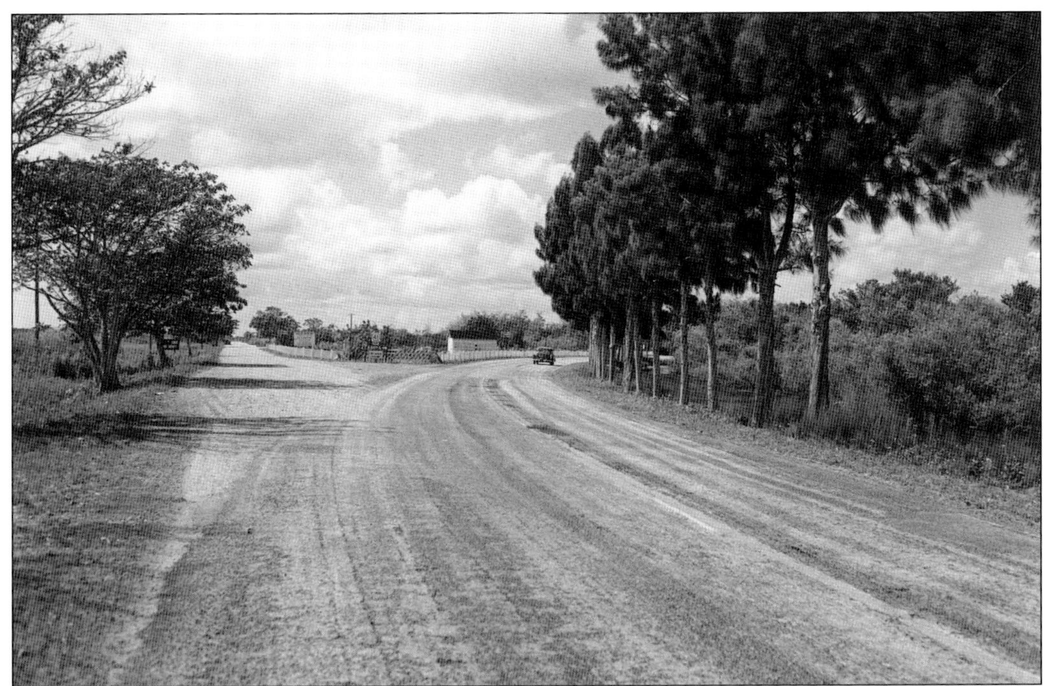

There was no welcome center at Big Cypress's eastern border, as this 1953 image of 40-Mile Bend shows. Through the 1950s and 1960s, the trail hosted evolving Collier-built stations, new Indian Villages and residences, and new businesses like George Hunter's Trail Center, where the three county lines met. It was a gas station, food stop, and a rendezvous point for hunters, truckers, and two county bus lines. (SLAF.)

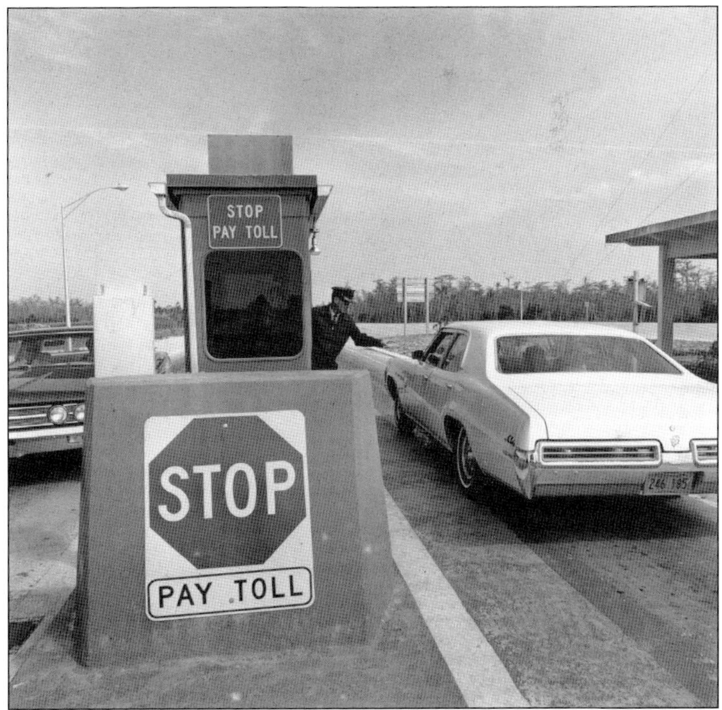

Opening in 1968, a second east-west road divided Big Cypress drainage, crossing 50 miles of the swamp. The Everglades Parkway was controversial, including its location, access, and tolls (toll booth shown). Derisively calling it Alligator Alley, the American Automobile Association declared the two-lane, canal-bordered, unlit, unfenced, poorly culverted road an alley for alligators and a killing ground, which it was for both wildlife and people. The Alligator Alley name stuck. (SLAF.)

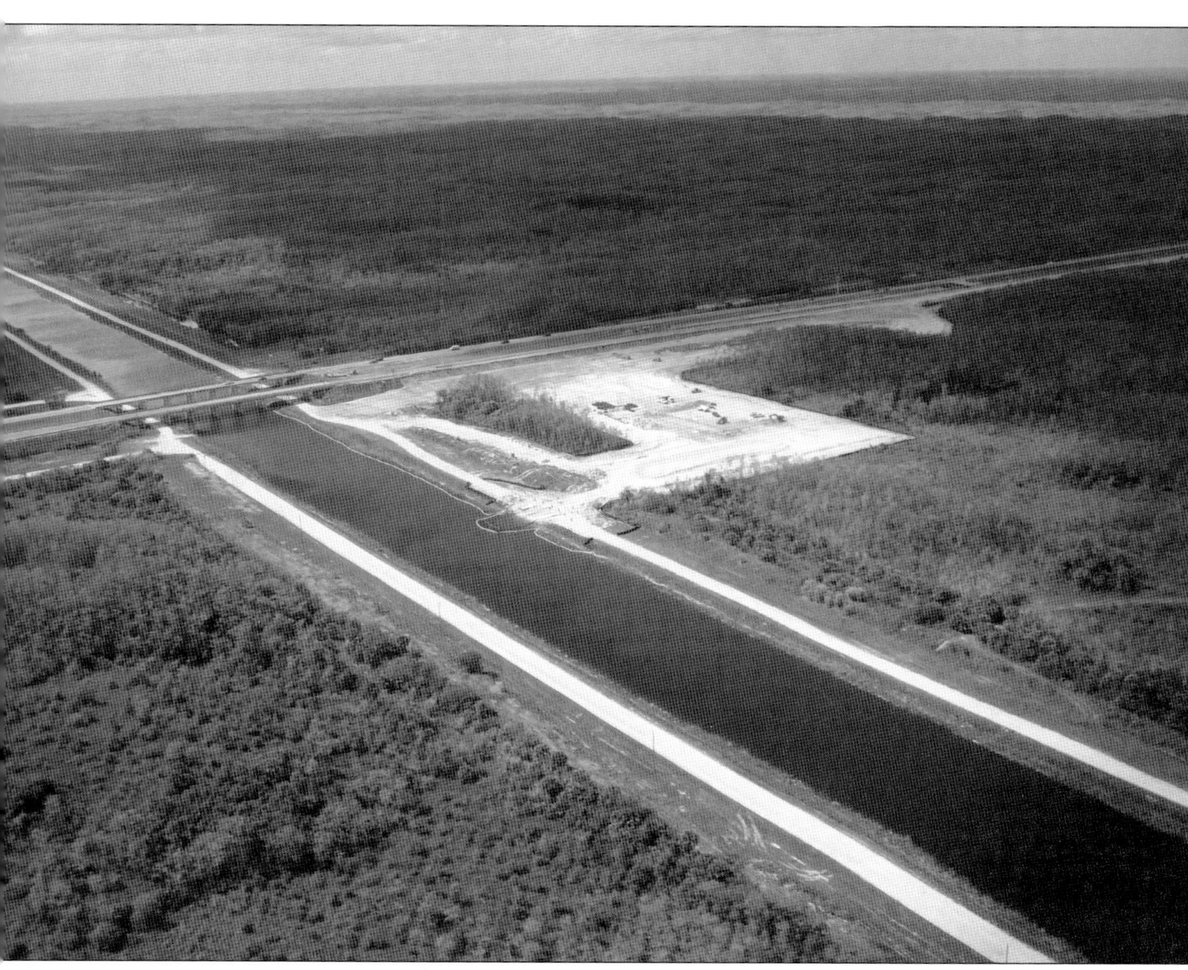

By the 1960s, two decades of canal-digging and levee-building had their effect. To encourage development, Birdon and Turner River Roads were extended. Canals drained the adjacent swamp and cut off the headwaters of the nine-mile-long, historic Turner River. Farther west, by the early 1970s, the Faka Union Canal had drastically reduced water levels in the Fakahatchee Strand. Tamiami Trail, Loop Road, and Alligator Alley continued to impede seasonal water flows. By 1963, the remaining Everglades had been walled in by 150 miles of levees, including L-28 bordering the Big Cypress (shown at the intersection with Alligator Alley). The levee affected water levels in areas traditionally used for Seminole ceremonies and, probably not coincidentally, areas of interest to the Dade County Port Authority. A seven-mile gap allowed Big Cypress water to flow through Mullet Slough into the Everglades but not back into the Big Cypress, cutting off natural water flow under Tamiami Trail and Loop Road to Lostmans Slough and the Big Cypress estuaries. (SFCMC.)

In 1966, Golden Gate developers bought Fakahatchee Slough but, in the early 1970s, transferred almost 10,000 acres to the state in a mitigation agreement. Philanthropist Lester Norris secured Big Cypress Bend, dedicated in 1970 (Norris left, Nathaniel Reed speaking). Starting in 1974, the state began buying the rest from 17,000 owners, establishing Fakahatchee Strand Preserve State Park. The conservation movement was led by Mel Finn, Jan Parks, and others. (CCM.)

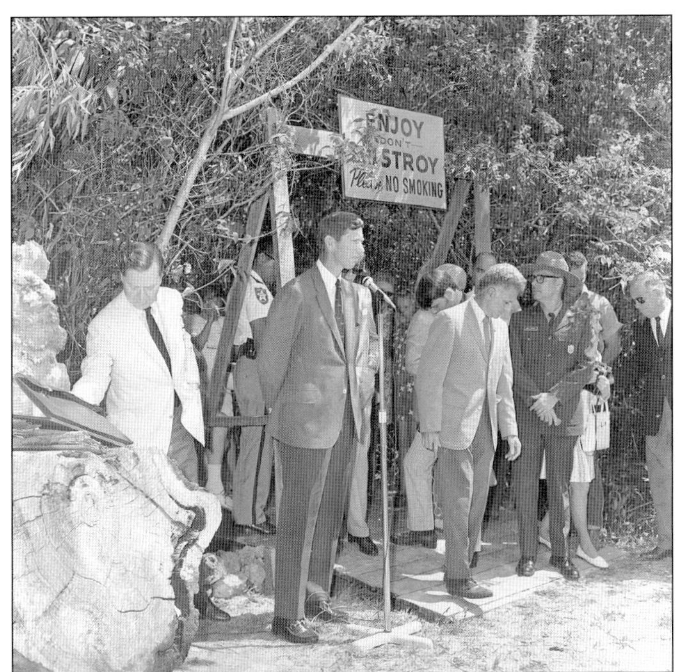

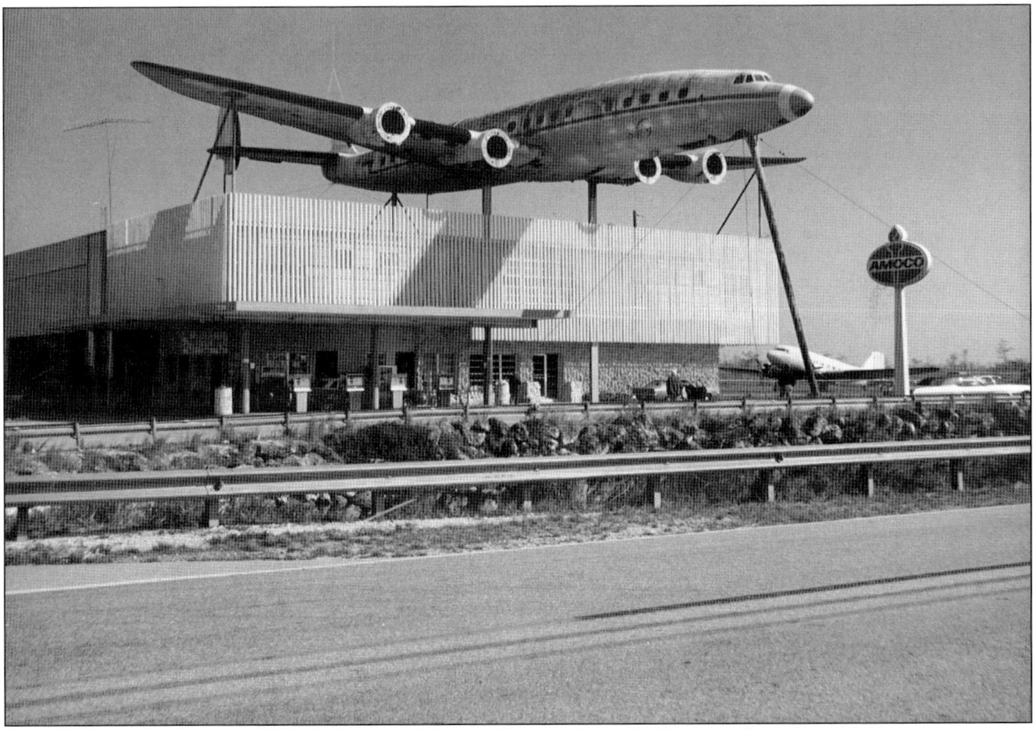

In the 1960s, airplanes became prominent in Big Cypress life. For quick access, camp owners built short airstrips. Airplanes were used illegally to spot deer and law enforcement and to drop drugs. The largest private facility was Aero Oasis Airport, starting in 1960 as an aircraft salvage shop. It had an airstrip, an administration-hangar building, an owner's residence, a gas station, and an attention-getting rooftop Lockheed Constellation. Its facilities never quite got finished. (SFCMC.)

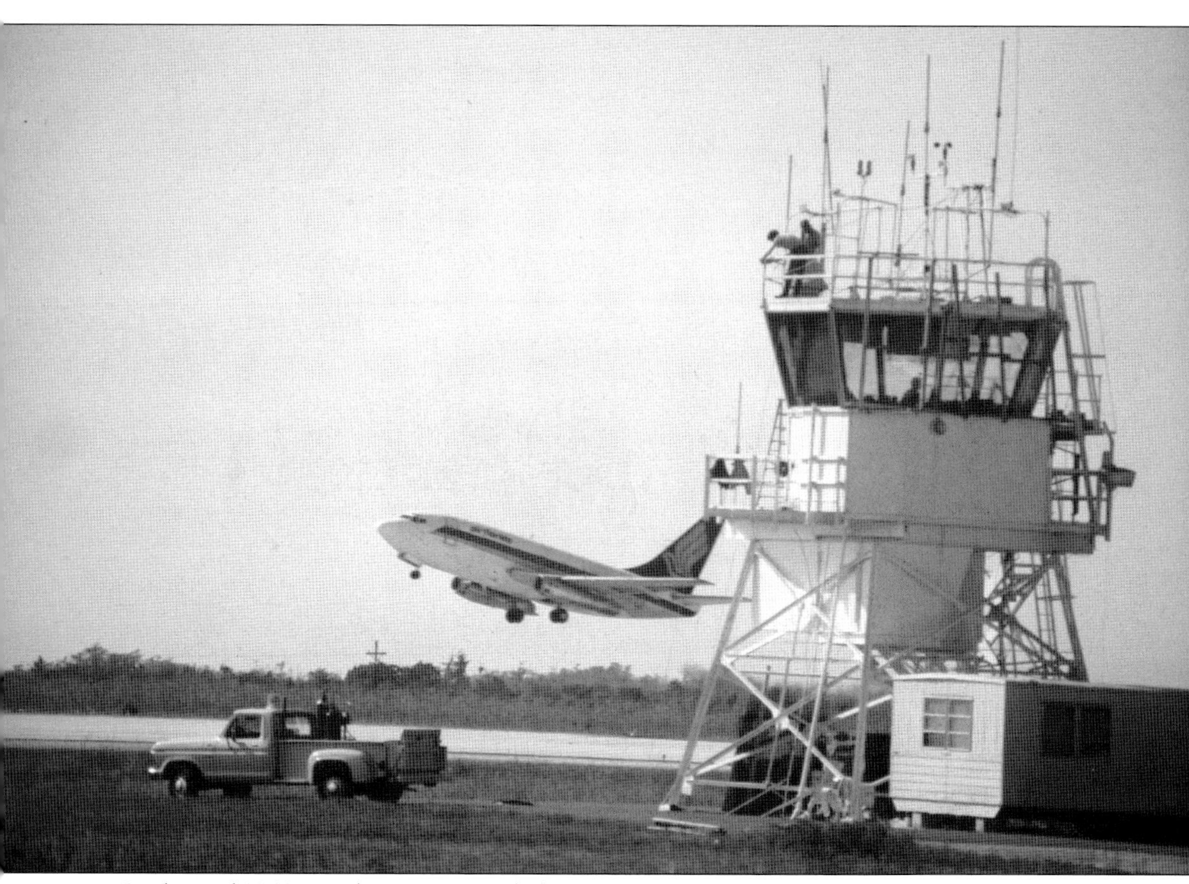

In the mid-1960s, Dade County needed a new airport, and federal aviation authorities wanted a flight-training facility. With minimal publicity, the Port Authority purchased 39 square miles of the Big Cypress to create the world's biggest airport, six runways for 300-passenger supersonic jets serviced by a rerouted Interstate 75, monorail, pipelines, and massive ancillary development. The jetport was six miles upstream of Everglades National Park. Dredging and filling the swamp began in 1968. The airport was approved only for touch-and-go training, with the rest of the plan mostly disguised. It seemed like a done deal; one completed runway was used for training until, in later years, it was superseded by flight simulators. Citizen-led efforts intensified, and the jetport controversy ensued. In the end, agreement among federal, state, and local officials produced one of the most significant and successful environmental campaigns of the 1960s environmental era. (SFCMC.)

The conservation side of the jetport controversy had many supporters, including National Audubon Society's Joe Browder (seen right in 1976), hunting and camp owners such as Johnny Jones and Cal Stone of the Florida Wildlife Federation, Buffalo Tiger of the Miccosukee tribe, and Robert Padrick of the flood control district. State support was led by Nathaniel Reed (below, left) and, belatedly but firmly, Gov. Claude Kirk (below, right). Federal supporters included Everglades superintendent John Raftery, John Ehrlichman, Interior Secretary Walter Hickel, Russel Train, and, in the end, Pres. Richard Nixon. Author John D. MacDonald wrote an influential piece for *Life*. To keep conservation interests united, Frank Marshand and others created the Everglades Coalition. Stories from the controversy include an overnight houseboating trip in Everglades National Park by Kirk and Hickel and a blown-up press conference in February 1969. (Right, HMM; below, SLAF.)

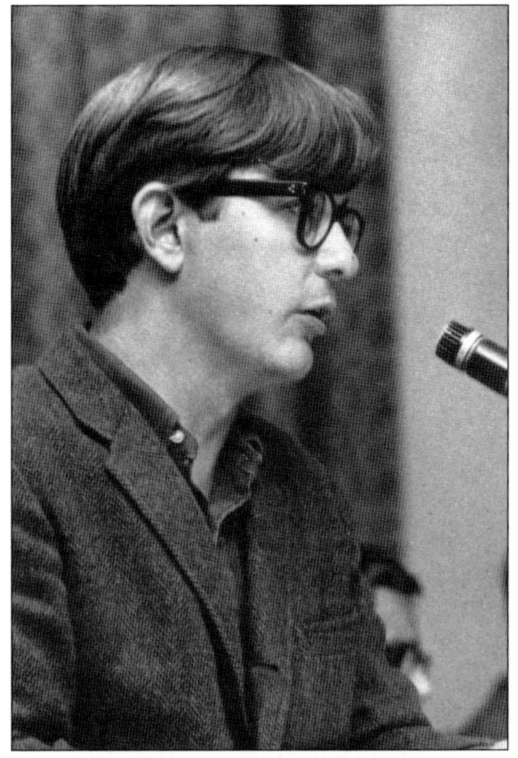

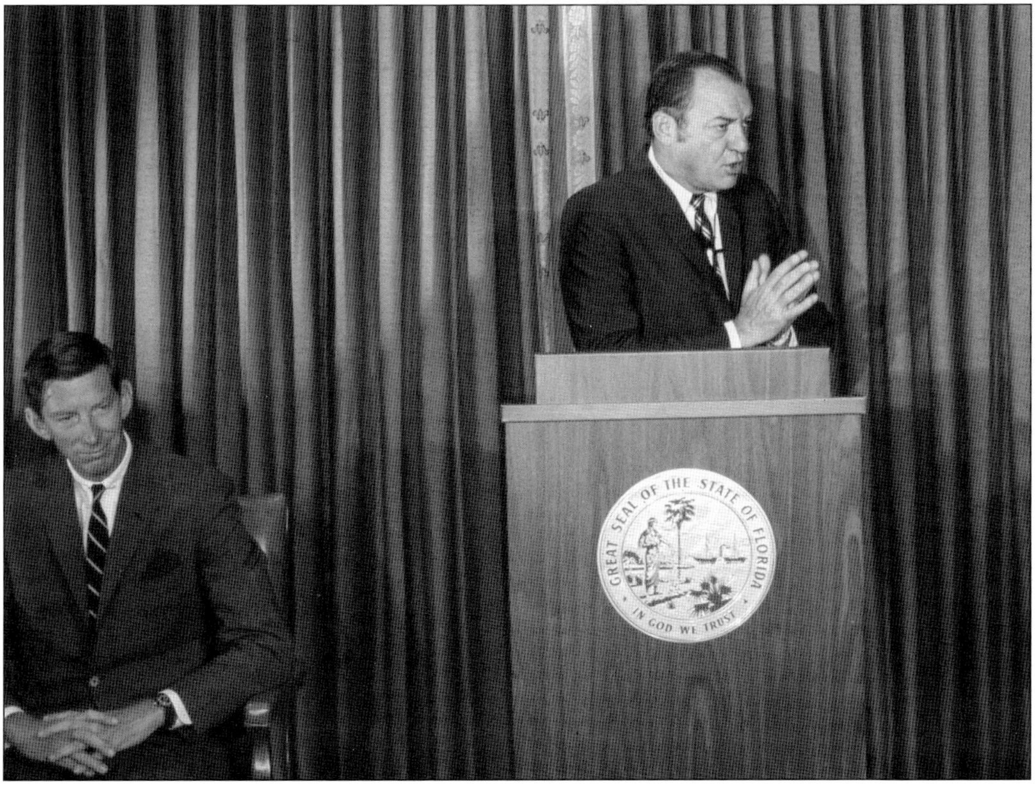

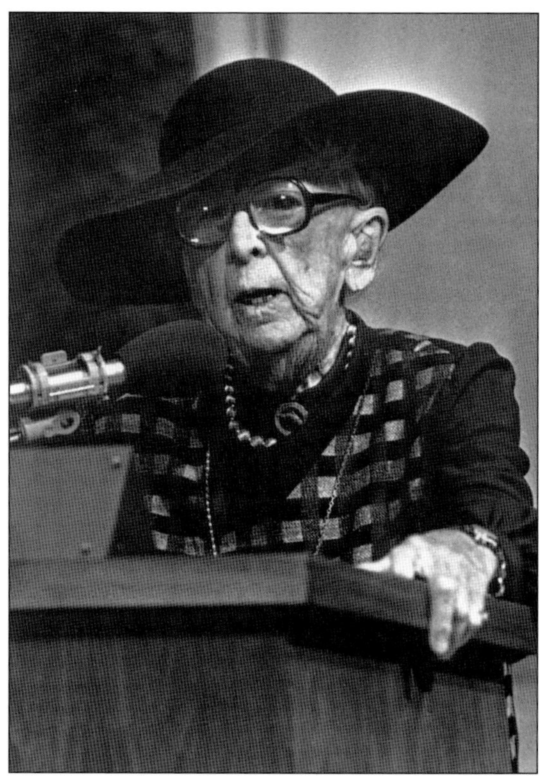

In 1969, Joe Browder famously recruited Marjory Stoneman Douglas to the cause. Then, at 78, the author of the 1947 book *River of Grass* began a new career as an environmentalist, lasting nearly 30 years more. She founded and ran a grassroots membership group, Friends of the Everglades, and provided the face of the movement, gave speeches, cajoled, retorted, and scolded anyone she thought might not be doing enough. (SLAF.)

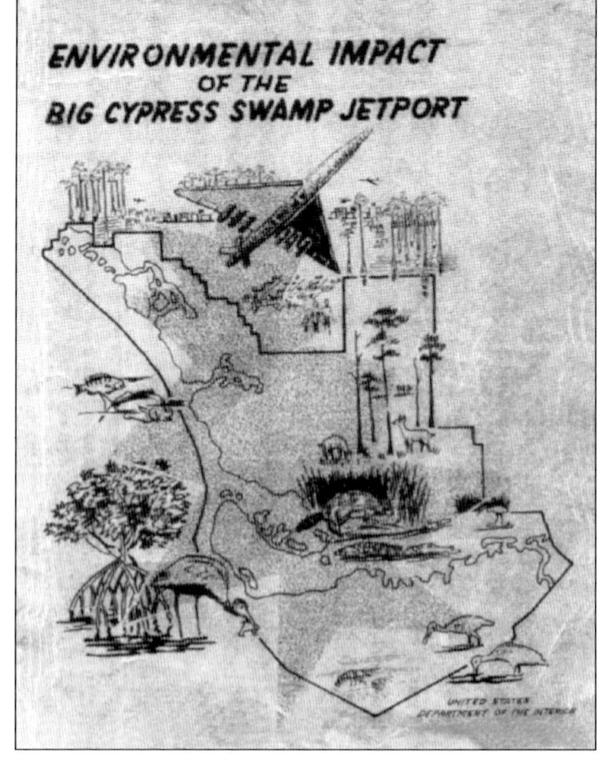

Technical studies were key to the government's decisions. The most influential of three studies addressing the jetport's environmental impact and possible mitigation was initiated by Russell Train, Interior Department undersecretary, using federal scientists led by Luna Leopold of the US Geological Survey and Arthur Marshall of the Bureau of Sport Fisheries and Wildlife. The Interior Department report definitively opposed the project; other reports were more equivocal. (UF.)

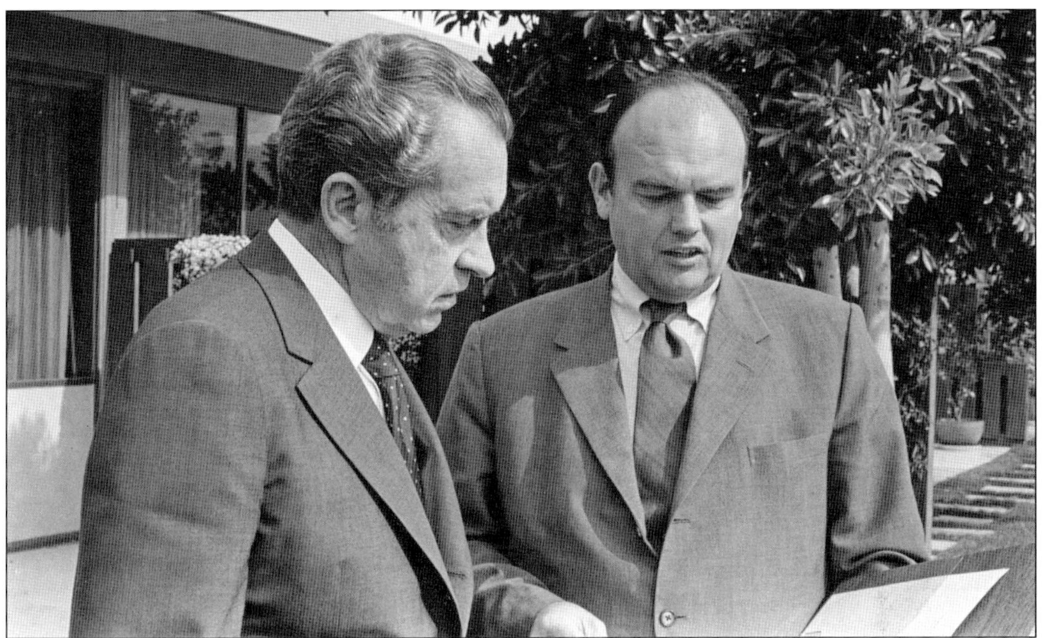

In late 1969, advised by John Ehrlichman (right) and Walter Hickel, Pres. Richard Nixon (left) decided to pull federal funding and approvals for developing the jetport. His cabinet secretaries began implementation. In January 1970, federal, state, and local interests signed off on the Everglades Jetport Pact. Construction halted. A multiagency search for a replacement site ultimately failed; Miami International Airport was improved instead. The airport's future threats were considered abated. (RNPL.)

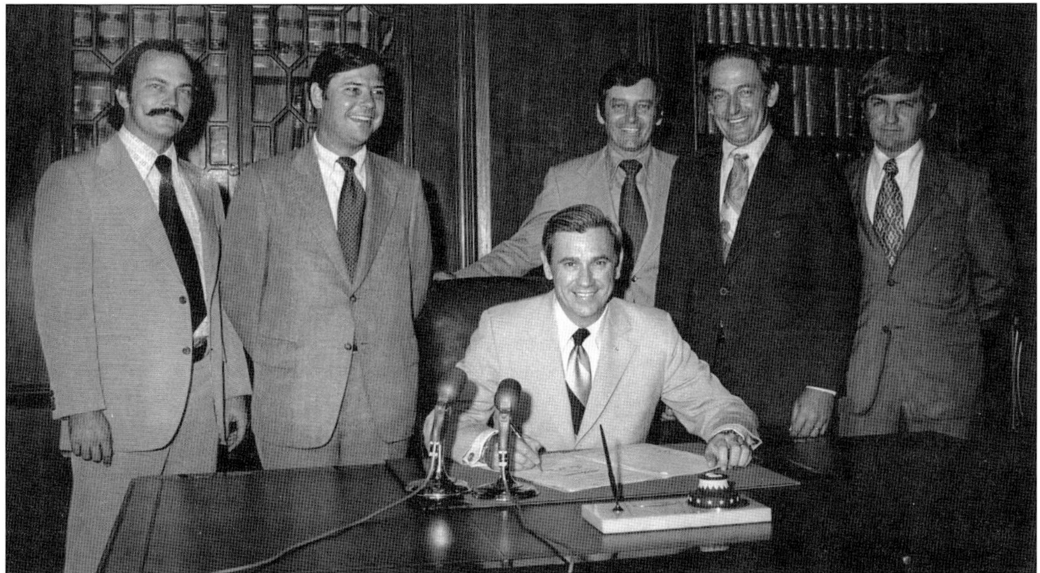

Left undecided was the future of the newly appreciated Big Cypress. Many worried about losing their particular use of land they owned—or did not actually own. Florida stopped oil exploration, made it an Area of Critical State Concern, and passed the Big Cypress Conservation Act in 1973. Shown is the signing by Gov. Reuben Askew; future governor Robert Graham is behind to the left. (SLAF.)

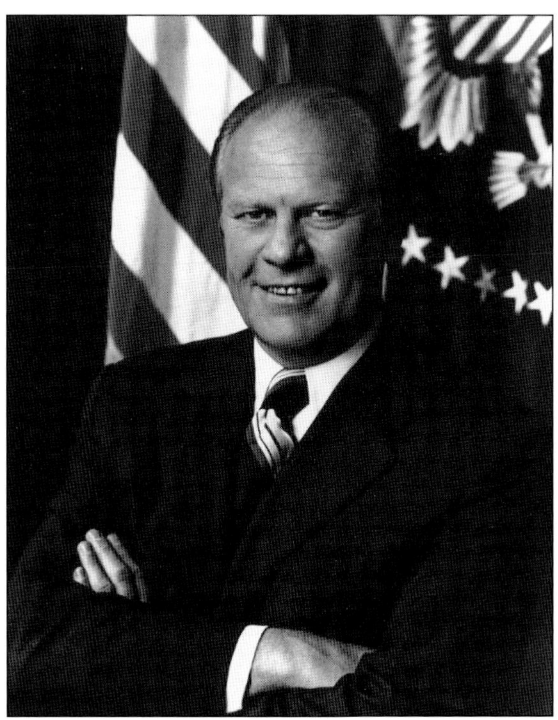

Senators Lawton Childs and Henry Jackson, Interior Secretary Rogers Morton, and assistant secretary Nathaniel Reed wrangled for federal acquisition. In 1971, and in his address to Congress in 1973, Pres. Richard Nixon proposed the acquisition of a national reserve. On October 11, 1974, Pres. Gerald Ford (pictured) signed the bill establishing Big Cypress National Preserve. (LOC.)

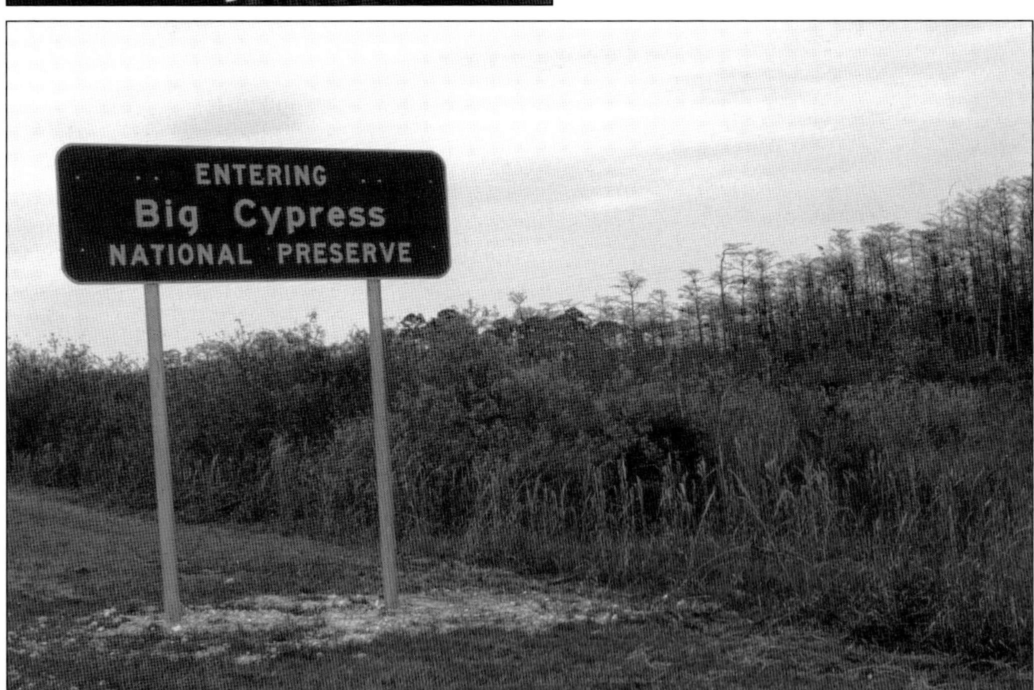

Initially covering 577,000 acres, over 900 square miles, a large portion of the Big Cypress was now the National Park Service's responsibility. This was not a national park but an area protected for multiple uses, including private inholdings, hunting, fishing, trapping, grazing, oil exploration and extraction, ORVs, and traditional uses by the Seminole and Miccosukee people, while also protecting the swamp and its hydrology. (SLAF.)

Five

People and the Swamp
The Big Cypress National Preserve

With the Big Cypress National Preserve established, the first order of business for the National Park Service was acquiring the land, initially the state's land and funds. There were over 40,000 other owners. Processes were established for purchases from willing sellers and acquisitions from those not so willing. Defensive civic organizations emerged, such as the Landowners Association of Big Cypress. Homes and other legal buildings constructed before November 1971 and oil rights could be retained; hardship exemptions could be granted. Most full-time homes were on the trail, but over 500 remote camps became problematic, notably those on property not owned by the occupants. Unincorporated settlements of Ochopee and Pinecrest were included within the boundaries and continued their declines. Reservation land of Seminoles and Miccosukees neighbored the preserve. Their customary uses and exclusive concessions were to continue. Everglades City found a renewed source of commerce, smuggling. Oil was extracted at three sites, and exploration continued. In association with the preserve, the Florida Fish and Wildlife Commission was to manage hunting and fishing. The welfare of endangered species, especially the Florida panther that had suffered a dramatic population collapse, was a priority. Research and management led to a remarkable population rebound. Swamp buggies and airboats, both heritage-worthy but creating undeniable habitat damage, soon became controversial. Concerned citizens and user organizations engaged. Populations of deer and hogs, prime hunting targets, fluctuated. Alligator Alley became Interstate 75. The preserve expanded to 729,000 acres with additional land protecting its northern watershed. The preserve established visitor centers at Oasis and Ochopee and headquarters at the previous Golden Lion Motor Inn. Visitor use increased and diversified with hiking, paddling, camping, and wildlife observation opportunities.

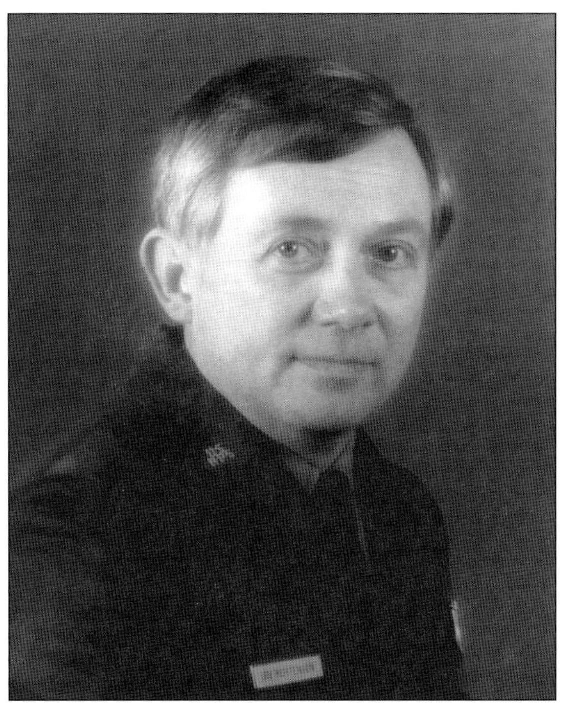

Irv Mortenson, then Everglades National Park Gulf Coast District ranger, was appointed as the site's first manager (pictured). James Sewell led the acquisition process. He started with donated state land and the purchase of big tracts. Collier's nearly 77,000 acres and the University of Miami's 6,000 were acquired in 1976, minus oil rights. There were over 40,000 other private owners; it would not be easy, and not everyone would be happy. (BICY.)

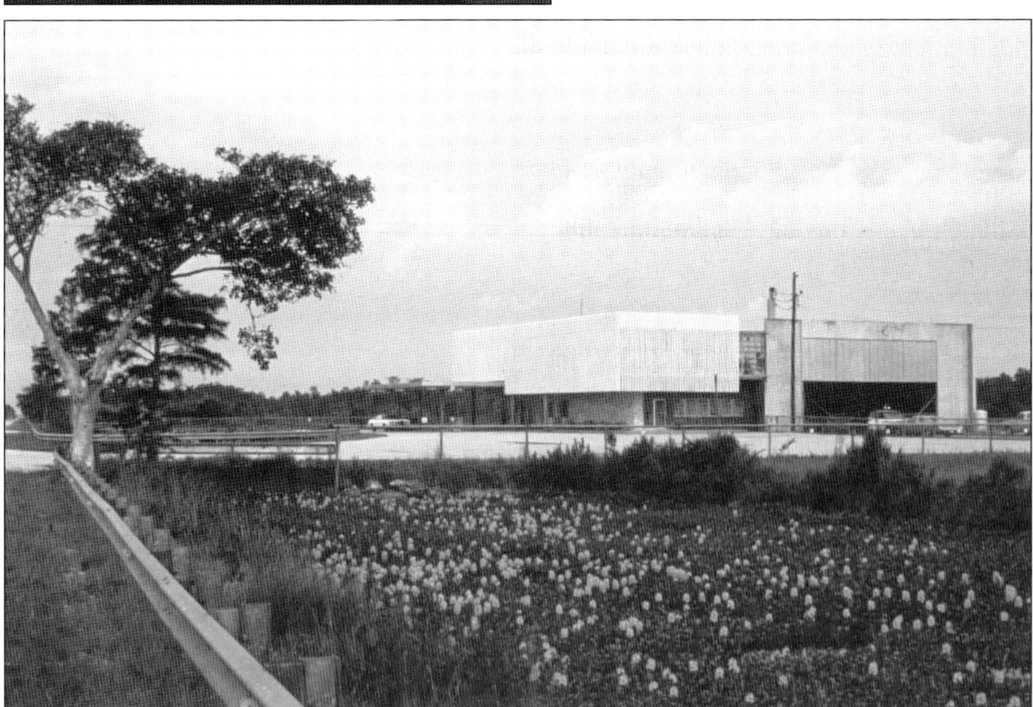

It needed to be sorted out which properties were exempt from acquisition by being legally improved before 1971 and do appraisals, make offers, and, if rejected, attend to condemnation procedures. Many exempt residences and businesses were on the Tamiami Trail. Aero-Oasis was acquired in 1977, becoming a ranger station (pictured). Most owners were quite willing sellers. With such a large inventory, acquisitions moved more slowly than some owners wanted. (SFCMC.)

Camps were part of Big Cypress's swamp heritage. Some had been used by families for a generation or more; others were new. Some were well-developed; some not so much (right). Over 400 of the 500 camps were on property not owned by the occupant. Owned camps could be kept or sold to the government. The question of the future of unowned camps ended up in court. Over time, the preserve had to learn approaches that worked best. General agreement is that early eviction actions and notices against "trespass camps" were unpopularly zealous. The image below is of Holiday Inn Camp south of the Loop, used by the family of James Kushlan, an author of this book. Here, Bob Ruff, posed for a newspaper photographer, gives an idea of attitude. Today, the remaining privately owned camps are appreciated as part of the heritage of the Big Cypress. (Right, HMM; below, KH.)

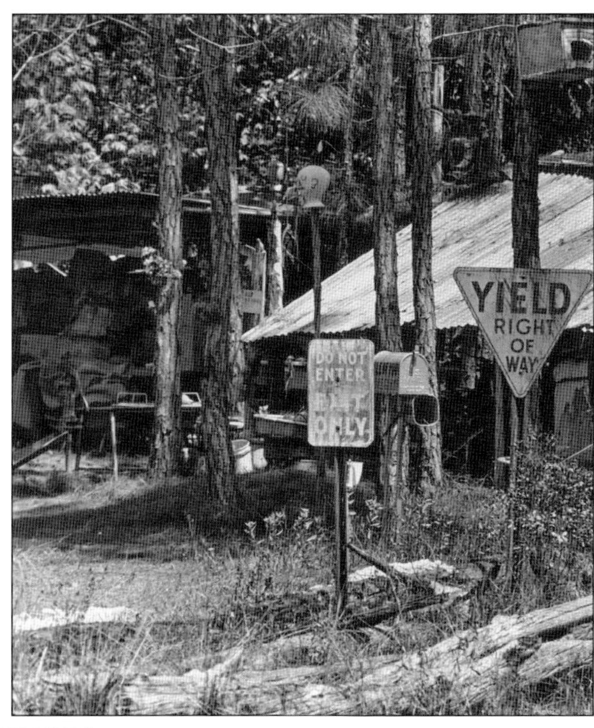

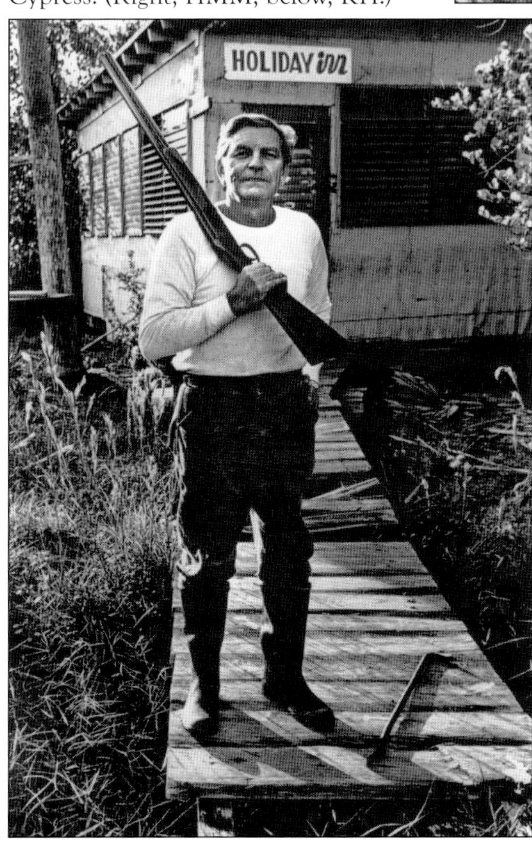

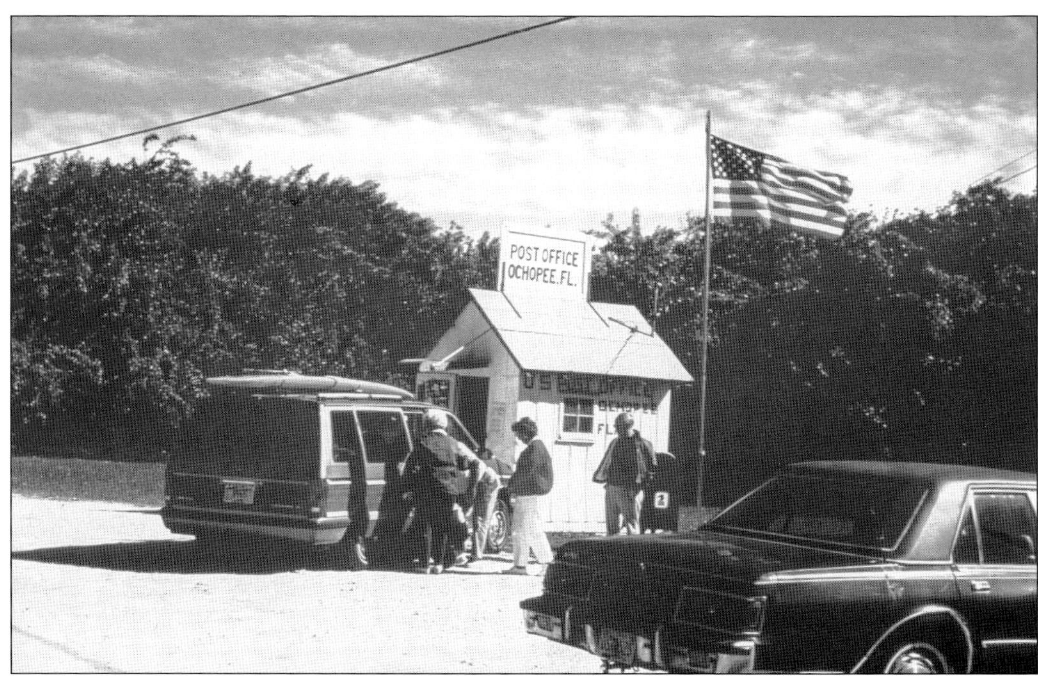

Ochopee was also difficult. Initially, there was much to recommend against its being incorporated into the preserve, but development activities were increasing. Individual parcels were purchased one by one. The Whichello family, for example, sold their house, but the government declined to buy their motel, concentrating on larger tracts and at-risk properties. The motel closed, was auctioned for back taxes, and purchased by the National Parks Conservation Association in 1985. Jeff Whichello tells his family's side of the story in his book *What Happened to Ochopee*. With decreased economic opportunities, the Ochopee population moved on. Little of the settlement remains visible. The famous Ochopee Post Office (above) and popular Joanie's Blue Crab Café (below) occupy old Ochopee farm structures, the oldest buildings in the preserve. The former motel was renovated into the preserve's headquarters. (Above, SFCMC; below, KH.)

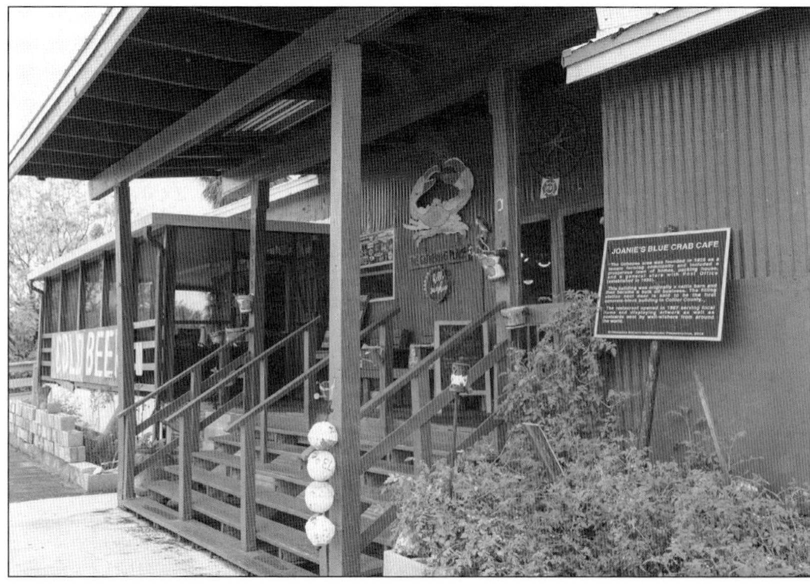

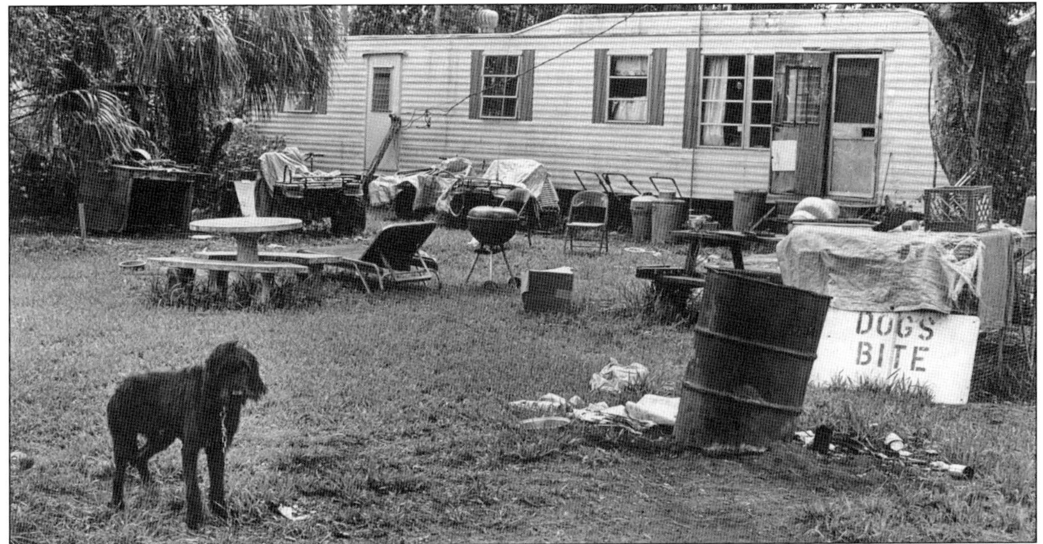

After its reanimation in the 1960s and 1970s, Pinecrest began its final decline. People departed; neglect and hurricanes had their impact. Gator Hook Lodge was sold to the preserve in 1977. Remnants and private homes remain along Loop Road, which became a scenic drive passing old Pinecrest, Tree Snail Hammock, Mitchell's Landing, ORV access at Pace's Dike, Sweetwater Strand, and Gator Hook Slough Trail. (UM.)

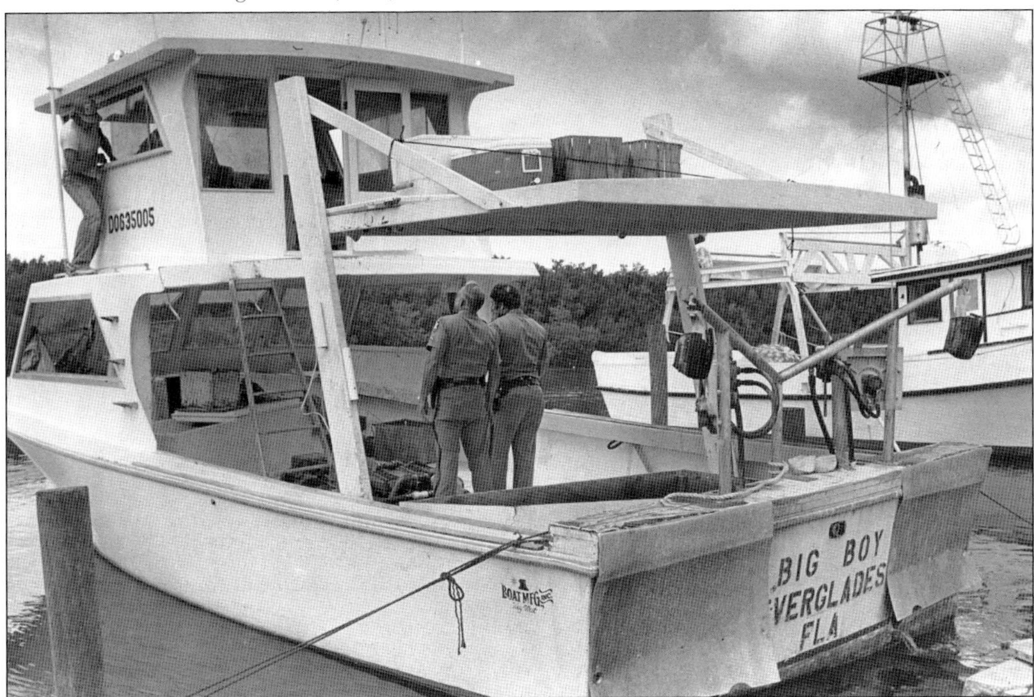

The 1970s and 1980s saw a burst of prosperity in Chokoloskee and Everglades City from a historic business as commercial fishermen turned to smuggling "square groupers" of marijuana. Captains met boats offshore; planes used camp airstrips. In 1983 and 1984, Operation Everglades arrested many of the townspeople and confiscated their boats (shown is one in 1983). Evolving stories feature such players as Totch Brown, Saltwater Cowboys, and Ghost People. (HMM.)

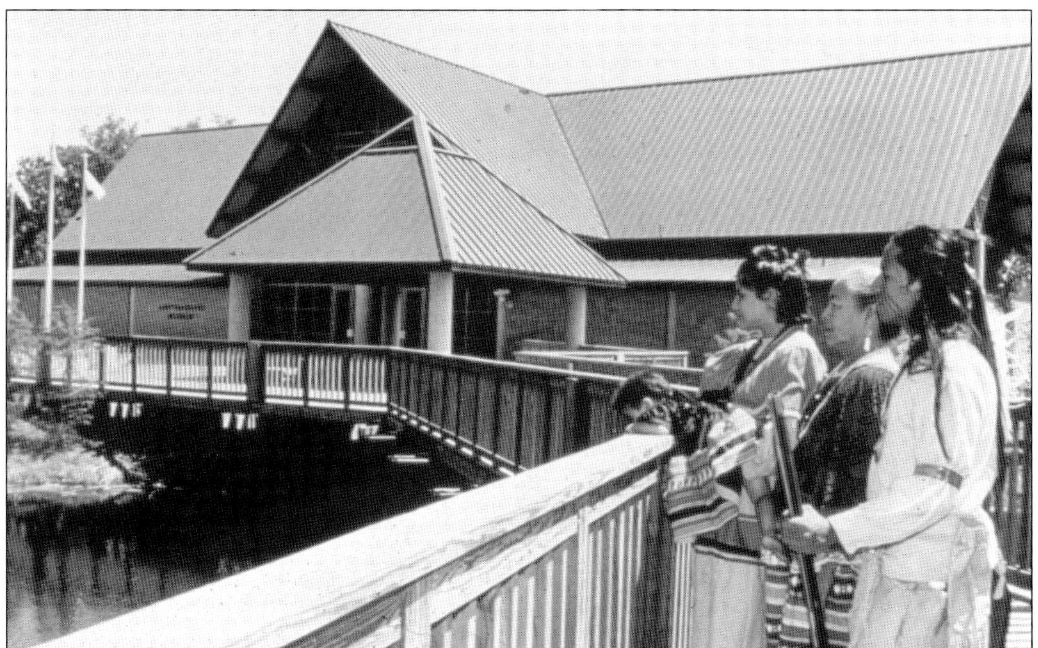

The new preserve was neighbored by the Big Cypress Seminole Indian Reservation of the Seminole Tribe of Florida to the north. In 1993, Seminole leader James Billie, who supported Seminole tourism, started his Billie Swamp Safari at the reservation. The Ah-Tah-Thi-Ki Museum, opened to the public in 1997 (shown in 1999), houses hundreds of thousands of objects as well as displays of Seminole history and culture. (SLAF.)

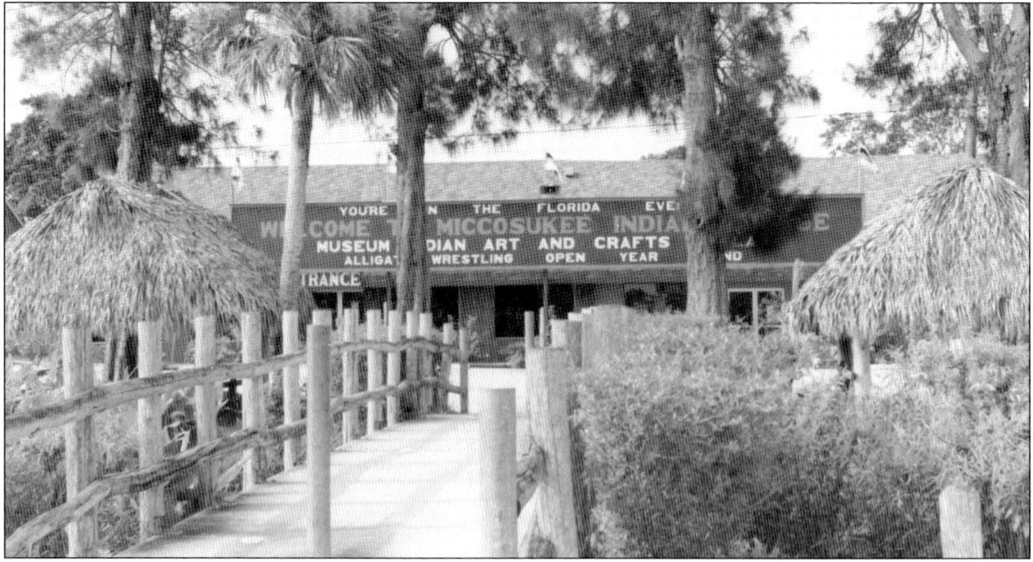

Two Miccosukee reservations adjoin the preserve. The Alligator Alley (Big Cypress) Miccosukee Reservation includes the Miccosukee Service Plaza at Interstate 75 and Snake Road. Tamiami Trail Reservation (Miccosukee Reserved Area) has tribal headquarters, a museum, a tourist store (shown in 1983), and other facilities. Its housing extends down Loop Road, crossing into the Big Cypress Swamp. The Greater Miccosukee Service Area through the Big Cypress encompasses Miccosukee tribal members, Independents, and Seminoles. (CCM.)

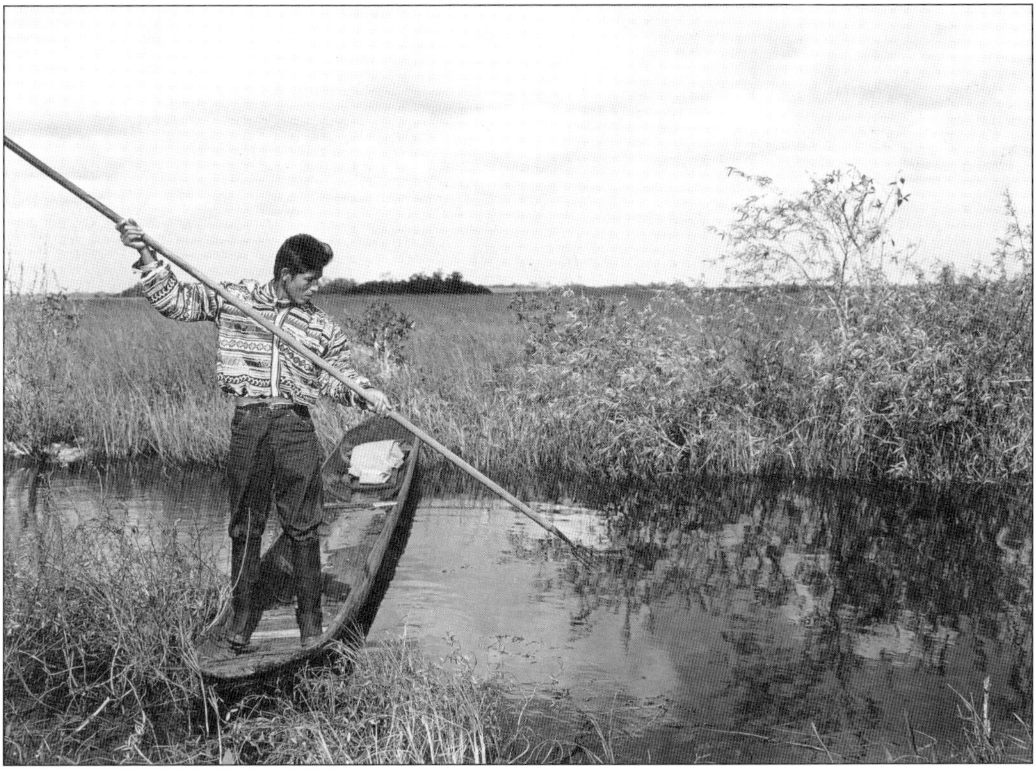

Seminoles and Miccosukees were authorized by the preserve's enabling legislation, subject to reasonable regulations, to continue their traditional and customary use and occupancy, including for hunting, fishing (pictured), and trapping on a subsistence basis and land use, including for ceremonial reasons, such as Green Corn Dance sites. Other traditional uses include harvesting plants for medicine and food and small cypress trunks for personal chickees. (SLAF.)

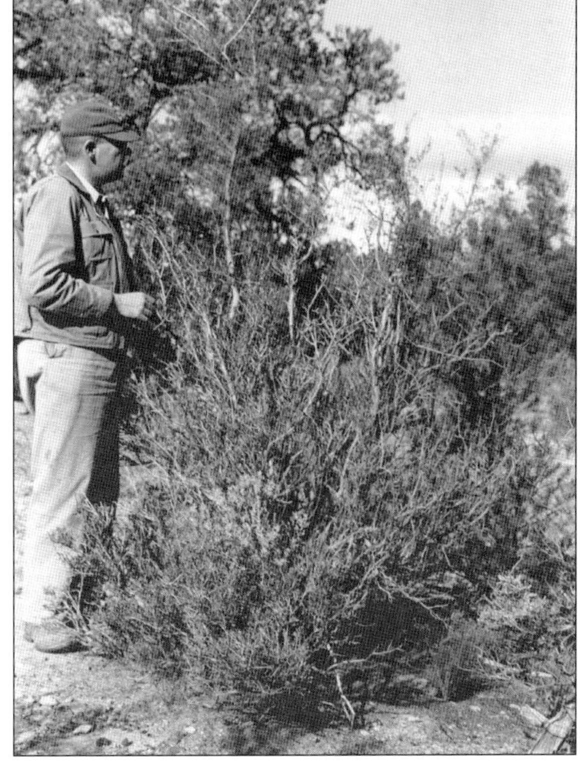

In 1981, the Big Cypress National Preserve got its own superintendent, Fred J. Fagergren, and began planning to operate the preserve independently of Everglades National Park. By 1982, a total of 96 percent of private tracts had been acquired. The issue of unowned camps took longer, with lawsuits through the 1980s and removals for another decade. Many other visitor-use issues and further understanding of resource issues needed to be sorted out. (NPS.)

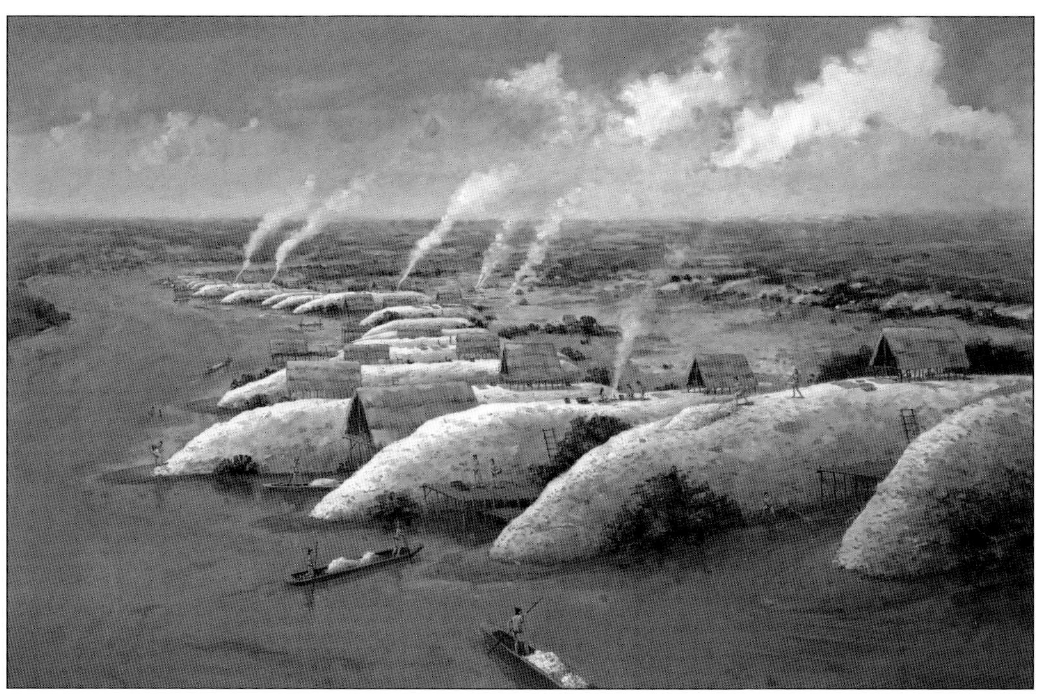

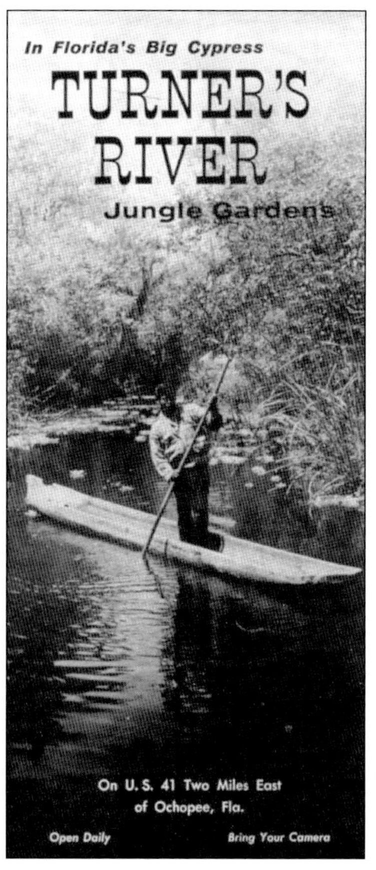

Surprisingly little was known of the preserve's historical resources when it was established. By 1982, nearly 400 archeological sites had been identified, 18 eligible for the National Register of Historic Places. The locations of most are undisclosed for security. But the well-known sites along Turner River provide excellent examples of the long history. The Calusa-era sand mounds at its mouth, in Everglades National Park, were first noted scientifically in 1900 and placed in the National Register of Historic Places in 1978 (drawing above). Calusa habitation mounds continued upriver. Later settlers farmed the mounds, pioneer Dick Turner farmed the sand mounds, and Chokoloskee's C.G. McKinney farmed the upriver soil mounds. In the 1920s, a Collier's service station was built on the Tamiami Trail. Ingraham Billie established his Indian Village alongside. In the 1950s, Turner's River Jungle Gardens provided tourist cruises on the river (left). (Above, MP; left, CCM.)

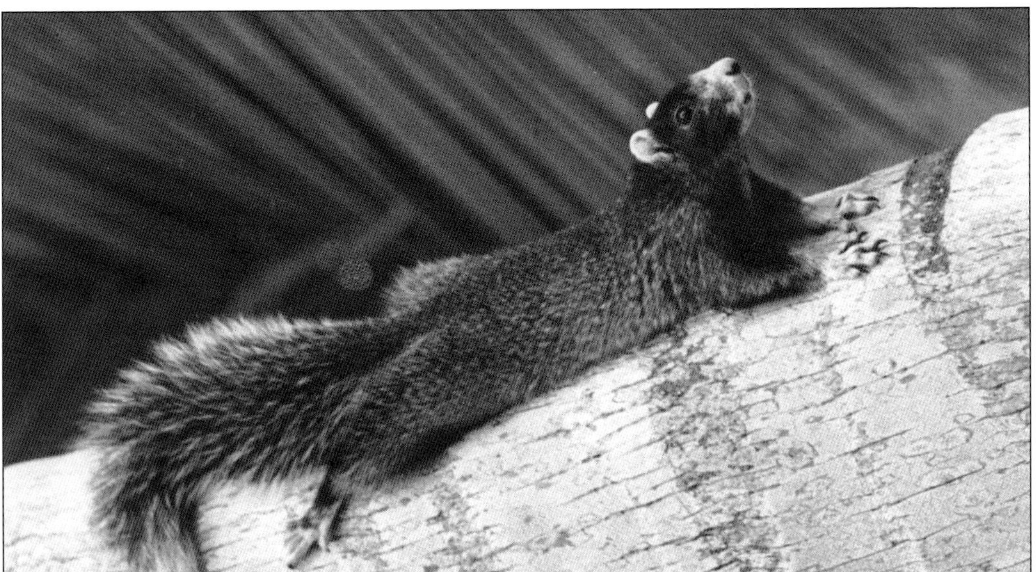

Similarly surprising, little was known about biological resources. A biological inventory and other studies were conducted in the late 1970s by Michael Duever. The National Park Service and the Florida Game and Freshwater Fish Commission were to manage wildlife in partnership. The preserve is also the state's Big Cypress Wildlife Management Area. Concerns identified early included hunting, ORVs, and species of concern, such as the Big Cypress fox squirrel, shown in 1954. (OPN.)

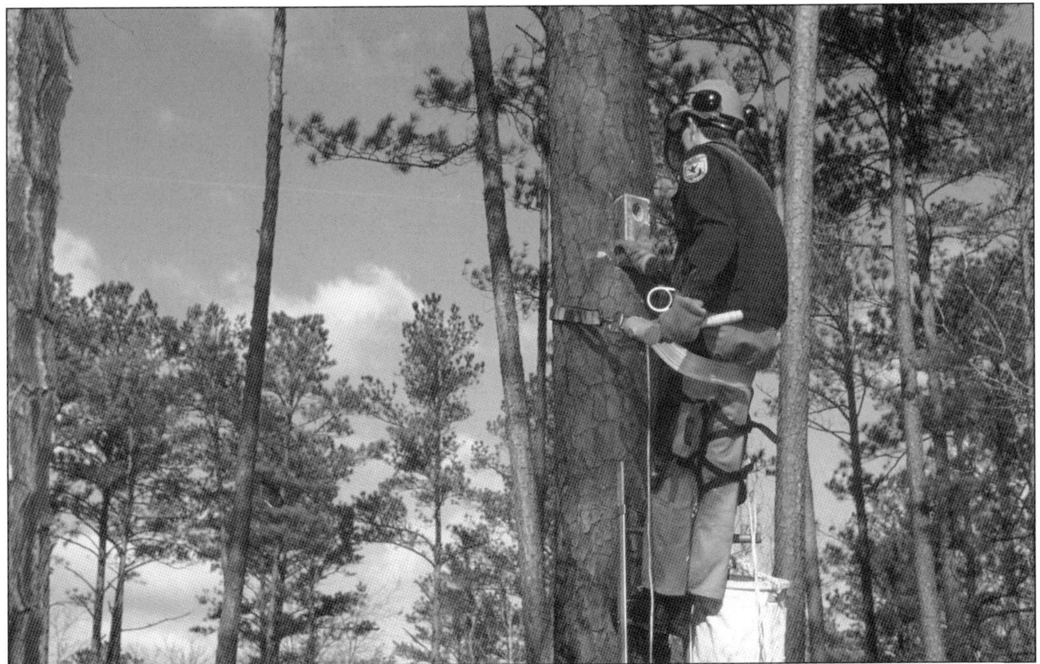

Among the endangered species, the late 1970s inventories found red-cockaded woodpeckers in the preserve. This species lives in family groups and nests in holes in living, old pine trees. Historic lumbering reduced such trees throughout the bird's range. In the preserve, open pine habitat was maintained through prescribed burns. This image shows a tree-climbing researcher installing a nest box; a high proportion of these are successful. (USNA.)

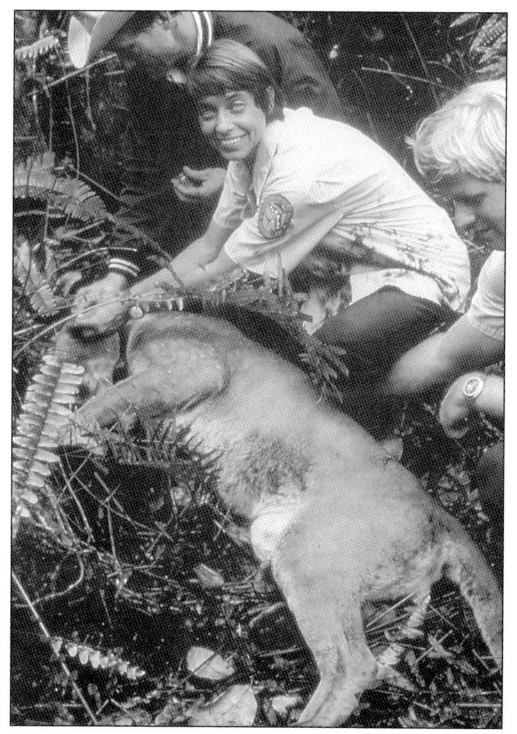

To save the Florida panther, a recovery plan, which James Kushlan, an author of this book, cowrote, was approved in 1981. Studies were undertaken by the state and preserve, the latter led by Deborah Jansen (left, center), shown examining her first panther for a radio collar. Trained dogs, under the guidance of Roy McBride (seen left in the left image), located and treed cats for capture and study (below). They found that males' territories may exceed 200 square miles and that Big Cypress provided the largest remaining contiguous habitat. Gov. Rubin Askew's Florida Panther Technical Advisory Council advised managing food supply, hunting dogs, and ORVs. Eight Texas mountain lions were temporarily released to strengthen the population's genetics. The population increased markedly to over 100 animals and expanded its range. Additional protected areas were set aside, including the Florida Panther National Wildlife Refuge adjacent to the preserve. (Both, RA.)

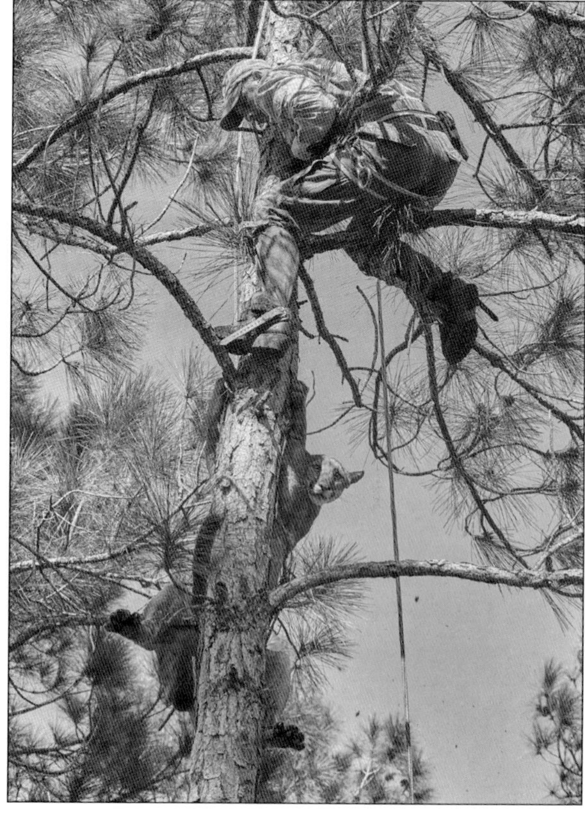

Plants too have become threatened, including Everglades bully, giant air plant, cigar orchid, and ghost orchid, owing to over-collecting, pollination and establishment challenges, non-native pests, and habitat changes. Over 30 orchid species occur in the preserve; over 40 occur in the Fakahatchee. Fewer than 700 reproductively active ghost orchids (pictured), made famous by Susan Orlean's book *The Orchid Thief*, are estimated to remain in Florida, all around the Big Cypress. (USFWS.)

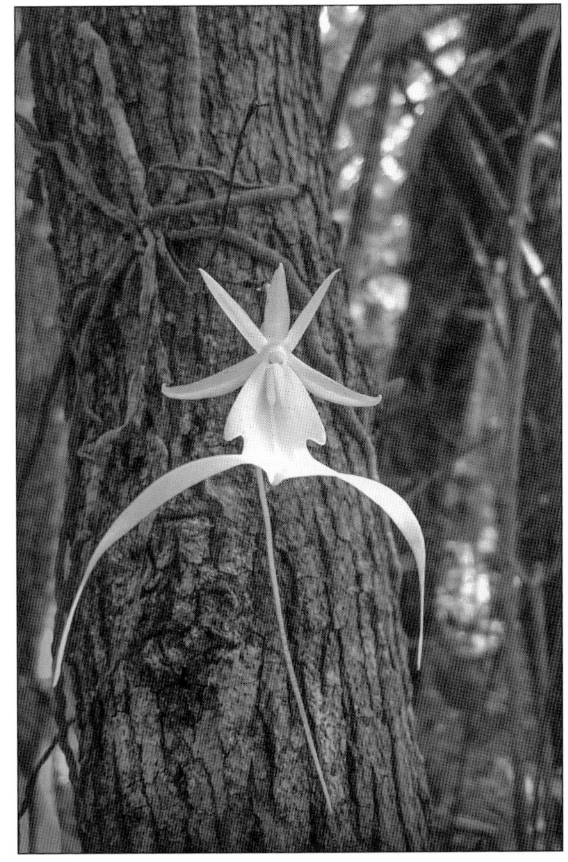

Wild hogs, although not native, have been in the Big Cypress for centuries. They were historically an important food source for panthers, Seminoles, and pioneers and today at the Everglades Conservation and Sportsman Club's annual Wild Hog BBQ (although no longer wild-sourced). They have been hugely destructive to habitat, plants, ground-nesting birds, and other animals. In recent decades, populations declined, possibly coinciding with panther population increases. (USFWS.)

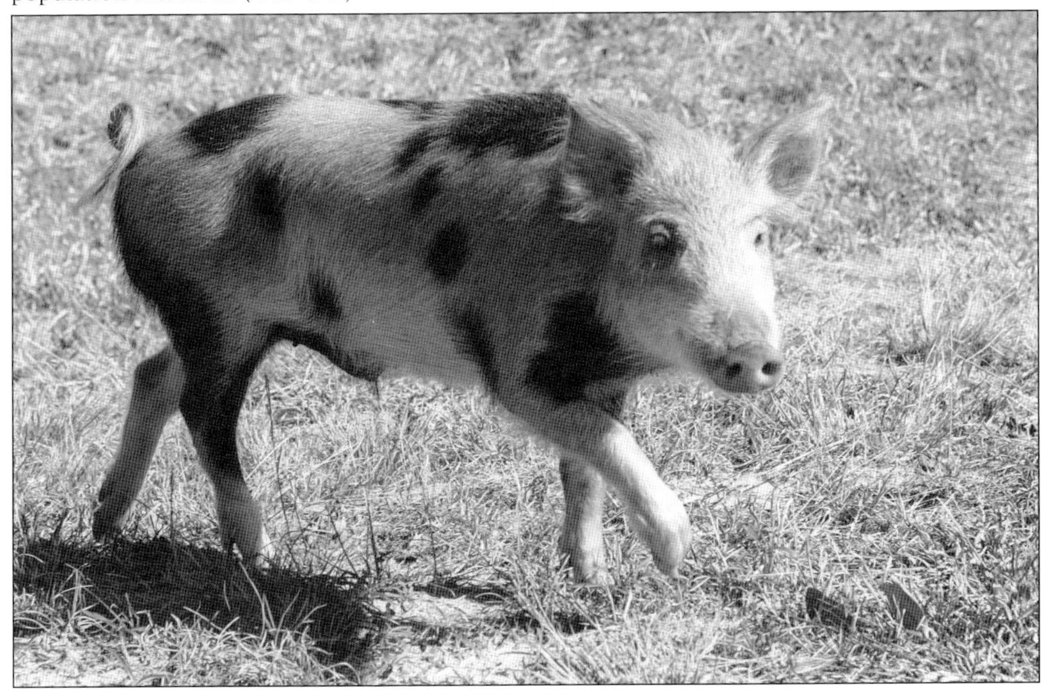

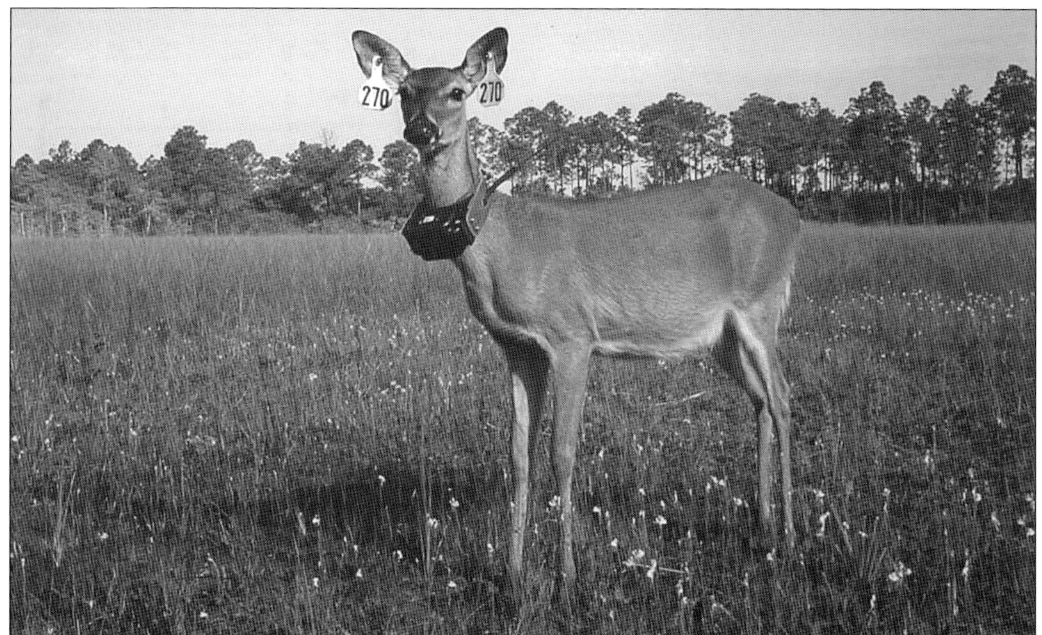

White-tailed deer are the primary large herbivore in the preserve. Studies showed deer were, as suspected, the main prey of Florida panthers and bobcats. From the 1990s, the population was reported to decline in some areas but not others. In addition to deer and hogs, turkey, quail, gray squirrel, rabbits, and migratory waterfowl are also hunted. Supporting hunting distinguishes the preserve from national parks. (FWC.)

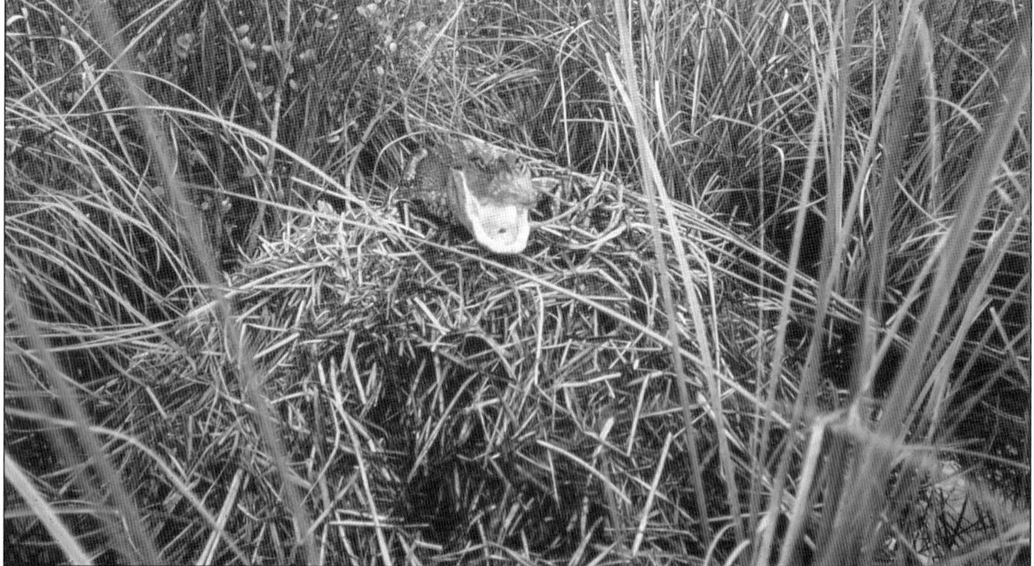
Alligators, having recovered from hide-hunting and 1950–1960s drought years, regained their abundance in the Big Cypress. An author of this book, James Kushlan, studied alligators in the Pinecrest area in the 1960s–1970s. This image is of an alligator defending her nest. Canals and borrow pits also became attractive, especially in the dry season. Although protected in the preserve, with their Florida population recovered and harvest allowed, alligator bites began appearing on local tourist menus. (KH.)

Fishing using gigs was a subsistence activity in the Big Cypress (shown in 1951). In the 1920s, the Tamiami Canal immediately became a fishing attraction, continuing today in the preserve. Florida bass, sunfish, and Florida gar are characteristic natives; walking catfish, Orinoco sailfin catfish, peacock bass, and other cichlids are non-native. Tarpon work their way upstream from the estuaries. To survive, Big Cypress fish are adapted to dry seasons. (SLAF.)

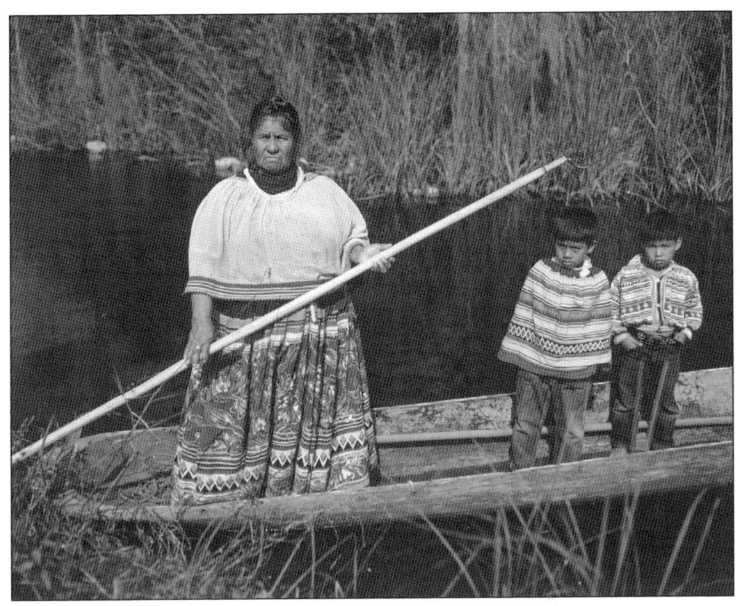

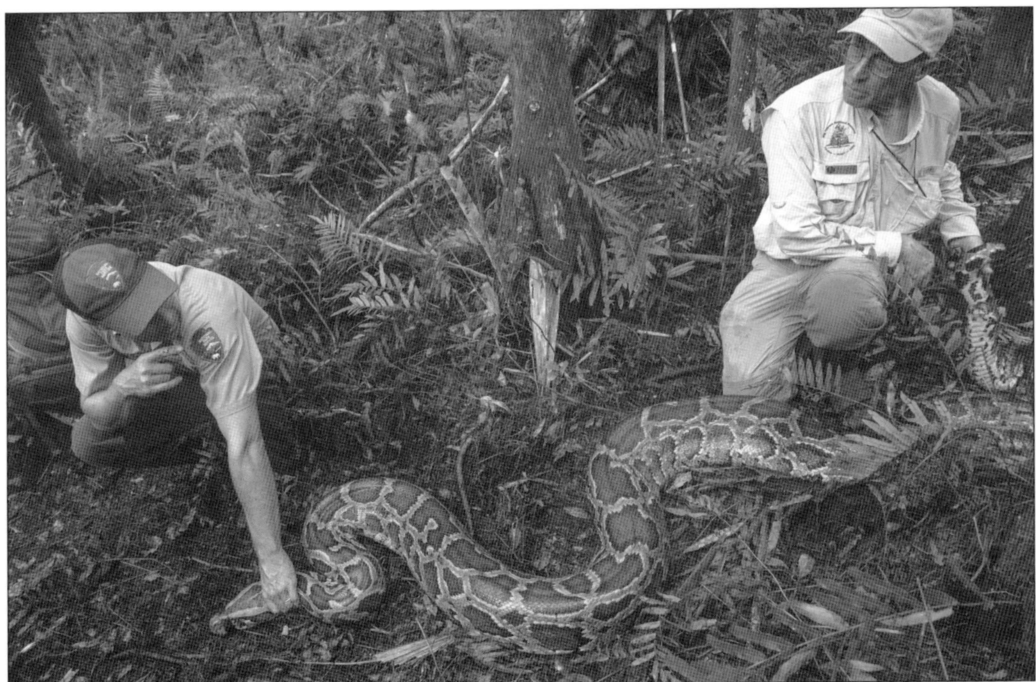

The Big Cypress Swamp has always been snake country; cottonmouths, rattlesnakes, and various water snakes were once abundant throughout, sufficient to support decades of market hunting. One non-native has changed things. Wild Burmese pythons were first found in the 1990s and have since spread into the Cypress. This image is of the preserve's research team. Adaptable to an aquatic life, pythons eat almost everything. Small mammal declines coincided with their spread. (KH.)

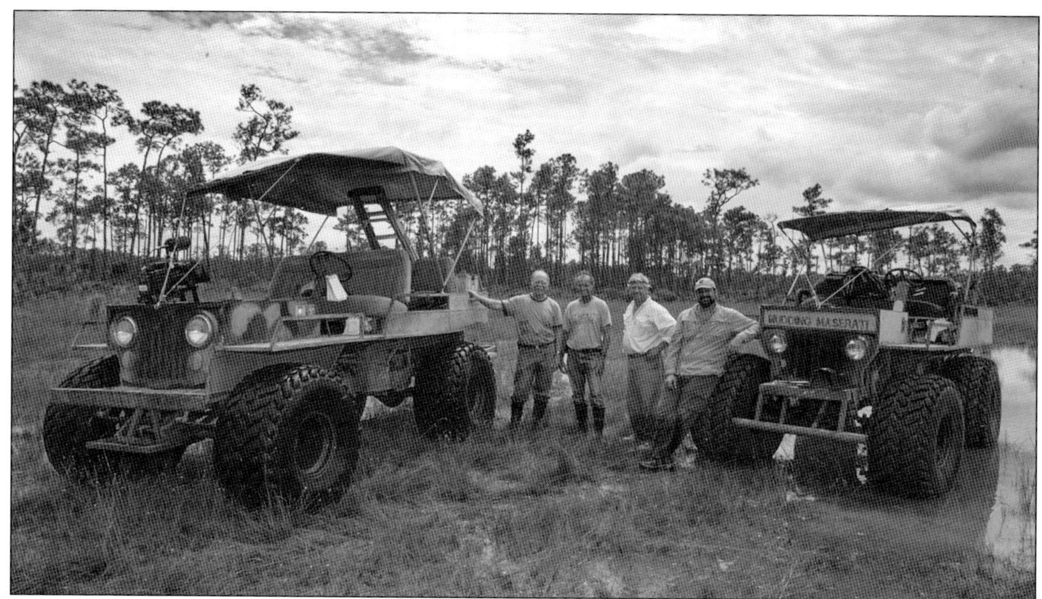

The preserve is huge and mostly roadless. For decades, off-roading in ORVs—swamp buggies (above), airboats, ATVs, UTVs, and street-legal 4X4s—was the way to hunt, explore, and access private camps. In the preserve, concerns arose early about disturbing wildlife, especially panthers, and the possible environmental effects of widespread travel (below). After the preserve's establishment, differing opinions of Big Cypress users became apparent, resulting in prolonged legal disputes. To channel ORV use, a system of designated trails was created. Buggies were built to be light, with wide tires to distribute weight, with mufflers, and with flame arrestors. Airboat use continued in wetter areas, such as south of Loop Road. One thing that has not changed is the need for users to have fix-it abilities. (Both, SFCMC.)

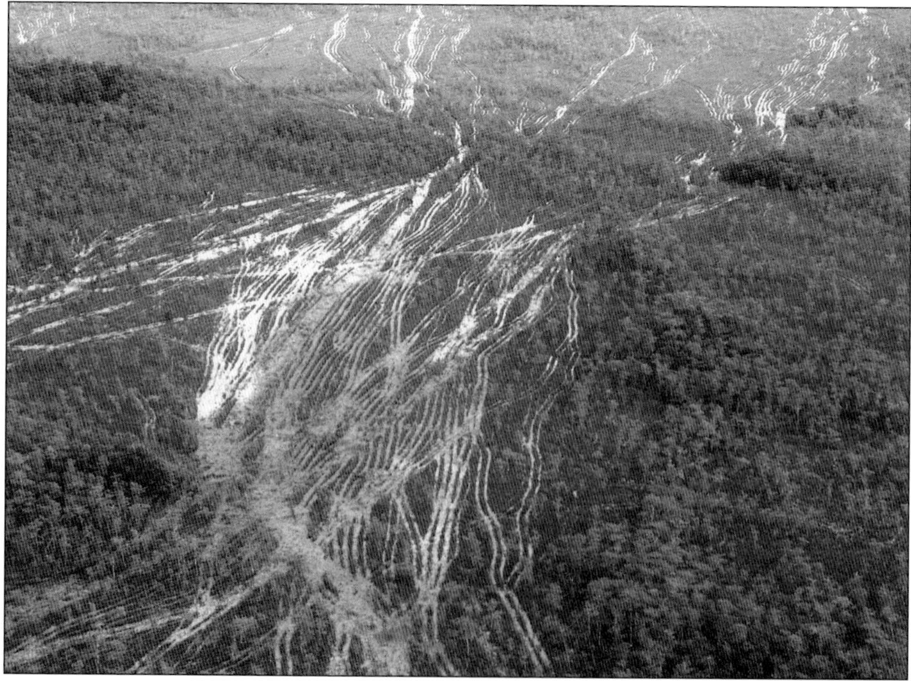

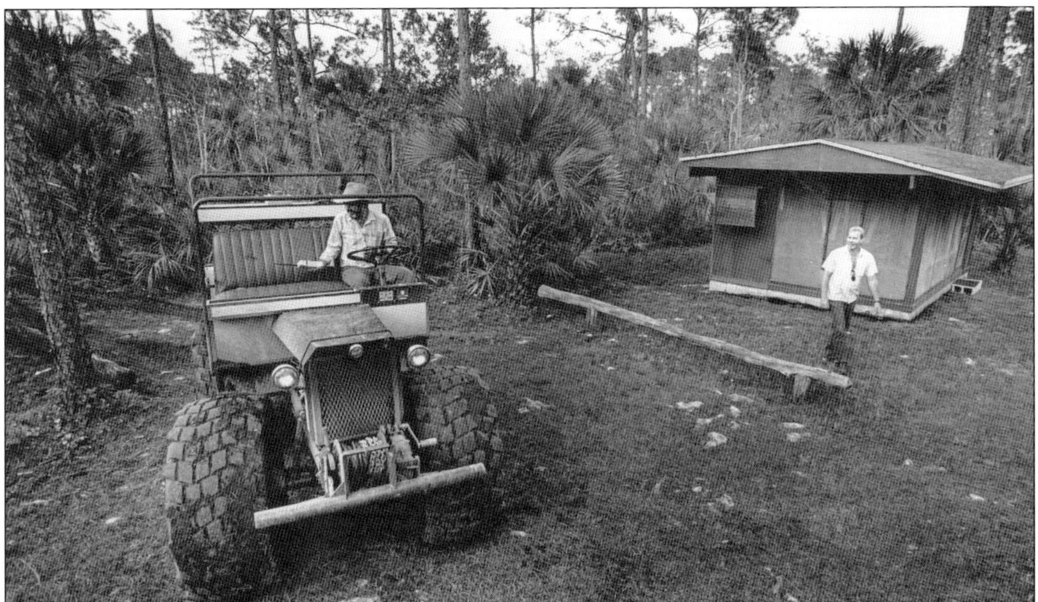

Hundreds of private camps accessible by swamp buggy (one shown) remained scattered throughout the Big Cypress and continued to be used, many on private properties that had been improved before the preserve was established. They covered up to three acres with authorized ground access and maybe an airstrip. Some camps had been owned for a generation or more. Camps remained an integral part of the swamp's heritage. (KH.)

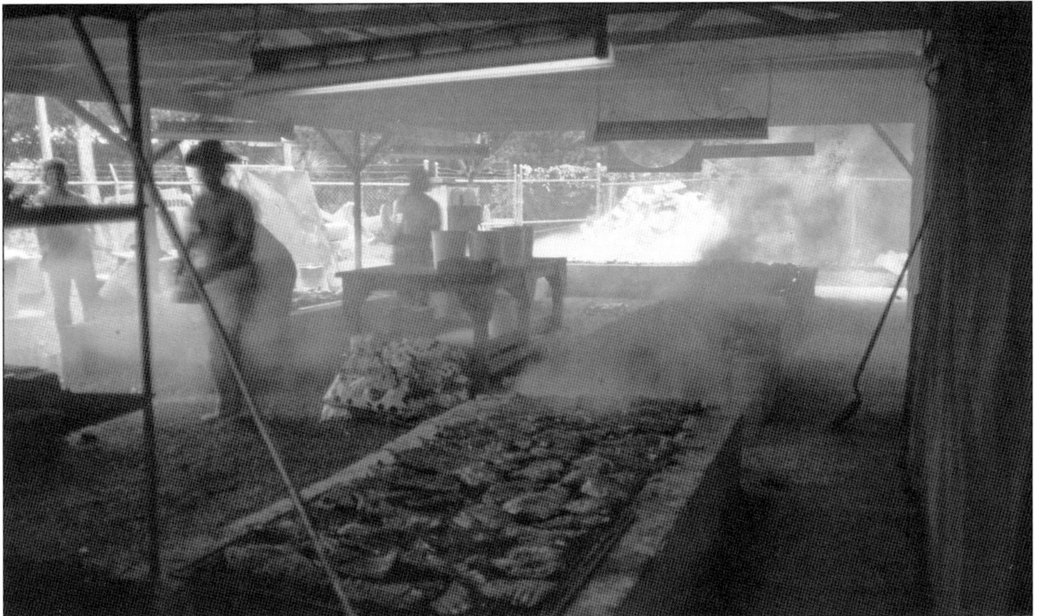

The Everglades Conservation and Sportsman Club was founded in 1950, dedicated to conservation and public use of the Big Cypress. Its famous annual Wild Hog BBQ (pictured) also started in 1950. The club's headquarters, service buildings, buggy storage, and campground were established on Loop Road at the Monroe Station intersection. The club represents the evolution of the swamp heritage of the Big Cypress. (SFCMC.)

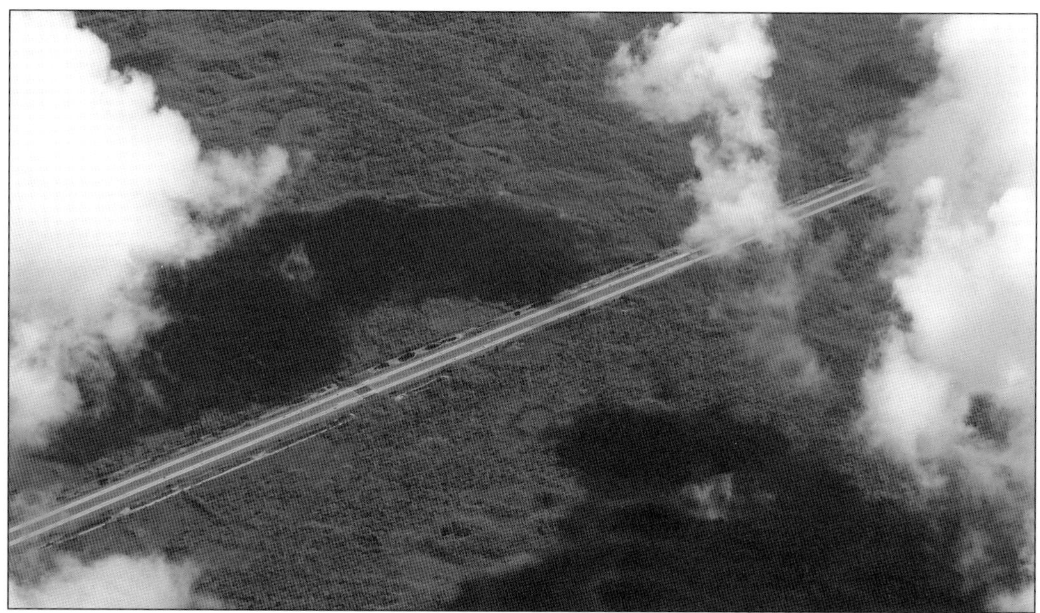

In 1986, Alligator Alley was transformed into Interstate 75, engendering significant controversy, including alternative routing such as by Tamiami Trail or servicing the jetport, a car-testing track, and access points, such as to the Miccosukee and Seminole reservations and the preserve. It is one of the few interstate highways passing through National Park Service lands. Divided four lanes, culverts, fencing, and wildlife underpasses tamed some of the earlier roads' environmental detriments. (FN.)

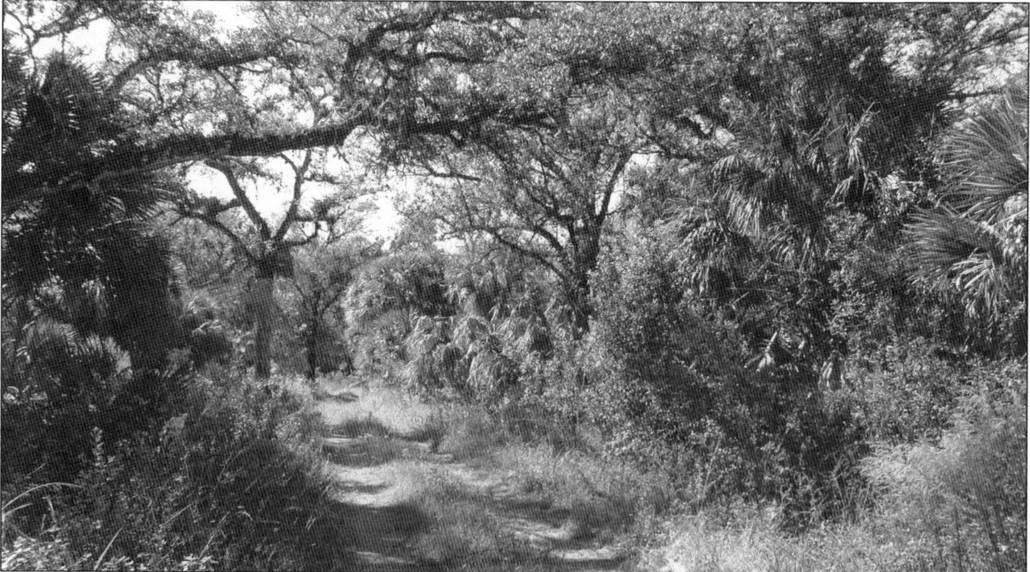

In an exceedingly complicated undertaking in 1988, Collier interests traded Big Cypress lands along the preserve's northern (pictured) and western boundaries to the federal government. Enlarging the preserve to over 1,100 square miles, these additional lands provided habitat connectivity for wide-ranging species, such as the black bear and panther, and secured the preserve's northern watershed. Acreage also added land to the Ten Thousand Islands and Florida Panther National Wildlife Refuges. (SFCMC.)

The long history of oil and gas development in the Big Cypress, begun in the 1940s, continued intermittently for the next decades. When the federal government procured lands in the preserve, belowground oil and gas rights were retained by some previous landowners, including Collier Resources. Oil was found at Bear Island in 1972 (right) and at Raccoon Point in 1978, which began production in 1981 and expanded in 1992. If wells were abandoned, pads were restored. The image below shows rangers inspecting a restored pad site. The state and federal government have attempted to buy these rights but failed owing to uncertainties as to ownership of all the mineral rights that might be affected. Options for the future of privately owned oil rights have continued to be proposed. (Right, SLAF; below, SFCMC.)

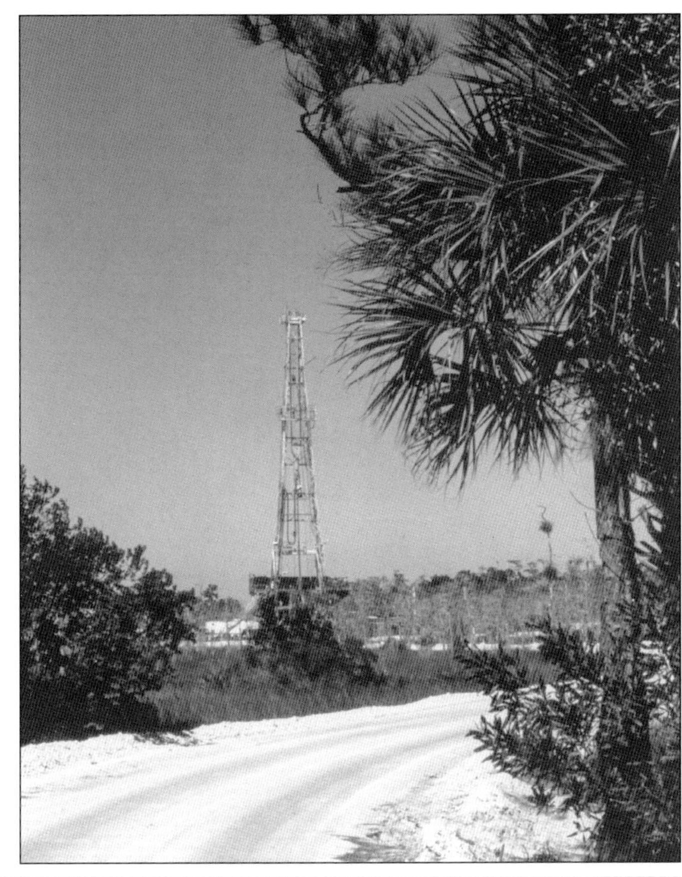

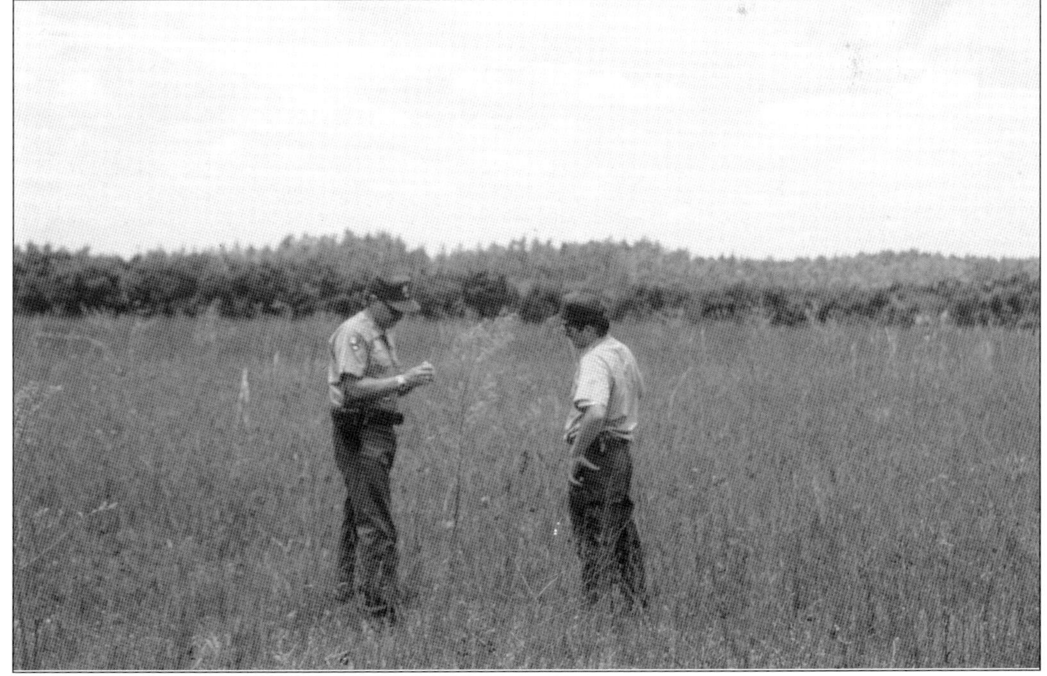

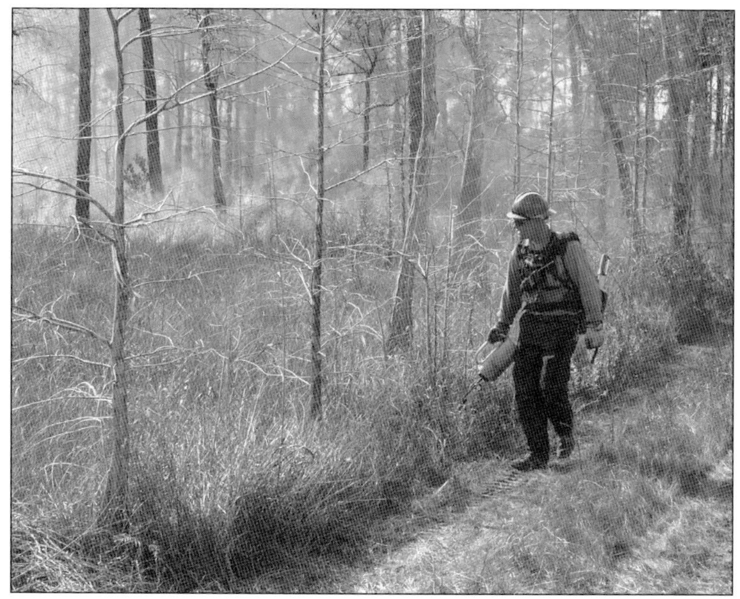

The Big Cypress burns, some habitats frequently, others hardly ever. Humans have always set fires in the Big Cypress. Initially, fires were suppressed in the preserve, but in 1981, a total of 160 square miles burned. It became understood that wild and prescribed fires maintain prairie, pineland, and endangered species habitat. The preserve developed one of the largest fire programs in the park system, burning 100 or more square miles each year. (SFCMC-GP.)

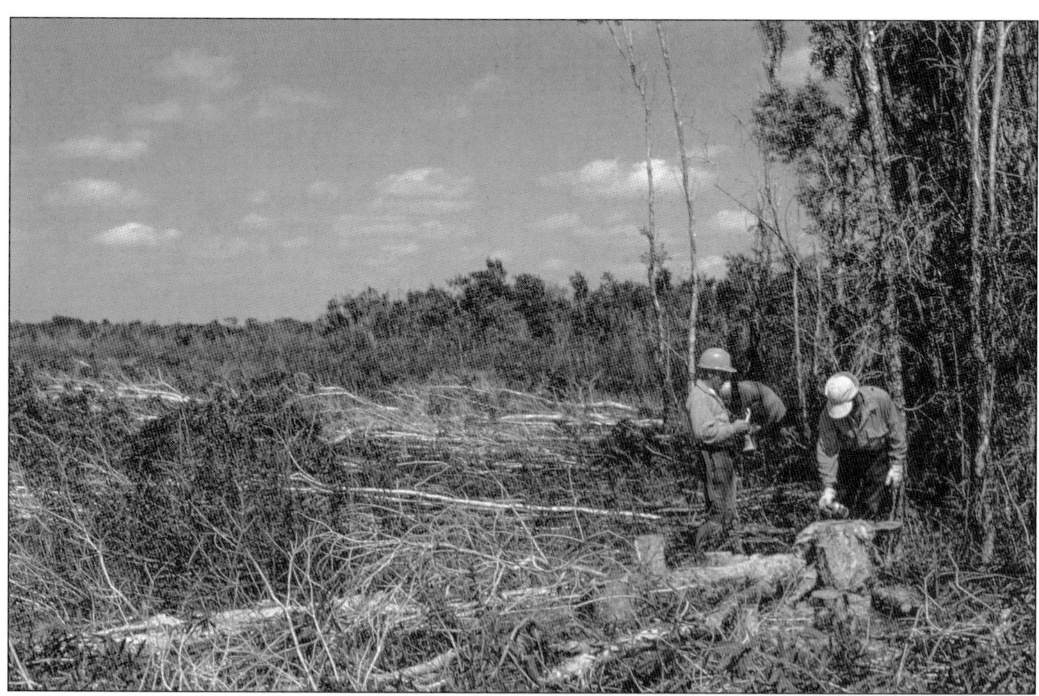

Along with pythons and fish, non-native plants, such as melaleuca, Brazilian pepper, Australian pine, and Old World climbing fern, proved to be major resource management issues. Progress against melaleuca was slow as controls had to be invented, but within a couple of decades, more than 15 million melaleuca trees had been removed from the preserve (pictured), and affected habitat began the process of restoring itself. (OPN.)

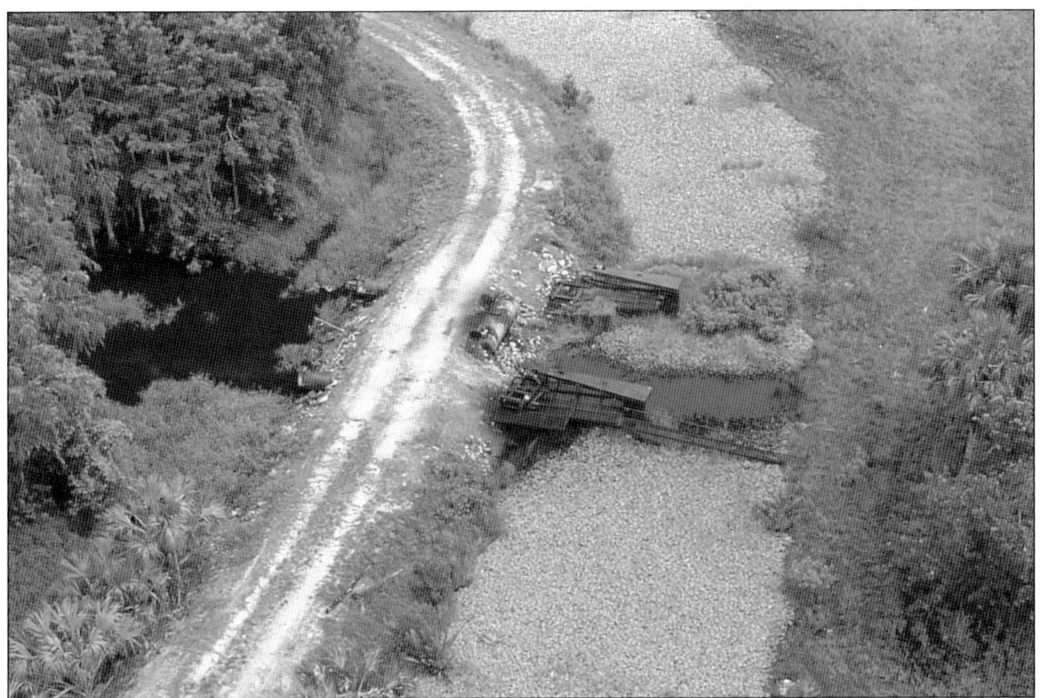

The Big Cypress's primary natural resource is rainwater. Providing upstream surface water for Everglades National Park was the reason for the Big Cypress gaining national attention and the national preserve's subsequent creation. The hydrology of the original preserve was predominantly driven by local rainfall. The addition of lands added protection for upstream inflows. The goal has been to restore a sheet-flow neutral environment, but the Big Cypress Basin had been afflicted with over 100 miles of primary canals as well as levees, various water-control structures, and culverts (above). Turner River and Birdon canals, L-28 canals and levee, and Alligator Alley and Tamiami Trail canals and roads all altered water flows, for which hydrology monitoring stations were set up (below). Upstream land uses affected water quality. The shunting of Big Cypress waters into the Everglades and then through its western gates persistently flooded Cape Sable seaside sparrow habitat. An important goal has remained to restore surface flows across the Tamiami Trail and Loop Road into Lostmans Slough. (Both, SFCMC.)

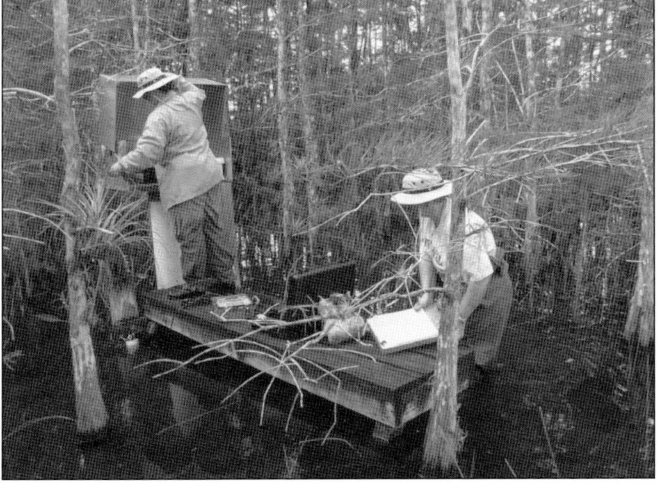

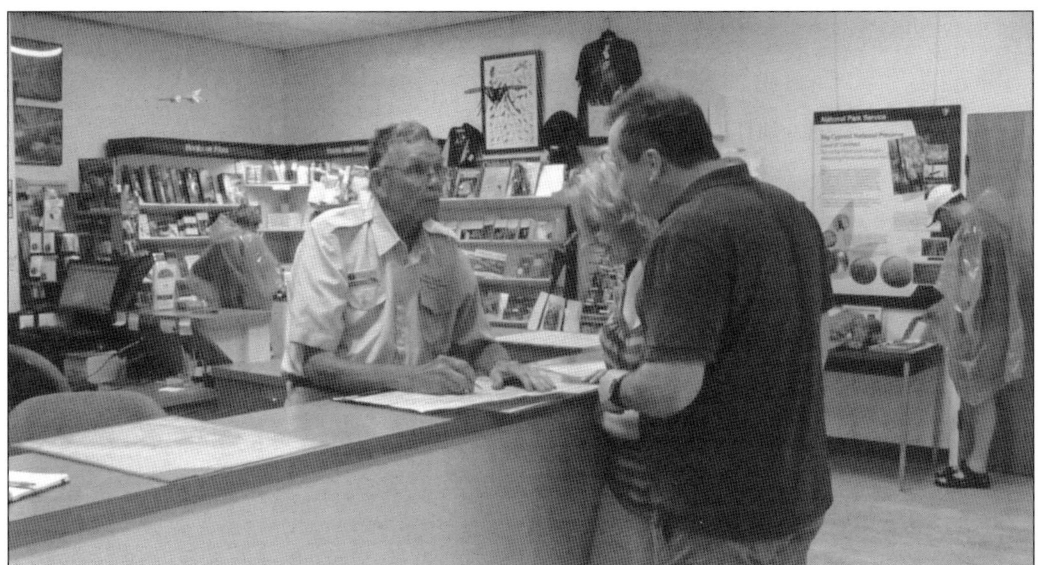

After the Oasis's airport was acquired in the 1980s, its eye-catching rooftop airplane was removed, and the building used as a ranger station. It was converted into the Oasis Visitor Center. Opening in 1985, the center, in addition to all-important restrooms, had a greeting lobby (pictured), exhibits, and an introductory film. The airstrip supported the preserve's aircraft operations. It also became the southern launching point for the Florida National Scenic Trail. (SFCMC.)

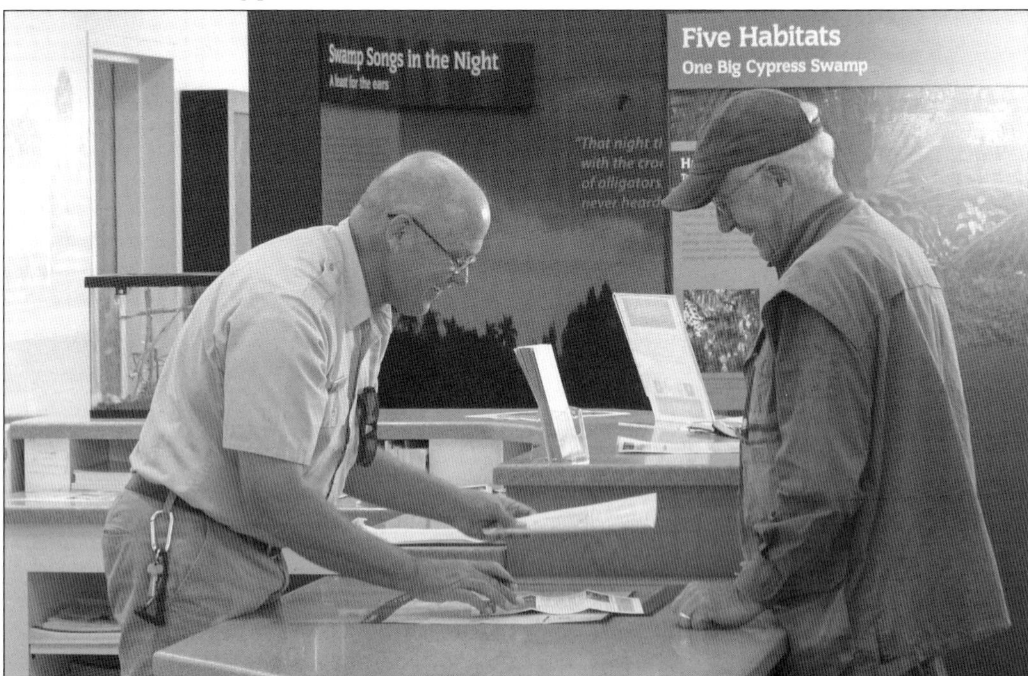

Near the old Collier County Welcome Center, the preserve built a western visitor contact station, later named for preserve supporter Nathaniel P. Reed (see page 93), after his passing. Its exhibits, some outdoors, describe the natural history of the Big Cypress and also human history, including farming and swamp heritage. Historic Halfway Creek provides a way for manatees to approach the boardwalk. (SFCMC.)

Along the Tamiami Trail, various attractions developed to entice passing motorists. Clyde Butcher opened his Big Cypress Gallery in the 1990s. It features the landscape photographer's black-and-white images of the Big Cypress. Butcher, who is pictured at right in 1991, has participated widely in Big Cypress conservation activities. His swamp walks were legendary; Pres. Jimmy Carter took one. The Shealy family continued and expanded on the traditions of the Trail Lakes Campground, adventure tours, and the skunk ape attraction (below). Continuing since the 1950s, Wooten's (see page 78) maintained the long-standing tradition of providing airboat and swamp buggy tours on their privately owned property. Tours into the swamp of various sorts continue to be developed by additional groups. (Right, UM; below, KH.)

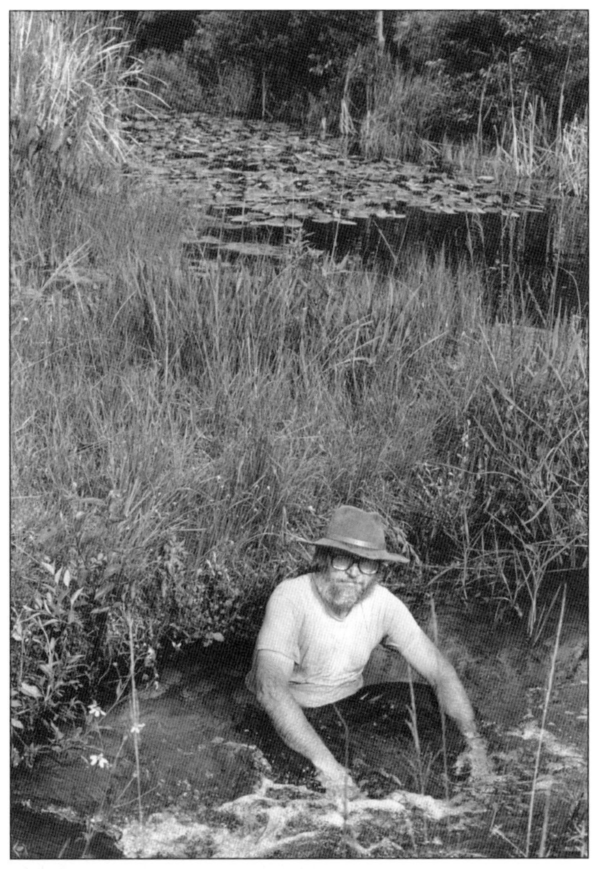

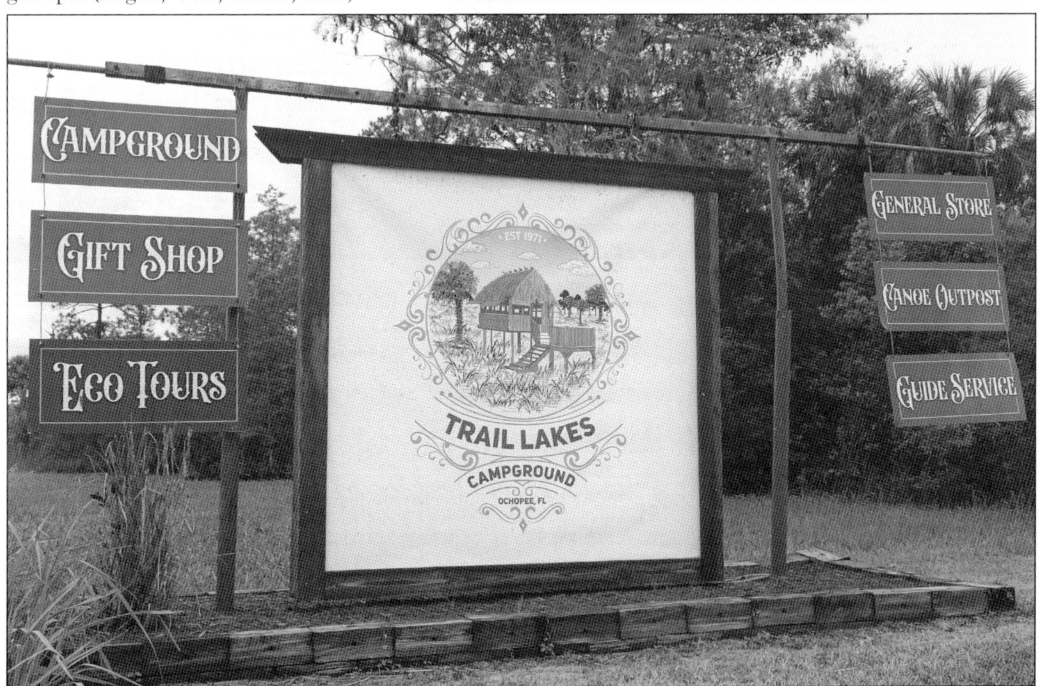

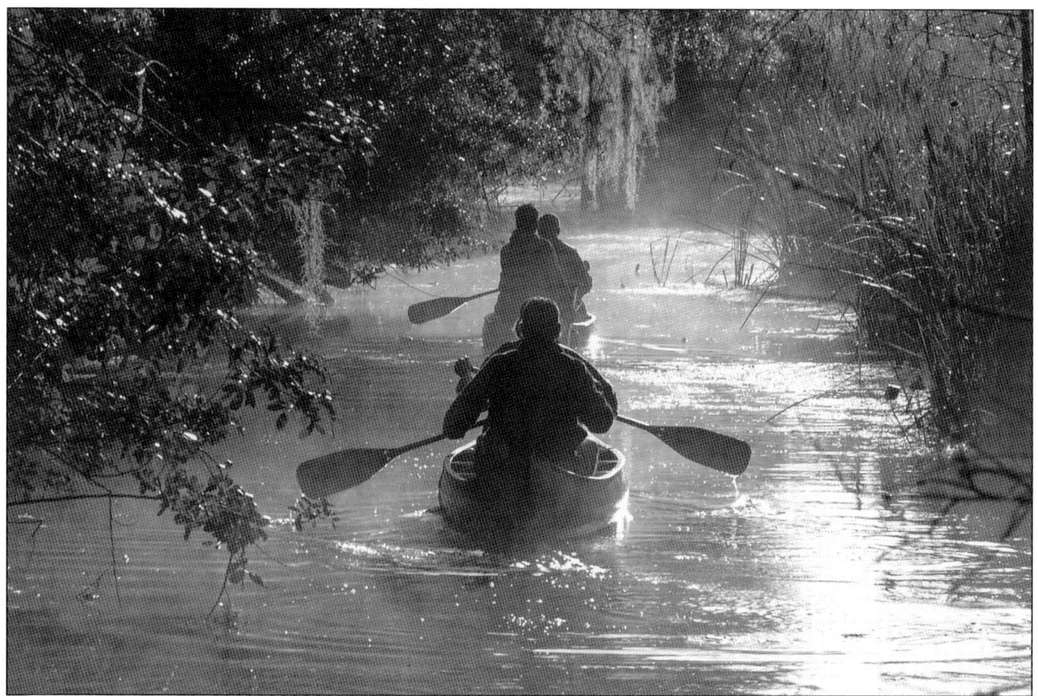

Canoes were the ancient mode of Big Cypress transportation. Trails were developed so that paddlers could follow routes used by Indigenous peoples, soldiers, and settlers at Turner River (pictured), Halfway Creek, and East River in Fakahatchee Strand Preserve State Park. Turner River's paddling trail benefited from restoration along the canal starting in the 1980s. It reestablished a more natural, seasonal flow to the river. (SFCMC-GP.)

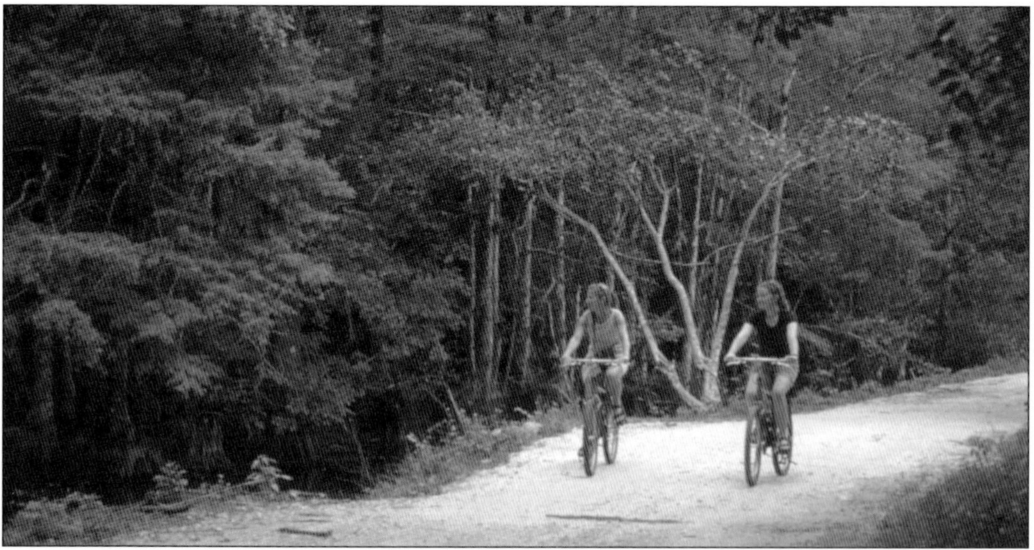

When the preserve designated trails, biking became more popular along roads and trails such as Bear Island Grade, Birdon Road, Loop Road (pictured), Nobles Grade Road from Alligator Alley, and Fire Prairie Trail from Turner River Road. More bike trails are available in the adjacent Fakahatchee Preserve. Biking is tidier in the dry season as many trails get muddy or inundated in the wet season. (SFCMC.)

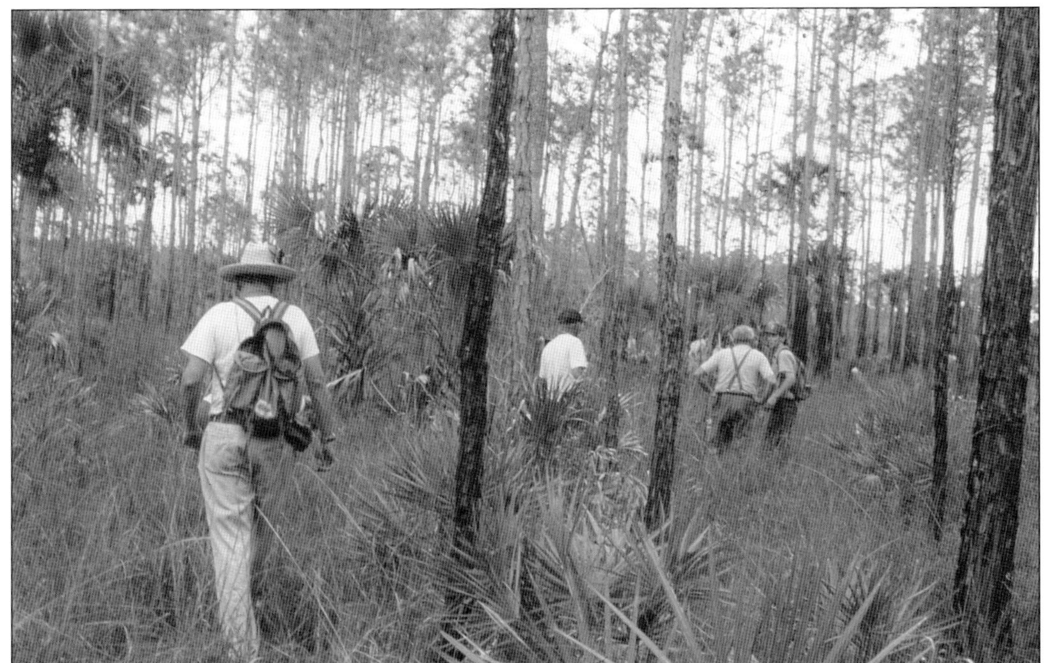

Although historically walking was how pioneers and gator hunters crossed the swamp in the dry season, non-hunting hiking took some time to catch on after the preserve was established (above). Although Big Cypress hiking has increased in popularity, it has never been a normal walk in the woods. The adventure is that treks are rocky, mushy, hole-ridden, and usually muddy. Initiated in 1966, the Florida National Scenic Trail, officially starting at Oasis Visitor Center, heads northward 1,400 miles, with six campgrounds in the preserve and access also at Alligator Alley. A former more southern section of the trail started at Pinecrest. Orienteering has always been hard, deep in a confusingly thick cypress swamp. Marked trails were established at Gator Hook off Loop Road and Fire Prairie off Turner River Road (below), but a hiker can head out anywhere. (Above, SFCMC; below, KH.)

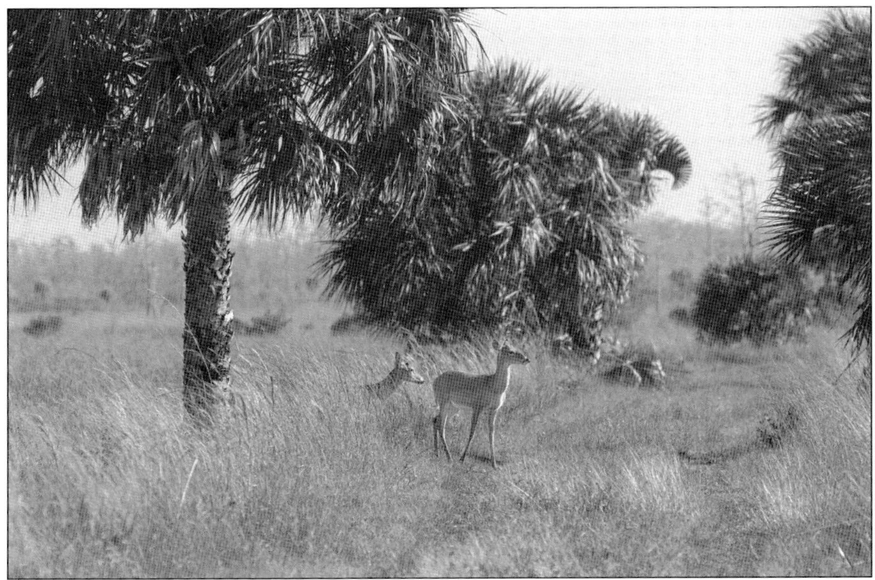

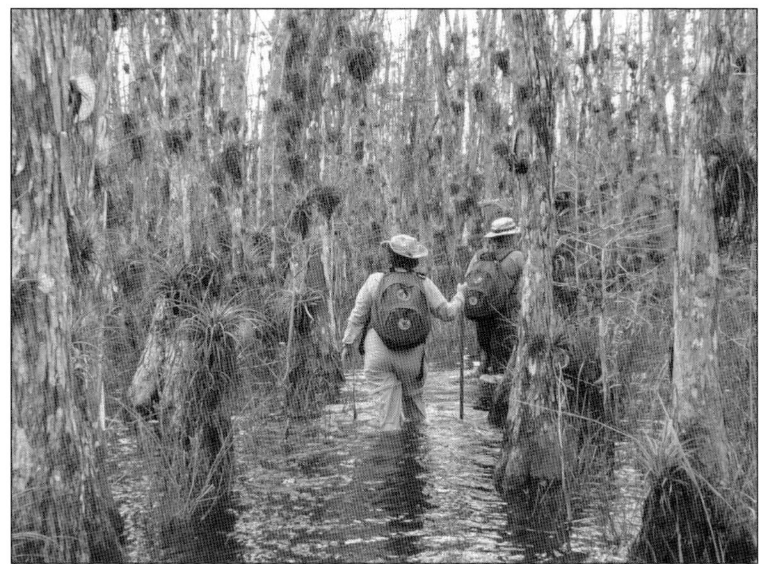

Most walking and hiking in the Big Cypress have always ended up as a swamp slog, wading through ankle-deep to chest-deep water. The classic slog wades through sloughs, prairies, and deep into cypress forests. Sweetwater Strand (page 23) off Loop Road has been a favored wet-season, deep-water slog. In fact, nearly any pathway will turn into a swamp slog in the wet season. (SFCMC.)

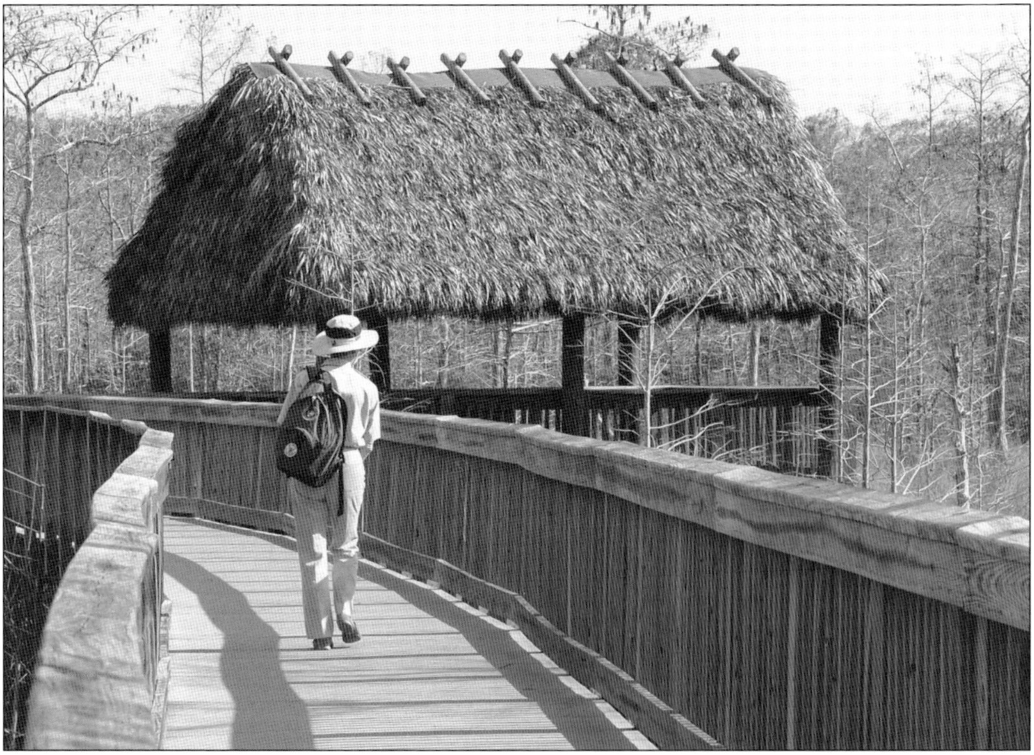

The Big Cypress's first boardwalk at Fakahatchee Big Cypress Bend was constructed in the 1960s (see page 91). Walkable and accessible viewing locations were also later developed at visitor centers, the Ten Thousand Islands Marsh Trail and tower, and the historic wayside parks such as Kirby Storter (pictured). Creating boardwalks meant that serious hiking and swamp slogging were not necessary to see Big Cypress's wildlife, plants, and habitats. (SFCMC-GP.)

The Big Cypress has always been for the birds, particularly large waterbirds that underpinned the swamp's economy for half a century. Hundreds of bird species occur, as illustrated by an author of the current book, Kirsten Hines, in her field guide, *Birds of Florida*. Migratory birds pass through in fall and spring, while wading birds move about following seasonally changing water levels. The preserve was placed on the Florida Birding Trail, having dozens of recognized birding hotspots. (SFCMC.)

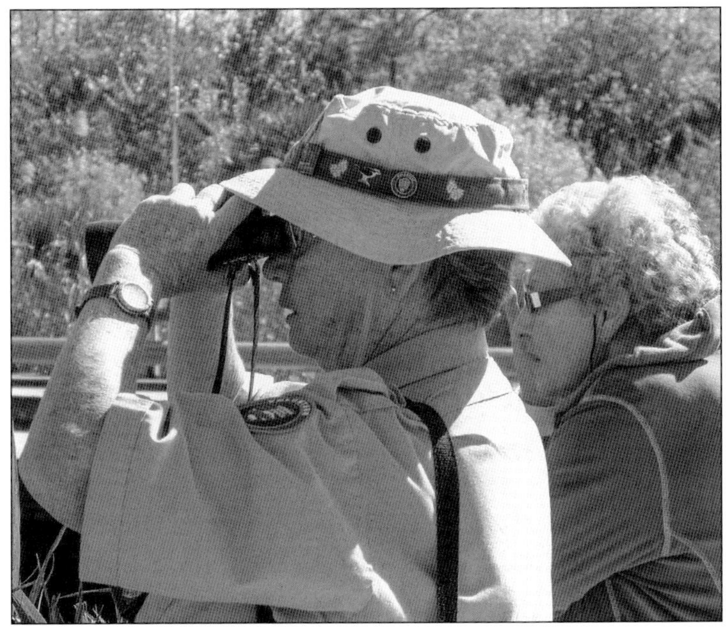

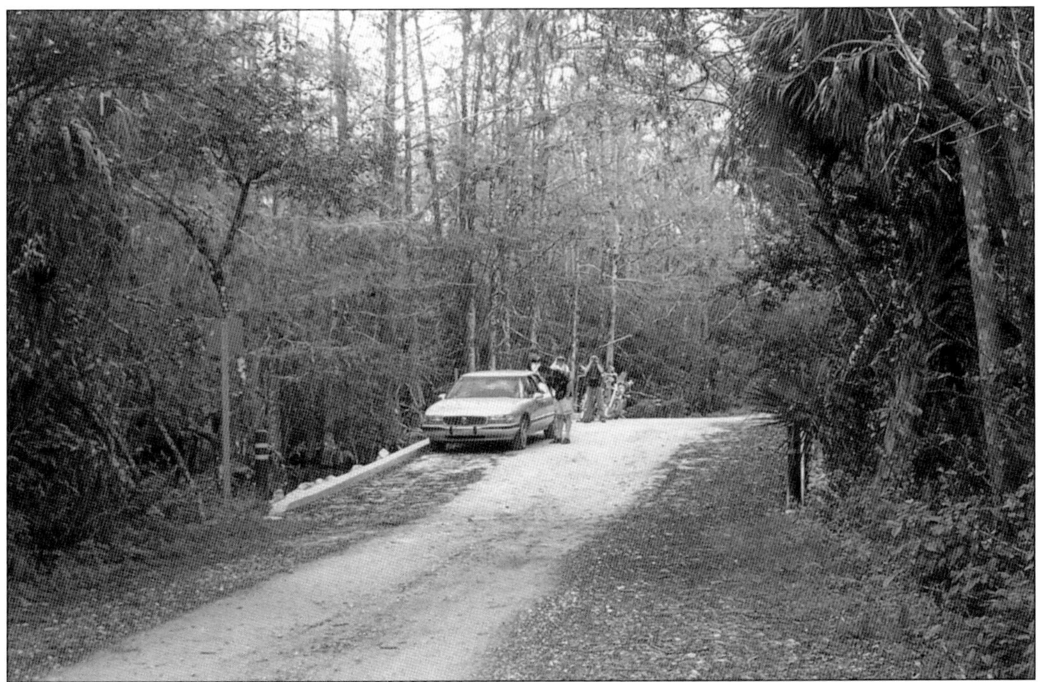

Although almost entirely a roadless wilderness, from the opening day of the Tamiami Trail in 1928, driving has been how most people experienced the Big Cypress. In the 1960s, the legislature named wayside parks honoring Collier-corporation road builders, Homer P. Williams and Kirby Storter. The preserve's roads, such as Loop Road (pictured) and the Turner River/Wagon Wheel/Birdon Roads, are scenic drives. (SFCMC.)

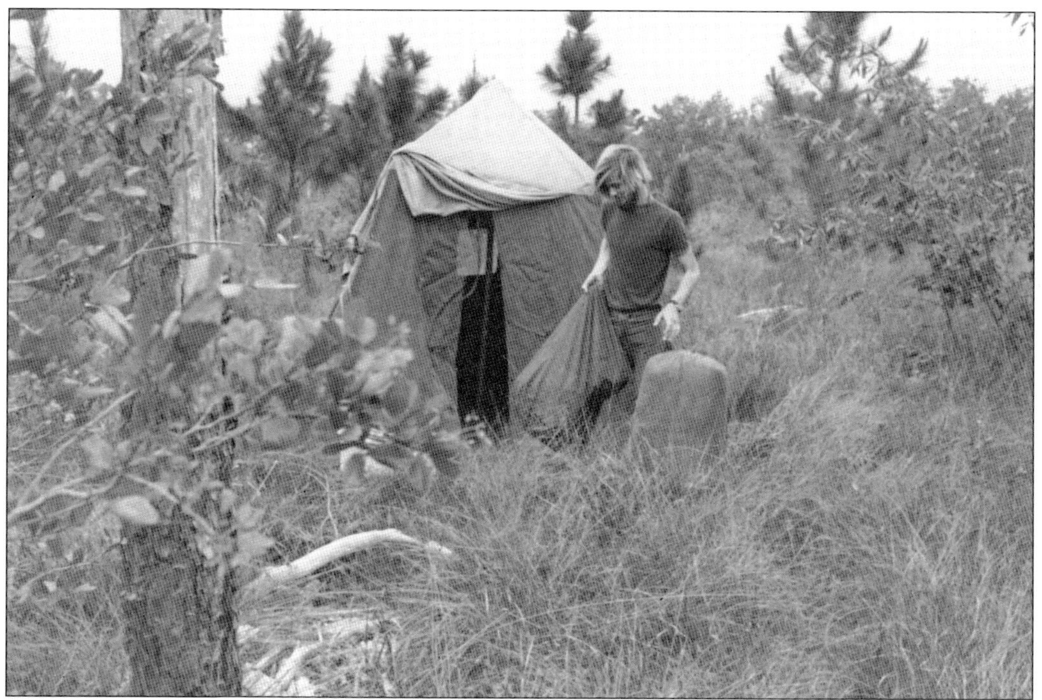

From pioneers in palmetto-topped lean-tos and gladesmen in makeshift shelters to permanent cabins and visitors in RVs, camping is the historic way to spend the night out in the Big Cypress Swamp. Camping is an example of the continuation of its swamp heritage. The tent camping image above shows James Kushlan, an author of this book, camping in the Big Cypress in the late 1960s. The image below shows a campfire with RVs in the background. Eight major official campgrounds were developed in the preserve. Pink Jeep, Gator Head, and campsites south of the Loop can be accessed only by ORVs. Campsite 10 south of the Loop is the site used by James Kushlan's family from the 1970s. The group campsite on Loop Road is at the location of the previous University of Miami field site. (Above, KH; below, SFCMC.)

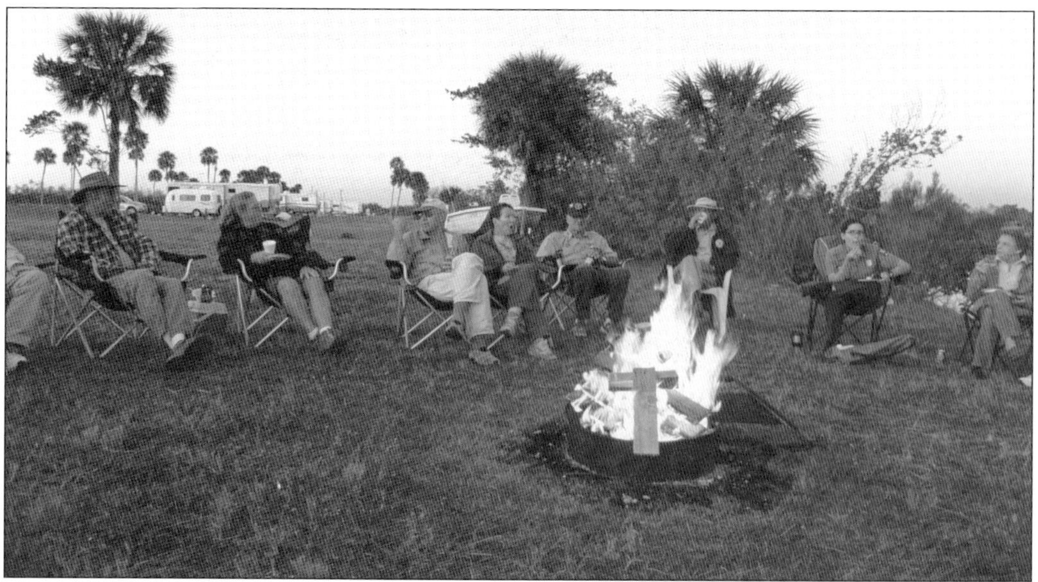

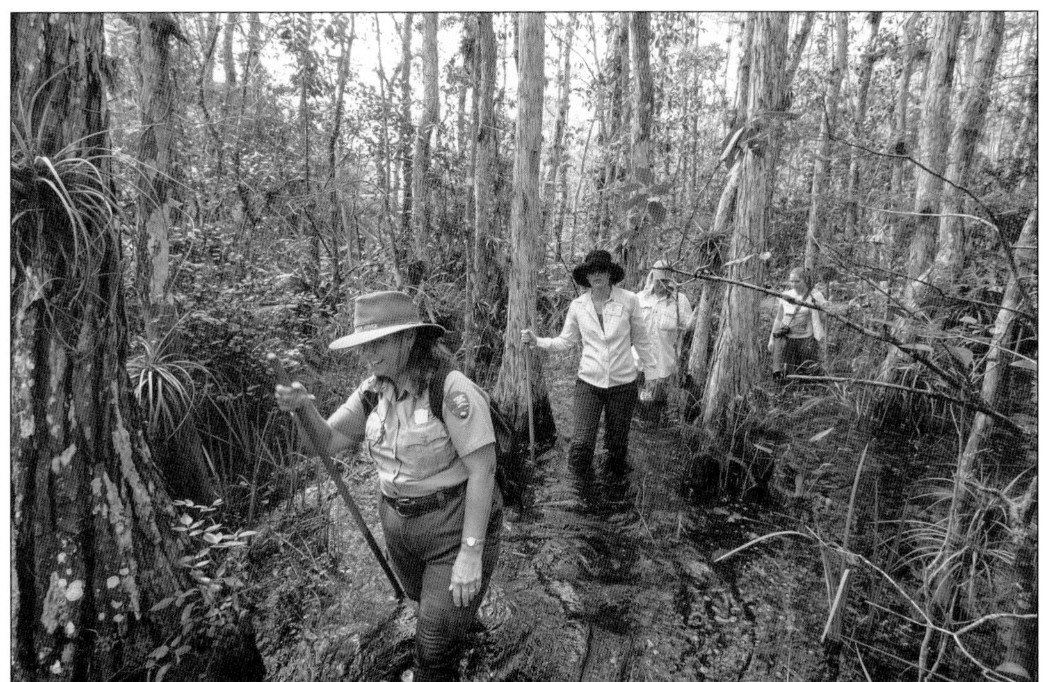

Initially, the Big Cypress National Preserve was expected to continue to be used by backcountry hunters and campers rather than attracting the more usual national park visitors. The first interpretive specialist did not arrive until 17 years after the preserve's establishment. Signage, displays, and ranger-led programs expanded and evolved with time (a ranger-led swamp walk is shown above). Among their many other contributions, volunteers in the Volunteers-In-Parks program shared their knowledge with preserve visitors (below). The Big Cypress Institute, established along with the preserve in 1974, also provided immersive, educational, and interpretive experiences. Loop Road Environmental Education Center, part of Everglades National Park, started in 1977. The Big Cypress's many stories are there to be told. (Above, SFCMC; below, SFCMC-GP.)

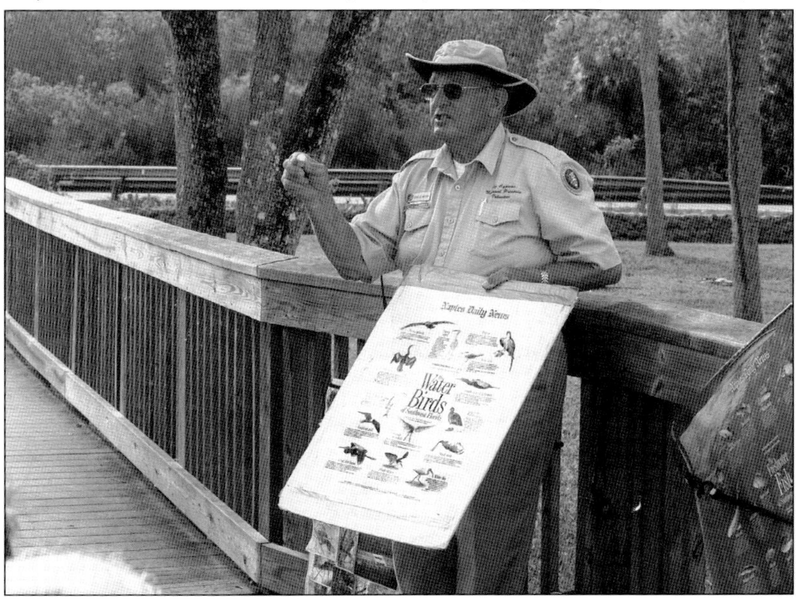

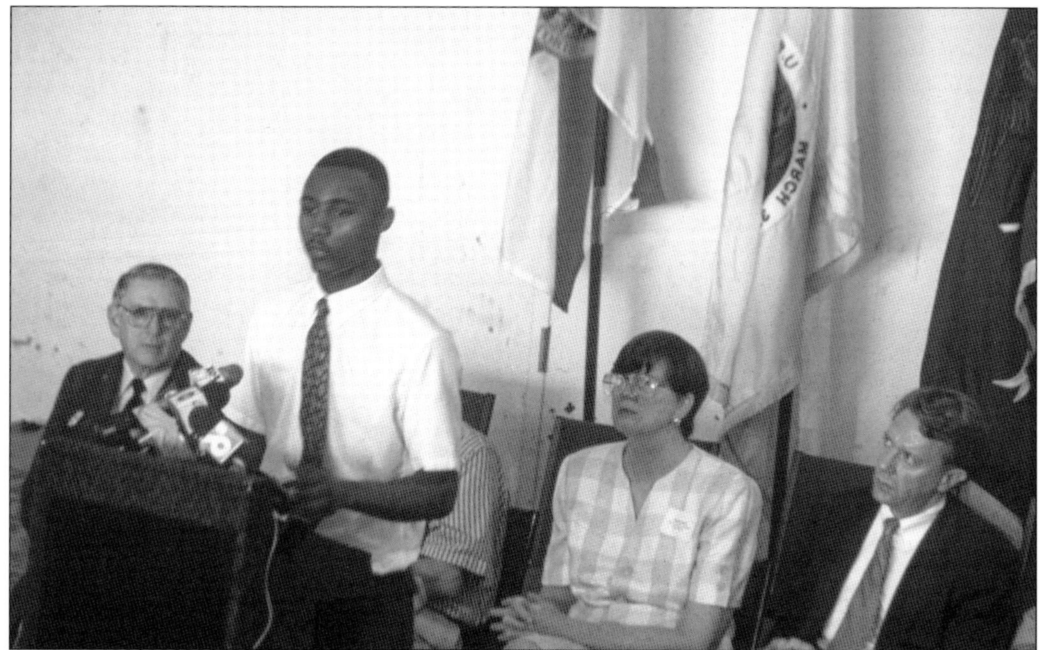

Formal education has been a much-cherished historic imperative in the Big Cypress, where schools were founded as soon as settlements reached a required number of children. The first school in what was to become Everglades City was established in 1893. Chokoloskee children came by boat. Pinecrest children were bused to schools in Miami or Everglades City from Trail Center. In 1994, Secretary of the Interior Bruce Babbitt (above, right) and Attorney General Janet Reno (above, second from right) established their Youth Environment Services' Swamp Camp for youthful offenders, dedicating the institution at Oasis (above). The preserve's Swamp Water and Me Program (SWAMP) started in the 1990s, integrating into Collier County's sixth-grade curriculum, providing classroom and field experiences such as taking and evaluating environmental readings and demonstrating radio-tracking (below). (Both, SFCMC.)

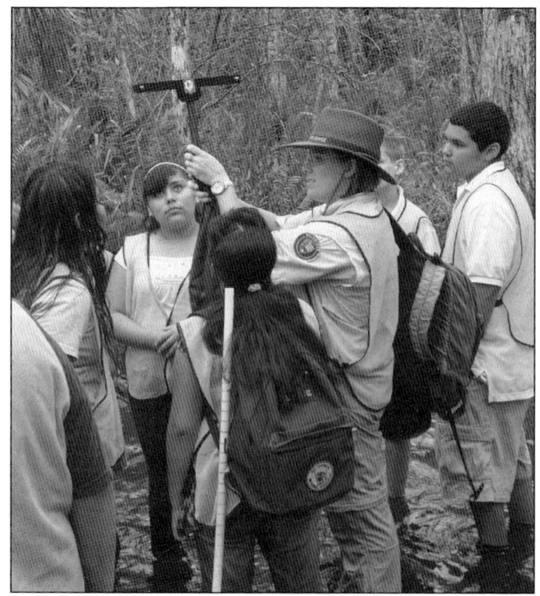

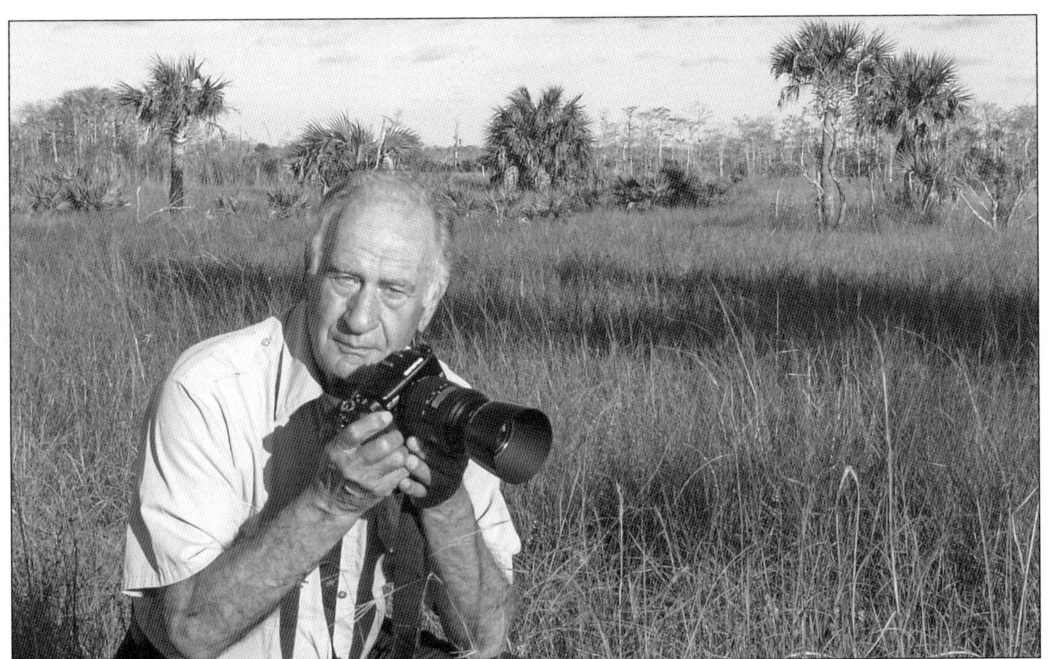

With its seasonally changing treed landscape, the Big Cypress Swamp is visually inspiring. Artists working in various media have been attracted to interact with its rough-barked, epiphyte-festooned cypress trees, quirky cypress knees, orchids, sunning alligators, wading egrets, and posing storks. The NPS Artist-In-Residence program has brought select artists to the preserve to be inspired and to share their work and talents with visitors. Kirsten Hines, an author of this book, had this opportunity, and this book is one result. From Clyde Butcher's large-format camera to a visitor with a quick cell phone shot, photographs stop action (above). Video captures it. Painters are inspired by elevated views from boardwalks (below) or by slogging deep through the water. (Both, SFCMC.)

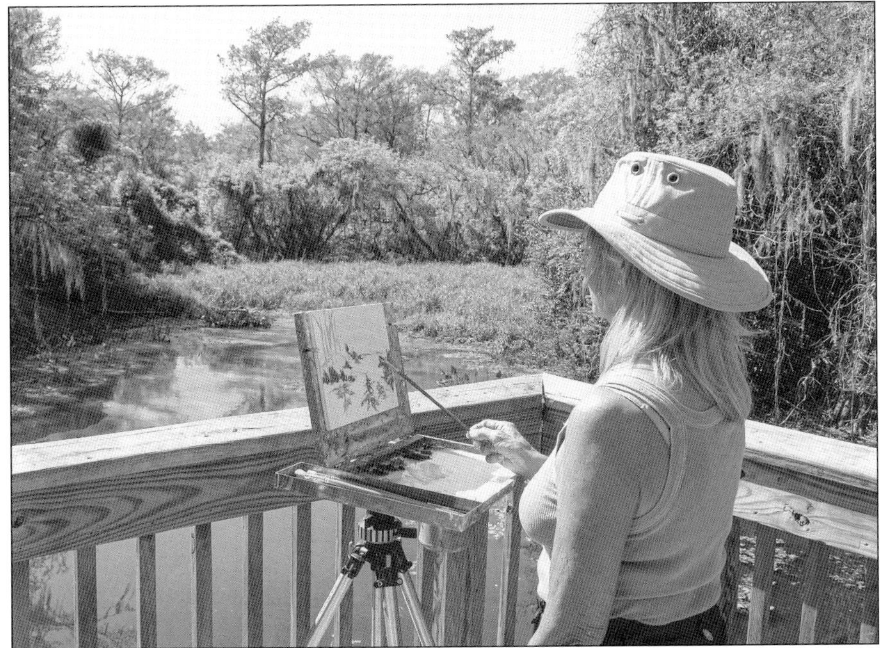

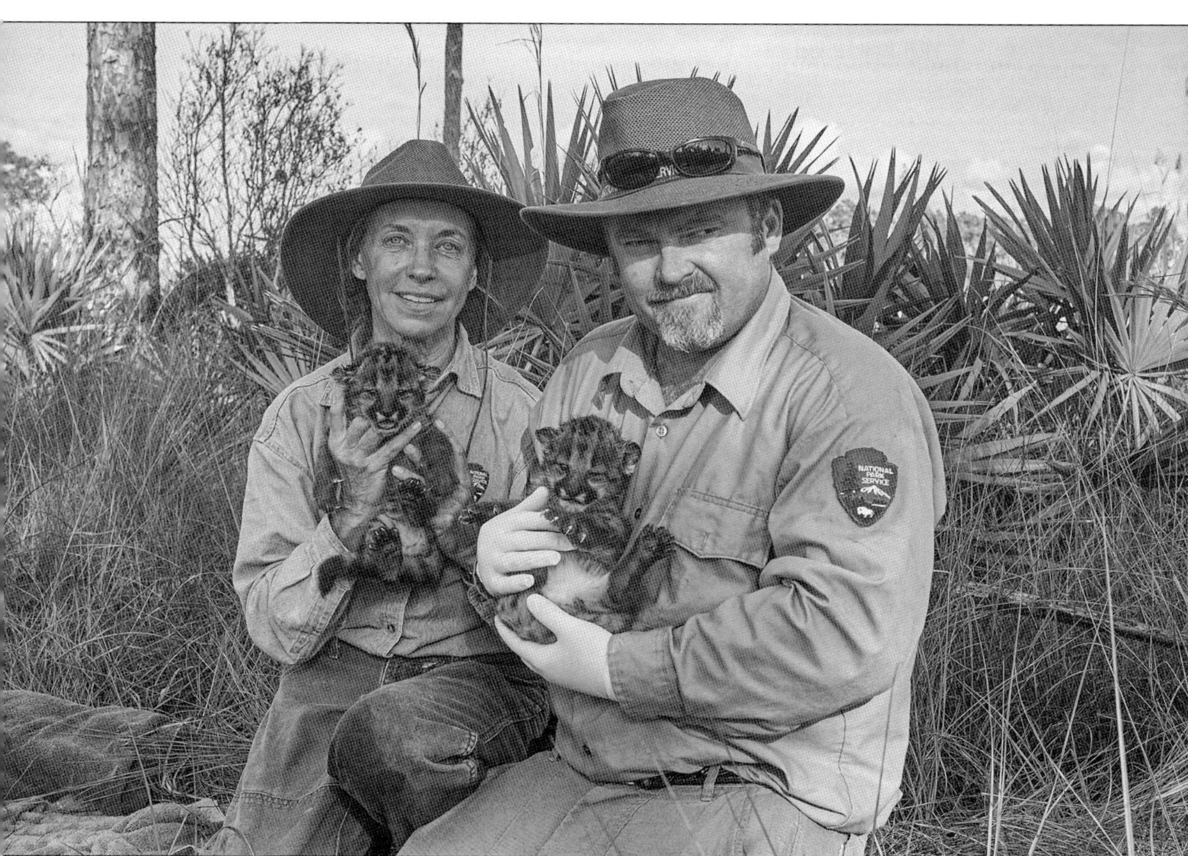

The Big Cypress Swamp and its Big Cypress National Preserve are a place of deep biological and human history, protecting a unique landscape and its iconic animals, such as the Florida panther. The kittens shown above with preserve biologists Deborah Jansen and John Bellam, and the kitten on the following page, which grew up to be the wild adult featured on this book's frontispiece, are encouraging evidence of successful management to bring a species back from the brink of extinction in its near-final refuge. (RA.)

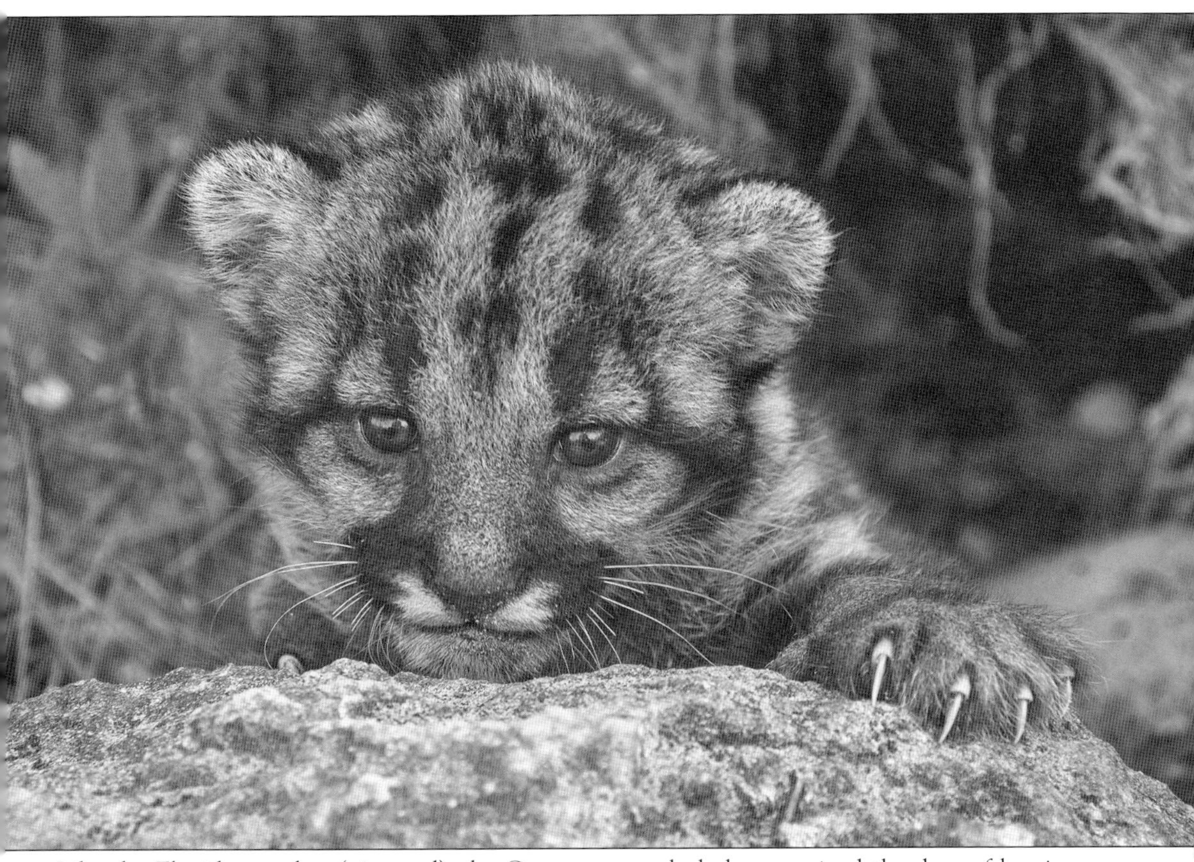

Like the Florida panther (pictured), the Cypress as a whole has survived the days of logging, farming, development, drainage, and roadbuilding. Although the Big Cypress Swamp is not as it was when Calusa occupied the land or when early pioneers arrived in the 1800s, it is also not as it was in the heavily used 1960s and not as it would have been had the world's largest airport taken it over. The Big Cypress Swamp remains, slowly restoring itself and providing habitat for its rare and typical plants and wildlife, and being used with environmental sensitivity by increasing numbers and diversity of visitors from around the world, experiencing the wonders of the Cypress. (RA.)